THE EVENT OF THE QUR'ĀN

THE EVENT OF THE QUR'ĀN

Islam in its Scripture

Kenneth Cragg

London · George Allen & Unwin Ltd
Ruskin House Museum Street

First published in 1971

ISBN 0 04 297024 5

Printed in Great Britain
in 11 point Fournier type
by Unwin Brothers Limited,
Woking and London

For
Arnold
and
St Justin's House, Beirut,
his
birthplace

Preface

The future, it has been said, is not what it was. Change is all about us and with it the expectation of change, self-compounding. And confounding, too. So some men turn instinctively to the old and the enduring to ask how it means to endure further. The central documents of religion generate in men a new wistfulness and a new anxiety, a fresh temper of anticipation and yet, of apprehension. What is the meaning, and what the prospect, of their continuity? In this interrogation of their heritage, there develops nowadays a new liveliness between the religions, liable as they all are for the interpretation of man and for achieving in the real world what they say of him.

The general source of this present study in the Islamic Qur'ān, and its pre-suppositions, are outlined in the Introduction and the Conclusion. It had its beginnings in the academic activity of the Department of Philosophy in the American University of Beirut, Lebanon, in the forties, and came into its present form in the tenure of a Bye-Fellowship at Gonville and Caius College, Cambridge, from 1969. The dedication salutes the student hostel of those years among Arab undergraduates and our great domestic joy there. The years between, in many travels and conversations, contributed to the reflections that inspired this essay. In November, 1968, I had the privilege of four Lectures in Lake Forest College, Lake Forest, Illinois, USA, home of the Bross Foundation, with the title: *The Fascination of the Qur'ān*. The present book contains the larger material on which they drew. It is now published within the Bross Library, in which it is the twentieth in a sequence which began in 1880, with Mark Hopkins' *Evidences of Christianity*. The Library and the Foundation, with its ten-yearly competition of manuscripts, and its selected publications, exist to foster religious studies, under the terms of the will of William Bross, of Chicago, in commemoration of his son, Nathaniel Bross, who died in 1856. Outstanding early volumes in the series were Josiah Royce's *The Sources of Religious Insight* (1911) and F. J. Bliss' *Religions of Modern Syria and Palestine* (1912). Recent publications have been Amos N. Wilder: *Modern Poetry and the Christian Tradition* (1952); John A. Hutchison: *Language and Faith: Studies in Sign, Symbol and Meaning* (1963); Michael Novak: *The Experience of Nothingness* (1970) and Charles C. West: *The Power to be Human* (1971). *The Event of the Qur'ān* is honoured to be in this good sequence and to extend it, for the first time, to the central theme of Islam.

It does not claim to be more than a gesture of concern for a large and demanding task. It needs—and may perhaps elsewhere have—a companion study, thinking further from its conclusion. Its aim is to focus on what happened in the Qur'ān, in the primary and ultimate encounter of Muḥammed with Arabian pluralism both of belief and tribe. It aspires to know what manner of phenomenon the Qur'ān was, looking for the answer to its question in the authentic quality of the Book itself, its geographical setting and locale of metaphor, its literary shape, its historical bearings, its personal *Rasūliyyah* and its great *Risālah*.

These chapters, then, are an exercise in religious enquiry and in trans-religious openness of heart. They are meant as a Christian's deep reckoning with his neighbours' Scripture, in the common context of our single humanity and our separate histories. Their attitude is much concerned with scholarship: but it is not indifferently academic. For they have to do, in the end, with that worship which searches all the self-interests of religions that it may authentically transcend, and yet inhabit, them. In this enterprise we have need of each other, as we are, such as we became, such as we are becoming.

Gonville and Caius College, Cambridge KENNETH CRAGG
June 1971.

Contents

Introduction

What happens in the Qur'ān is a question which it is important to formulate and fascinating to answer. There can be no doubt that it is the right, the inclusive, question to ask, more apt and certainly more vivid, than enquiries about more static concepts. For the Scripture of Islam is emphatically an event as well as a document. Historical perception has to apprehend the one in the texture of the other, to seek beyond the episodes and occasions for the central phenomenon itself. In all its psychic, political, social and religious elements, it constitutes a single dynamic reality, as elusive in its origins as it was revolutionary in its issue. The necessary concerns of exegetes and scholars have meaning only in the wake of the great experience itself. They are the other tenses of the present active. To this the historian must go. Events *in* the Qur'ān yield their relevance, and the primacy, to the event *of* the Qur'ān. To find it and to search it is to read aright.

Reading that way is to be aware of a fourfold thing. The event of the Qur'ān lives in an intense personal prophetic vocation. As such it moves with eloquence and poetry in the mystery of speech. It speaks a corporate solidarity, awakening a stirring sense of ethnic identity. These, in their progress, and their climax, are none other than the claim and the vehicle of a total religious demand and surrender. In each the quality of all is intertwined. We separate them only for purposes of study and for reasons of exposition. Together they comprise the prophetic, the literary, the political and the spiritual, character of Islamic revelation. There is the book in its recipience in the heart of Muḥammad, in its nature as the Arabic classic, in its authority as the Arabs' Scripture, and in its summons as the voice from heaven. The Qur'ān is a fusion, unique in history, of personal *charisma*, literary fascination, corporate possession, and imperative religion. In the continuity of its reception since the event we have perhaps the largest and most sustained expression of what might be called documentary faith. Throughout we have to do with revelation as literature and with literature as revelation.

Islam lives by the centrality of a Scripture for which the prophet-ruler is the means, and by an obedience-community, responding in worship and polity to its contents and its claims. Though it takes its antecedents back to the beginning of time, the operative years are few, intense and local. The narrative with which the revelation moves has to do with a single representative encounter of hardly more than two decades, a decisive encounter, with pagan idolatry. It happens against a long background of patriarchal precedent. But it ensues in a sharp, politico-religious drama, ranging truth against falsehood in climactic terms. There are internal problems of chronology inside that drama or, rather, in relating to its sequence the pages and paragraphs of the Quranic text. Some of these are faced in Chapter 7 below. But of chronology in the inclusive sense of location in time there is no doubt.

Nor is there of location in territory. The *sitz im leben* of the Islamic Scripture yields its metaphors and suggests its parables. Chapters 5 and 6 are concerned with the imagery of the Qur'ān in both its nomadic and its urban, its desert and its mercantile, environments and of the caravans that link them. But, further to these literary consequences, we take the date and place of the event to justify a deliberate decision here to concentrate on the pagan arena of Muḥammad's mission. Since it is fundamental to the whole scope and logic of this work, this proposal deserves careful statement. It involves disengaging Islam in its Quranic sequence throughout the Prophet's life from the encounter with the Jews and Christians.

It is incontestable that his supreme purpose was to terminate idolatry and establish the sole worship of God, acknowledged as God alone. Islam was the faith about God to end gods. It was the revelation to finalize revelation. It was the call, in rugged simplicity, to let God be God. This could only be by letting Islam be Islam, which meant, in turn, allowing that the Prophet be the Prophet. The three demands, unity, community and prophethood, were mutual and inseparable.

In all their aspects they engaged Islam in relationship—both positive, even dependent, and controversial—with the earlier monotheisms, namely Judaism and Christianity. To these 'people of (their) book', as we must argue in Chapter 3, Muḥammad owed the prototype and the incentive of 'a Scripture for the unscriptured', a book for the Arabs. On this count alone, it is impossible to detach the event of the

Qur'ān from a Jewish-Christian matrix or ultimately to exclude the attendant controversies from its significance. Muḥammad's personal history certainly unfolded, both before and after his initial call, in a constant relation to Jewish and Christian beliefs and people—a conviction not affected in itself by how the many puzzling questions are resolved that have to do with the distribution of these faiths, and the shape, duration and quality of his contacts with them. In its origins and development, Islam was profoundly affected by the presence, the example, and the provocation of the antecedent Semitic religions. Many interior patterns and decisions seem to have turned upon aspirations towards, disappointments from, and tensions with, the 'other theists'. The consequences are evident both in doctrines and institutions.

Nevertheless, our present intention, without ignoring and in no way reducing these involvements, is to isolate the pagan direction of Muḥammad's calling and of the Qur'ān. We propose to study the iconoclasm and the 'education' into Islam which transformed a heathen Arab society of the seventh century into the first generation of Muslims. By every criterion this was the preponderant realm of action, whether we assess by numbers, by effectiveness or by finality. It is the contra-pagan theme which is central to all else. By this Islam was made Islam, in its own newness, its own momentum and its independence. In a sense even the inter-theistic issues—straining our terminology—were part of this fundamental Islamic mission. There exists no explicit Quranic controversy with the earlier faiths which is not implicit in the main contention between Muḥammad and his pagan Arab context. It was undoubtedly this which fashioned his supreme vocational dilemma by dint of its Meccan persecution of his word and person. It was this which required the *Hijrah*. It was this which was at stake in the conflict with Mecca and its capitulation. The events which are pivotal in the Qur'ān are those that relate to the struggle with idolatry. Others, however vital, are only contributory.

There is, furthermore, a better hope of focus on the ruling terms and concepts of the book if exploring them can be relieved of the antagonisms incurred *vis-à-vis* the Biblical communities. These have too long monopolized attention or diverted it from the kindred objectives evident when the Qur'ān is primarily seen as a mission to retrieve idolaters for a true worship. Our silence here on Old and New Testament matters, except as they arise within the other priority, is, therefore, no improper silence and certainly no tactical one. It will be found in the end to relate Islam more vitally and positively to Biblical concerns. It is simply a consistent intention for an open, historical awareness of Islam. We are reaching for the sense of an event, not the springs of a polemic.

All that follows, then, is based on the view that the crux of things Quranic lies in the confrontation by Muḥammad of the world of the Quraish, the custodians of the city of his birth with its shrine and pilgrimage. This was the human constituency of his public mission through its decisive years. It was the scene of the double battle for recognition of prophetic status and divine word. As the encounter deepened in the setting of hostility it grew into the very argument of divine Lordship with the obdurate world. Muḥammad's experience—one could say his personality—was itself the ground where vocation wrestled with society for a due hearing on behalf of God. The personal conviction of instrumentality from God became one with a struggle for the right acknowledgement of the divine Name. The Qur'ān is the document, almost in a sense the sacrament, of both aspects in their unity—God and His messenger. The living context is Arabian paganism, where the prophetic duty must be done, in order that the undivided Lordship may prevail and so *islām* come to pass.

By this deliberate focus on the Qur'ān in its time and place we no doubt incur a suspicion which it will be well to discount in advance. It is that a firm emphasis on seventh-century actuality, as the book reveals it, implies some intended consignment of the Scripture to that distant past. Nothing in fact is further from the mind of these pages. The deep relevance of the Qur'ān to contemporary man is the more eloquent for being rooted in contemporary realities as they were to the Prophet. Our purpose is to take the measure, in its own context, of a phenomenon which bears urgently upon our own age but which can only address us in the authenticity of its original quality.

This conviction has therefore to counter resolutely all pleas, however pious in their inspiration, to have the Qur'ān timeless in an arbitrary sort of way. There have long been those who interpreted the Qur'ān's authority and status as somehow absolving it from historical conditions, who have even cited its traditional non-chronological arrangement in their support. As the eternal and final revelation the Scripture is, no doubt, in history. But once in, by divine decree, it disengages from mere time and possesses a kind of absolute, historically unconditioned, quality which makes a sense of its context superfluous.

Such assumptions, of course, jeopardize—indeed disqualify—the whole possibility of revelation itself. As we must note in detail in Chapter 7, they also imply an entire misguidedness in the whole instinct of Tradition to draw guidance from the time and place of Muḥammad. They also overlook or mistake the role of the context of revelation in its very content and the place of 'the occasions of *tanzīl*', or the points in the story at which *waḥy* interposed its message. For inspiration was not seldom an actual commentary on a situation or a response to an interrogative latent or articulate in events of the prophetic biography. The Qur'ān could not have been revelatory had it not been also 'eventful'. As itself a total event within events its study, like its quality, must live in history.

If it be asked, then, why, in the light of this, Muslim devotion has been so often tempted to exempt it from historical circumstance, the answer has undoubtedly to do with a legitimate religious anxiety—the anxiety that cares for the due 'eternity' of the Qur'ān. The wish to abstract it from the temporal order, or, rather, to have it within that order in unconditioned terms, was part of a fear for its abiding relevance. This fear is groundless. The significance of the Qur'ān is sure enough and abides beyond such nervous and mistaken defence. Indeed, defence in these terms proves in fact embarrassment. There is no need for the devout and orthodox mind to say within itself: 'In that time means only to that time.' Such may be perhaps the intention of some impatient ill-wishers, ready enough to relegate the Qur'ān to a sort of antiquarian realm of mere historical study. But these discredit themselves by their insensitivity and should not enjoy the kind of orthodox timidity which can play into their hands. To be firmly in the seventh century is not to exclude the Qur'ān from the twentieth. Rather it is to plant it there more intelligently. Historical and contextual study of the temper we intend in these chapters is calculated to have the book in its proper historical perspective *and* its abiding spiritual authority and to have it more powerfully so by refusing any separation however motivated, whether by academic historians or assertive dogmatists. Some effort will be made in the Conclusion to illustrate the substance of this belief.

'The Event of the Qur'ān' as a title has yet another broad consideration in view. It is the attempt to see the Qur'ān, as it were, in its own mirror. The chapters that follow stay very closely with the text itself and are not conceived as an essay in studies bearing on the Scripture from outside. These have their urgent place in Quranic scholarship and some of their results are incorporated in the argument. There are many fascinating issues that still await exploration as research develops. But the intention here has been to reflect on the book within itself and assemble its own implications about the nature of what happened in its genesis as a religious experience and in its battle for the realization in moral and religious community of the goals which it proclaimed. We are not, therefore, embarking on a commentary in the general sense of the term. We are aiming rather to inhabit a situation, to think within the elements, reviewed in the first four chapters, which constituted the inner prophetic event, and thence, via the landscape and the urban world in Chapters 5 and 6, to the corporate event by which Islam, in the Prophet's care of word and nurture and leadership, made its way in the penetration and persuasion of the pagan setting. This involves us in the pivot of the *Hijrah*, or great migration from Mecca to Medina. It means also an education and a discipline, studied in Chapters 9 and 10, turning on the sense of words and the progress of religion within the texture of customary society and the strife of vested interests. To speak in this context of 'the struggle to mean', does not argue any intentional compromise of the authority of the revelation, but rather to see it proceeding within the fabric of the real world. It may be possible here to see from a new and illuminating angle some of the persistent semantic problems of the Quranic text. To ask what the Prophet's hearers took him to mean is surely the right the way to measure the task implicit in what it was given him to mean and so to appreciate the tension existing between the two. Thoughts in this sphere may further help to raise, if not to clarify, the central issue of all revelation, namely the relation of language to truth. The Arabic of the Qur'ān, as we note in Chapter 2, was with a view to Arabs' understanding—a simple enough fact but one that more subtle conjectures have often overlooked. Traditional Quranic theory, or dogma, has long insisted that revelation must needs dictate language in bestowing truth. This conviction has determined the interpretation of prophetic experience and, with a kindred sort of 'dictation', decided the conceptions of verbally authoritative, even untranslatable, Scriptures. But the question persists whether such ideas of how meaning relates to words, and truth to its utterance, do not in fact omit the human element on the hearing end, whether they do not make a situation dual only, which is in fact triangular. There are not simply meanings and words: there are meanings and words and people. There is not only content and form: there is content and form and audience. If we are discussing revelation, not soliloquy, apostolate among men and not simply audition from heaven—as we certainly are in the Qur'ān—then the collective human hearing imposes its own necessities of awareness and interpretation. Even if we can imagine the spokesman inspired in the complete verbal form of his message, the inspiration, understood as so effectuated, does not extend to the hearing world. Its verbal terms, therefore, at that point, must operate, must connote and circulate, within the apprehensions the audience can bring them.

To keep this triangular situation always in mind—meaning, speech and hearing—serves to have the prophetic role in its full dimension as a communication to men as well as recipience from God. It may also serve to deepen the categories with which we understand this recipience itself. Does the human locus of the revelation become active only when he turns to his community of discourse, having been passive in the heavenly commissioning? Will it not be sounder to understand a parallel quality of active mind and spirit in both directions of his medial position between the eternal and the temporal, between the word given and the word declared? If so, shall we not be in the way towards a much truer, not to say more vital and liberating, concept of the prophetic reality and of the Qur'ān as its eventuation? If so, the eternity of what on earth we must speak of as 'eventuation' is not compromised or betrayed. On the contrary, it is more radically acknowledged. For revelation, *ex hypothesi*, is most fully affirmed as real when it is known to be received. Such receiving was its very purpose. There is no prophecy, honoured or otherwise, without a country of the mind. Muḥammad's country had its character. It was there the Qur'ān was heard.

But in a profound way it also made a homeland of the heart that has endured these fourteen centuries. So there devolves upon the modern reader outside Islam the question whether it can be really understood, or even rightly studied, beyond the frontiers of that resulting world. To face this issue is the remaining business of this Introduction. It is our duty to state the terms in which we see the Qur'ān belonging validly beyond the borders of the Muslim community of faith. Can it be properly read and pondered without commitment to Islam as its institutional consequence and meaning? Is it duly handled by external readers whose concern is with academic enquiry or with the broad religious heritage of man and the scriptures of history?

Certainly the Qur'ān did not, and does not, exist in order to be 'interesting'. It was, and is, a living summons asking a personal response and requiring a corporate participation. The first obligation of any study is to be commensurate with that situation. The Qur'ān can never be authentically known in neglect of the sensitivities, the emotions, the spiritual property in it, of Muslims. There have been pursuits of western scholarship unhappily careless of these courtesies. For all their admirable erudition and equipment of criticism, they have nevertheless disserved their own cause by failing to reckon with the human responsibilities of the clash of culture and of thought in which they were involved. A scholarship that exempts itself from the patient toils of due relationships is liable to forfeit in real intellectual achievement what it may attempt in bare analysis. Our hope, in these pages, is more specifically 'religious', using the term in no restrictive sense. It is to seek the event of the Qur'ān with a steady awareness of centuries of devotion, of personal existence and collective possession, gathering around it through the long generations of Islam. For the Qur'ān as event in the seventh century has become an unbroken history of patient, jealous, tenacious recollection and religious existence. As such it is a document of faith looking for a faith to receive it. The scholar must be alive to it as such. Its nature must come within his strictly academic reckonings if these are not to be finally inappropriate. To enquire genuinely into the Qur'ān is to live with the life of Islam.

Or should we rather say it is to feel with it? The belief of these chapters is that the Qur'ān is truly open to more than its formal community of institutional allegiance. Given the quality of sympathy that keeps them always in mind, there may well be a capacity of penetration that is the better for its being the outsider's search. Muslim possessiveness of the book has developed attitudes and skills which have in part obscured and impeded its fullest relevance. The history of classical exegesis shows many arts and subtleties which, though admirable in their pains, are wanting in perspective and imagination.

This is not the place to venture even the briefest characterization of an intricate and tedious subject. Rather, the idea of seeking out the event of the Qur'ān is precisely to cut through a mass of extraneous material gathered in its margins. This is a situation readily reproduced in quite other religious traditions. Like these, the Qur'ān cannot well be left as a world private to its customary possessors alone. To live with these open-mindedly is at the same time to reserve a freedom of thought and of criticism which, in the broad context of contemporary religious relationship, will be the truest form of recognition and of faith.

Such an aim, taking the Qur'ān in its own seriousness and with respect for, and yet independence of, its own faith-system, suffices to cover in a practical way the vexed question of authority. Orthodox Islam, of course, requires an intellectual assent to the doctrine of *tanzīl* as a true miracle of divine initiative bestowing both meaning and word upon a recipient having them wholly from without by virtue of such bestowal. Therein lies the established doctrine of the 'illiterate prophet' and the otherwise total inaccountability of the Qur'ān, in that it could not have been but by such intervening action—an action dispensing, for better attestation of itself, with all co-operating circumstances of mind or of environment.

This understanding, which still dominates the theology of Quranic commentary, has long deterred the minds of non-Muslim students of the Scripture. It seems to point to a fundamentalism that misses, even depreciates, the personal genius of Muḥammad, and to involve by the same token a misconception of the ways of the divine spirit with the human psyche. The reverent reader, therefore, asks himself whether he may not well come to terms with it as embodying, not the essence of the phenomenon itself, but the form of the Muslim security in the sense of that phenomenon, and in the trust of its meaning. It is not seldom that faith erects a dogma where it would better hold a confidence. The *I'jāz* of the Qur'ān, its miraculous quality, is then the form by which Muslim conviction possesses its relevance. The outsider then can take it pragmatically in this way without holding it credally. In doing so he will differ from, and with, orthodoxy, but only about the form in which orthodoxy receives the significance he aims to share and, indeed, to revere.

In stating himself this way the outsider will no doubt alarm or dismay the doctrinaire mind. For the latter does not always take comfortably to the distinction we are making between the reality in his belief and the shape of his security in it. Yet the distinction serves to obviate both an impatient, external dismissal of the mystery of the Qur'ān and a mutual alienation of sympathy and spiritual converse. A reverent religious study of the Qur'ān becomes possible, which allows the Muslim still to safeguard the doctrinal formulation of what the book is to him and to his, and to do so as long as he wills. But it also allows the non-Muslim to come adequately to the same Scripture, in concern for what lies within that formulation, yet unimpeded by its embarrassment to his integrity.

It may be held, as it is in Islam, that divine revelation is more truly, more credibly, divine by its being independent essentially of human partnership, that—to phrase a simple formula—the more a thing is God's the less it is man's. It may also be held that, on the contrary, the more emphatically it is God's the more fully, vitally and energetically it is man's. But this debate about the incidence of revelation and of prophecy need not of itself preclude a common openness to their content and their summons. A care for the Qur'ān, as that which happened, can be separated from dogma about its occurrence, at least until the sense of the event no longer needs the protection of the dogma in its rigorous form.

That time may be still distant in some segments of Muslim thinking. In others it may be near at hand. Even in medieval Islamic thought there was a steady, if intermittent, emphasis on the superlative role of the human Muḥammad and indeed on prophecy in general as coinciding with human excellence and capacity of mind. Revelation, by these criteria, is a supreme occasion of intelligence and wisdom, always of course instrumentally to the divine initiative but yet eminently at work themselves. Much mystical veneration of Muḥammad points in the same direction. His 'ordinariness', in the classic doctrine of his role, can, therefore, be understood as the emphasis of a faith assuring itself, by that means, of the suprahuman origin and authority of that on which it vitally relies. So the Muslim's Qur'ān can be the non-Muslim's with a difference that divides their standpoints but need not debar a unity of attention.

Perhaps in certain circumstances, to which both must contribute, that attention can be co-operative. There are urgent reasons in the common world of today why it should be so. What happens in the Qur'ān, as these pages hope to indicate by exploring it, is deeply related to the travail of our time, and we need the Quranic word in face of it. This would be true, of course, if only for the reason that multitudes of mankind, to be guided or persuaded about modernity at all, will need to be guided and persuaded Quranically. And they are peoples and nations close to some of the most desperate and pressing problems of the human family, having to do with peace and war, with nationhood and minorities, with justice and compassion, with population and development. Even where secularity has gone far among them or irreligion presses, their judgements and their sanity, their priorities and ideals, will always be in large measure within the mind of the Qur'ān whether for definition or for impulse and will.

But that practical, domestic role of the Qur'ān in the direction of its immediate community does not exhaust its relevance. Muḥammad has to be seen to be at the heart of seventh-century forms of human argument and destiny which belong insistently with this one. Muslims are no exception to the fascination of numbers and have traditionally thought of renewal with the turn of the centuries. They are now in the last decade of the fourteenth in the sequence since the *Hijrah*. However the sects or the custodians or the poets celebrate or anticipate the incidence of the spirit and the calendar, there can be no doubt where their mutual bearing lies. Some will doubtless cry for a more determined conservation of the old, a more insistently rigorous loyalty to dogma and the past. Others may urge as the old century runs out their own versions of adaptability and *ijtihād*. New Iqbāls may arise to castigate the decadent and the moribund in Islamic society, identifying either by criteria of their own devising. There will be health and adventure as well as timidity and impatience in the debate. The five pillars of religion and the great sources of the *Sharī'ah* will all be diversely involved. Continuity will be in living encounter with change and conservation with circumstance.

Yet, through all these themes proper to Islam and intimate to Muslims, there abides the ultimate and universal business of man, his meaning as man, the sanction of his institutions and the shape of his obligation in history, the mystery of his personal existence and the struggle to worship aright. It was these which, in the end, the event of the Qur'ān raised and registered with its own quality of drama and decision. To these the perceptive reader returns as the needle to its north. They lie within, and yet in their authority also beyond, the more familiar concerns of commentary and tradition. Chapter 11 below, with its effort after the immediate Quranic sense of history, forms a prelude to a purpose, in the Conclusion, to think them over afresh.

In the immediate world of the Ḥijāz and beyond, the impact of the Qur'ān consisted in a paradox close to the heart of all human history. It moved with an assured militancy of spirit sustained by steadfast belief in the consummating 'peace' of truth. Thus it brought into illuminating focus the whole issue of power in the service of faith. It was an insistent iconoclasm. Yet it eloquently conserved that sense of the wonder of the natural order which inspires all paganism and told it in 'the signs of God', as the grateful benediction of the divine unity through the plural world. It was a solitary prophethood in the utter singularity of the one apostle. Yet it kindled a phenomenal corporateness of conviction and shaped a whole new achievement of culture and society. From its rigorous confinement of time and of territory it emerged into a large destiny.

Taking thus into itself so many of the themes of history it becomes itself in turn a trial of their meaning and a drama of their making. We come, then, to the Qur'ān for the answers it exemplifies and enjoins. But we come also for the questions it discloses in deciding them. And we do so the better for the forthrightness of the Qur'ānic situation. Not here do 'the currents turn awry and lose the name of action'. In the event all is vigorous, robust and confident. The tasks of reflective thought are, therefore, the more clear and the more cogently defined. How does worship rightly displace idolatry? What do we mean by God over men and men under God and how is the meaning symbolized in religion and expressed in institutions? Are there limits to the competence of power in the care of truth? What, in the end, is politics under God? In what terms is human history amenable to the divine will?

It is finally in these realms that the Qur'ān happens. These are its eventfulness.

Chapter 1
THE VOICE SAID: 'CRY!'

After I had seen
That spectacle, for many days my brain
Worked with a dim and undetermined sense
Of unknown modes of being: o'er my thoughts
There hung a darkness, call it solitude . . .
But huge and mighty forms, that do not live
Like living men, moved slowly through the mind
By day, and were a trouble to my dreams.[1]

The hills of Wordsworth's 'Prelude' are as far removed from the mountains of Mecca as the poem from the Scripture of Islam. To suggest a parallel is not in mind. For it would be anathema to every loyal Muslim and dubious even to a casual observer. Yet the very instinct that rejects it stands to gain from the provocation, if only in coming vividly to the human reality of that which, otherwise, is so readily abstracted into the prose of historians and contracted into the terms of dogma. There is no doubt that Muḥammad knew the troubled dream and the overwhelming vision, that he lived by day and night with the solitude of 'huge and mighty forms'.

This is none other than a revelation revealed.
One of awesome might has taught him,
One endued with strength. Standing there
He was, away on the horizon;
Then he drew near, hovering down,
Two bows lengths away, nearer still,
And what He revealed to His servant He revealed.
The heart does not lie: he saw.
Are you disputing with him, with him who saw?

[1] William Wordsworth, 'The Prelude', i, 390 ff.

Here, in the most descriptive of passages, is the genesis of the Qur'ān (Surah 53: 4–12). It confronts us with the questions: What happened for Muḥammad? What happened in him? What was the experience by which he discovered, first, and then followed, the conviction of prophethood? Whence this solitary figure for whom 'the Power'

> . . . rose from the mind's abyss
> Like an unfathomed vapour that enwraps
> At once some lonely traveller.[1]

'Enwrapped' he was—we shall return to the Qur'ān's use of the word—out of the streets and shrines of Mecca and into the hills that stand in austere severity, with their sharp ravines and contours, around the suburbs of the Ḥijāzī capital. By virtue of what had he become a 'lonely traveller', ripe for that encounter?

These are the concerns that occupy this chapter. It has to do with the inner imperative of Islam, isolated, as far as is practicable, from the themes of Chapters 2 and 3, which relate to the Scripture as 'literature' and as 'leadership', and from the final, theological enquiry of Chapter 4. All these, in their unity, are the event of the Qur'ān. But it lives in what we may here call the event of Muḥammad. We are in search of the original meaning of prophetic *charisma*, before we move to its activity in word, in rule and in doctrine. What, if we may use the phrase, was the personal dimension of the Qur'ān, the relation—which Wordsworth may have helped us to reach for—between the event in the spirit and the event of the text?

The search begins and ends in the imperative. Hence the decision to borrow the familiar words of Isaiah 40: 6, from their different context: 'The voice said "Cry!".' The impulse that made the vocation made the utterance. Contemplation may have preceded it. But it was not a call to contemplate. Reflection may have aroused it. But it was not an invitation to reflect.

> Recite: in the Name of your Lord who created.

'Recite', 'rehearse', 'speak out' —*Iqra'* is the decisive word at the beginning of Surah 96, to which—even beyond Surah 53—all Quranic study traditionally turns as to the inaugural moment itself. The word is the active imperative singular, of the root *qar'a*, from which, as

[1] William Wordsworth, 'The Prelude', vi, 594–6

verbal noun, the word *qur'ān* derives. It could almost mean 'Quranize', if we are careful to clarify what 'Quranicity 'is. As 'read' is to 'reading', so *iqrā'* is to *Qur'ān*. It is akin to the Aramaic *Qeryāna* and the Latin *lectio* and so to the English 'lesson'. If Surah 96 does not mark, in fact, the point of origin of the contents of the Qur'ān, it certainly symbolizes the authority that in one act initiates both the personal prophethood and the actual Scripture.

> Recite: in the Name of your Lord who created,
> Created man from blood-mated.
> Recite: your Lord is most kindly,
> Who taught by the pen,
> Taught what men did not ken.[1]

What, in Muḥammad's consciousness, were the sources of that summons? How can they be elucidated, not in conflict or competition with traditional orthodoxy about celestial visitation, but in a patient attempt to understand the phenomenon to which that doctrine means to point. The Islamic faith about Muḥammad is not properly foreclosed, in sheer arbitrariness, to all that history, biography, psychology, may bring to the interpretation of its confidence, provided only that all such enquiry keeps faith with that faith in its own reverence and honesty.

There are, to assist the answer, many deeply biographical passages and hints in the Qur'ān itself. These must yield the material for such conclusions as may justify themselves. The Islamic Scripture, of course, is nowhere autobiographical. This is one of its sharpest points of contrast with psalmists and prophets in the Old Testament, who conversed boldly with God about their travail and perplexity. Such autobiography is quite inconsistent with Quranic views, where the divine address must be awaited, as it were, in personal 'neutrality'. Yet 'neutrality' in any final sense is impossible, if there is to be revelation. For revelation, *ex hypothesi*, is inconceivable in a total abeyance of receptivity. Nor is such abeyance itself possible in life and history.

[1] The three double, and two pairs of terminal, rhymes here are difficult to render. *'Alaq*, 'blood clot', means the early embryo in the womb. 'Blood-mated' seems a right poetic translation, since 'blood' is a synonym for birth and embryos result from intercourse and conception. The search for English rhyme, as in 'pen' and 'ken', is awkward. It is possible, too, that *'alaq* intends the origin of archetypal man *ex nihilo*, rather than the mystery of procreation, in which, however, the Qur'ān in many other passages is deeply interested.

The broad biographical context of the Qur'ān is the business of Chapter 7. Here we have to do with backgrounds and origins. It is important to ponder Muḥammad's vision and vocation of Surahs 96 and 53 and other passages, by starting with his birth. Muslim piety has done this in its own way. The man who stood in the mouth of the cave on Mount Ḥirā' had been an orphan within the 'Abd Manāf branch of 'the sacred family' of *Ka'bah* custodianship in Mecca. He had been a posthumous child and his mother died in his early childhood. 'Did We not find you an orphan and shelter you?' asks 93:6. The fact was a main element in his reassurance in a time of disquiet.

It was more. It lies, we may conjecture, within the whole sense of destiny and, perhaps, within the mysterious sources of prophetic yearning. The reason is not simply the marked solicitude of the Qur'ān for orphans (who are mentioned some twenty-three times), but the deep, dismaying, yet fortifying, sense that he might so easily have never been. 'Peace upon me the day of my birth', the Qur'ān has Jesus saying, and there is an identical phrase in the third person about John, son of Zachariah (19:15 and 33). Precarious circumstances make the same phrase fitting at Muḥammad's birth. Never to have known a father is to know that death failed only by a few short months to veto one's own existence. There is a haunting mystery for the sensitive in the near miscarriage, not of birth, but of conception, in the realization that, in the Qur'ān's vivid phrase, a father only just survived to 'spill the seed'.

The question might more readily be ignored were the Qur'ān not so intensely alive to the wonder of procreation, which it notes repeatedly as one of the awesome 'signs of God' (cf. 23:12–14; 40:67; 77:20–2; 86:5–7, *et al.*), and which recurs, notably, in the words of the *Iqrā'* command itself. Was there at the heart of Muḥammad's sense of himself this dimension of preciousness in existence, of what had come to pass awed by what might not have come to pass, had his father died too soon. To penetrate further into the psychology of orphanhood would carry us into fields of speculation from which it is wise to refrain. But it would not be strange if the genesis of the prophetic *charisma* we are pondering lay in the deep regions of those first crises of circumstance.

Further, the problem throughout is to know how far we can rightly read the present by the future, how far events in their unfolding shaped the personality at their centre and how far they simply disclosed and achieved an innate force of character and purpose. Even careful reservations here, however, if we suppose them to be necessary, cannot doubt the absolute centrality to Muḥammad's mission and personality of Mecca, its sacred house and its custodian family. His intimate emotions were wholly engaged in the complex of family traditions and discords around the shrine in the days of his youth. Despite the city's prosperity, there was an essential precariousness about its economy which may well have obsessed his mind. For there were contradictions at its core, which hinged on the idolatry it became his vocation to destroy.

Only a fraction of Mecca's inhabitants lived, or ever could live, off its own terrain. Its fortunes were finally hostage to the tribes around the caravan routes. These, it is true, sustained a flourishing web of trade and finance, the setting of which concerns Chapters 5 and 6. But their vulnerability to restless peoples on their flanks demanded constant vigilance and the wielding of prestige. Months of truce were not wholly adequate against the endless feuding and attempts had been made in the decades before Islam to reduce the incidence of blood revenge for the better securing of the vital commerce.

But these were only palliatives that left the real menace unidentified. For the whole system, both of the city's wealth and of its social scheme, turned upon tribal worships and pagan pilgrimage. Could months of truce ever give way to permanent security as long as the confusions of idolatry persisted? Was Mecca's very status built upon a negation of well-being? Could the idols be lifted from the backs of men without destroying its economy? Could they be retained without degrading their custodians? Was there a basic contradiction between the city's standing and the human meaning? Were these the inner tumults of mind which drove Muḥammad, as a scion of the custodian family, itself divided, into the caves and hills where its destinies lay bare to view? Surah 39: 29, a Meccan Surah, has a striking 'similitude' of a slave who is owned by many masters at odds among themselves. How different from the man devoted to a single master! If the picture did not originate in Mecca early, it seems to mirror what Mecca's situation meant religiously.

These economic areas in the hinterland of vocation merge into factors less readily defined but more deeply causal. They have to do with the movement of Muḥammad's mind towards the claims of divine unity in their positive pressure. This movement, of course, cannot be isolated from the impact of the antecedent monotheisms, though in its issue, as we must study in Chapter 3, it required to be independent of them. It was in the idea and the ideal of Scriptures, and of being Scriptuaries, that the main relevance of the Judeo-Christian communities to Muḥammad's mission belongs. Seeing that mission, here, as an apostolate to pagans in the call of the unity of God, we do not attempt to penetrate the many conjectures and questions that attach to the Jewish/Christian bearings of original Islam. Furthermore, there would appear to be less ground than scholars formerly assumed for any clear reliance on *Ḥanafiyyah* as a precursor of Islam.[1] What is here important in these monotheistic influences, postponing doctrinal discussion until Chapter 4, is the seminal idea of prophets in personal impact on their peoples, of 'warners' and 'apostles', staking divine claims within particular communities and their words, cited, recited and perpetuated, making God real in terms of demand and reply.

Those intimations of the prophetic however, could only be read from within the cultic preoccupations of the Quraish and the *Ka'bah.* Muḥammad could only know and feel them within the purview of the administrative functions, the ritual privilege and custodianship of the family from which his line came. To the Hāshim branch of 'Abd Manāf appertained the 'watering of the pilgrims'. In a late Surah at Medina comes the question: 'Do you make the watering of the pilgrims and holding the sacred mosque the same as believing in God and the last day and exerting in the way of God?' (9: 19). Late as it is, the query may be transposed without strain to the earlier context, if we render it back from the categorical into the conjectural, from the prophetic authority in its full tide to the prophetic awakening in its first stirrings. It was surely not only, or first, in war and politics that Muḥammad knew Abū Safyān[2] as the symbol of what he must question and subdue.

[1] The term *ḥanīf* is applied to Abraham as a *muslim* before Islam and *ḥanafiyyah* may well have been a term for Muḥammad's faith before Islam became the current word. But it is difficult to identify with certainty before Muḥammad any effective activity that could be denoted by this term in the later Islamic sense.

On the general theme see R. Bell, *The Origin of Islam in its Christian Environment*, London, 1926; C. C. Torrey, *Jewish Foundation of Islam*, New Haven, 1933; and G. Ryckmans, *Les Religions Pre-Islamiques*, Bibliothèque du Museon, xxvi, 2nd ed., Louvain, 1951.

[2] The question in the text is linked historically with the termination of pagan custody of the *Ka'bah* after its conquest. It is preceded by the famous Immunity decree of AH 9/10 which gave notice of the cessation of pagan pilgrimage altogether. 'Exerting in the way of God' is the traditional phrase for the military *Jihād*, but we need not confine the force of the indictment of Mecca's religion to that form or point.

Mecca's religion as unworthy and prophetic 'reminder' as divinely aroused seemed ripe for rendezvous. But—in whose soul?

Such, it may be claimed, were the factors in the heart that brought Muḥammad into the search which both ended and began in Surah 96, which drew him into isolation and solitude, away from the city's clamour into the gaunt perimeter of hills and caves around it. And night was their most proper hour. Though, as the sober Al-Suyūṭī is careful to note, it was by day that the Qur'ān was mostly given,[1] the early Surahs are intensely at home with night and the stars and the break of dawn. For they conspired with the will to silence and withdrawal. One might call Henry Vaughan to register their mood.

> Dear night, this world's defeat,
> The stop to busie fools: care's check and curb,
> The day of spirits: my soul's calm retreat
> Which none disturb . . .
> His knocking time, my soul's dumb watch,
> When spirits their fair kindred catch;
> Whose peace but by some angel's wing or voice
> Is seldom rent.[2]

Thus Surah 97, with the title of 'Authority' (*Qadr*), celebrates the 'night 'of Muḥammad's vision and commission, either symbolically fusing into one a series of experiences broken by interludes, or describing a single one of them (perhaps that of Surah 96) in token of them all.

> Truly we revealed the Qur'ān on the night of authority.
> Would that you knew what the night of authority means!
> Better than a thousand months is the night of authority.
> Thereon come the angels and the Spirit down
> By leave of their Lord, for every behest.
> It is a night of peace till the breaking of the day.

The ruling term *Qadr* here, for all the conjectures of commentators as to fate and decrees, means essentially the *imprimatur*, the authentic word, the declaration of the revelatory divine will, what God speaks.[3]

[1] *Al-Itqān fī 'Ulūm al-Qur'ān*, vol. 1, Cairo, 1941, p. 34.
[2] Henry Vaughan, *Silex Scintillans and Sacred Poems*
[3] On the range of the meaning of *Qadr* see, further, Ch. 9 below.

It is better in its single quality than all a thousand months could hold, eluding the full apprehension even of the recipient himself, yet indubitable to his conviction and urging him forth in the dawn to invoke the day: 'By the sun and the morning radiance. . .' (91: 1).

What are we to understand of this 'dumb watch' of night, with its compulsive awareness of the command to speak? What is the unpremeditated experience in the setting of the meditative search?

> By the darkening night,
> By the breathing dawn,
> It was truly the word of a noble messenger,
> Of one whose power is with the Lord of the throne,
> Obeyed and sure.
> Your comrade is not deluded:
> He saw him truly on the clear horizon.
> He does not scant the unseen. (81: 17—24)

Night—for watching, and watching out of questioning, and questioning out of yearning, and yearning out of all the personal past that Mecca shaped, and from all these a crisis, distinct but indivisible, in the self and in the whole. We cannot escape the personal equation. All that happened, happened as a conviction about himself as thus commissioned. Yet it had to do with what reduced the self to a bare agent of the eternal contention of God with the city and its world. The movement of Muḥammad towards vocation was, by the same token, a movement towards identity, just as the subsequent travail for a hearing became a struggle for recognition.

The impetus of the experience was towards a Scripture. The poetic and the 'national' within it we defer to subsequent chapters. Muḥammad at once understood the commission as relating to words already 'with God', and requiring to be 'recited' among men. Their presence in his mind and mouth linked him, and ranked him, with the historic prophets. His acceptance became integral to theirs. The messenger was in the message, inasmuch as the message was by the messenger. 'God and His apostle' became the due formula of the single Quranic fact.

This emerging theme of the theme, the crier in the 'cry', is continuous with the personal measure of the issues which it satisfied. Before responding to apostolate, Muḥammad had already become the inward focus of the public needs it answered, of the spiritual situation it addressed. To penetrate and portray this truth is perhaps the most difficult of all imaginative tasks in Quranic study. In the movement of Muḥammad's self-consciousness in the stresses of his people and his place, we measure also the momentum of his self-consciousness in the conviction of prophethood. The two are one progression. The need for the prophecy and the need to be the prophet converge into one. The unique status is the answer to the common situation. It is not pretentious and presumptive vocation that forces itself upon unrelated circumstance. Nor is it circumstance that provokes an opportunist answer. It is that the travail aroused by the Meccan context, in the manner of man Muḥammad was, became a responsive conviction of apostolate within the one and for the other.

In 'the enwrapped', 'the enmantled', figure of Surahs 73 and 74 we may see the image of this double fact. These two Chapters, though using different words, begin with address to Muḥammad as 'cloaked' or 'clothed', and the mantle becomes a focus of significance, almost of 'investiture'.

> O you that are enwrapped, watch almost the night long,
> Or half the night, or thereabouts
> A fragment less or more.
> Recite the Qur'ān with due recital.
> We shall entrust to you profound words.[1]
> Truly in the watches of the night
> Impressions are weightiest
> And words most telling.
> By day you have pressing business.
> Remember the Name of your Lord,
> Devote yourself altogether to Him.
> He is the Lord of the east and of the west.
> There is no god save He,
> Take Him for your trust.
> What they say bear patiently
> And go out from among them courteously.
>
> (73: 1–10)
>
> You who are enveloped in your mantle,
> Arise and warn!
> Your Lord magnify, your garments purify,
> And shun defilement.
> Give not with a view to self-increase
> And to your Lord be your patience.
>
> (74: 1–7)

[1] Lit. 'a saying, a heavy'.

Quite literal meanings have been given to these 'mantle' verses—the nights were cold in Mount Ḥirā', or the sense of inspiration produced sweat and tremor, or Khadījah, the Prophet's wife, tended him thus in solicitude for his travail and perplexity, or Muḥammad enveloped himself in awe and fear at the sight of the vision. Or, taking the passages as establishing or explaining a tradition, Muḥammad was accustomed to mark Quranic incidence with this external gesture in order to symbolize its authority and impress upon his auditors the special nature of the times and moments of utterance. It is even possible that *muzzammil* in 73: 1 has a suggestion of one 'ostracized', or 'withdrawn' by his own will within his own tent, so that he refrains from participating in the society or the battles of his tribe. The salutation would then be a confirmation of that stance. Or, in Al-Baiḍāwī's simplest suggestion, it may simply be that Muḥammad was 'enwrapped' for sleep.

But, in the immediate context of these verses the words *al-muzzammil* and *al-muddaththir*, which occur nowhere else in the Qur'ān, would seem to deserve an interpretation more integral to the situation than any of these prosaic senses. Mantles, of course, since Elijah, have been a symbol of prophetic and, indeed, of priestly authority, and there are traditions of similar ideas in the soothsaying of Arabia. But these apart, there is nothing more intimately personal than attire and the sense of it to the wearer may be, under imaginable circumstances, a focal point of self-confrontation. What the night and its vigil were deliberatively, the robe and the calling may have been figuratively. Is the address to 'the enmantled' the explicit form of the stirring of awareness and commission, guaranteed, as it were, by this token, *in* its content and *to* its bearer? The context certainly has to do with watching and seclusion, with recollection and devotion, with entrustment and patience. All these may be seen as represented in a wearer wearing his identity, a personality invested with his meaning. The robes have to be purified if God is to be magnified.

Effort has been made in some quarters to invoke these passages as evidences of a practising mysticism as the clue to Muḥammad.[1] The enmantling would then be seen as a deliberate technique, calculated to induce the state of trance and illumination familiar in later Islamic mystics. The garment, in that event, has to be visualized, not as a robe

[1] Notably by John Clark Archer, *The Mystical Elements in Muhammad*, New Haven, 1924.

merely, but as a 'tent' thrown over the head, to serve the abatement of sense distraction and to concentrate the mind wholly on the themes of contemplation. We must then imagine the lonely figure, swathed and hooded in the darkness, achieving by this means something of the intense focus of mind which the yogi attains by immobility of will in the rejection of sense, or the dervish by rhythmic and ejaculatory prefaces to ecstacy.

In the absence of firmer evidence, it is impossible to substantiate this thesis from the Qur'ān. It may be attractive, retroactively, to certain strains of Islamic mysticism claiming Muḥammad as their prototype, to be honoured, not so much in audition, as in imitation. But it seems remote, by the same token, and with its Persian and Indian overtones, from the rugged native Semitic genius that speaks in the Qur'ān. Nor is it necessary to explain the ecstatic quality of Muḥammad's eloquence which has ample roots elsewhere. It might make superfluous the natural enveloping of the night and the tradition of the cave. For these bestow a seclusion no devices can improve. And it is hardly adequate, in the end, to the 'weighty' mission into which it is required to lead. Nor can the impetus to such conscious contrivance of ecstacy be convincingly derived from Muḥammad's Meccan environment. There are more sufficient explanations of the phenomenon already to hand in the factors we have pondered above. It is hazardous to try to make Muḥammad fit the type of self-conducing mystics whom it took historic Islam to develop over the centuries out of men and moods very different from those of the Ḥijāz.[1]

Inadequate and dubious as a theory, the 'mystical' hypothesis has, nevertheless, the merit of pointing vitally to the central reality of the self intensely aware of itself and so identified with a meaning beyond itself. 'O you who are enwrapped, keep tryst,' 'O you who are enmantled, arise . . . '—the two salutations are one self-discovery. Through all that follows this remains the central fact. It fuses into one the orphan child, the son of the Quraish, the brooder of Mecca, the watcher for the day, who came to it out of the past, with the man of word and of action, of struggle and of warfare, who went from it into the future. The watershed was, it is true, a sequence and not a single occasion. But once the recurrence of the Quranic state was assured,

[1] For evidence tending to a contrary view however, see D. B. MacDonald, *Religious Attitude and Life in Islam*, Chicago, 1909, pp. 33–40, where emphasis is laid on a trance condition physically explicable.

its momentum was then also secure. The victory over incredulity once inwardly won in himself, the prophetic status was set for its battle with incredulity around.

'Would that you knew the night of authority,' Surah 97: 2 exclaims. There, in the very texture of the experience, is the still uncomprehending emotion, the entire surprise, it first engendered. 'What conception', as we might translate, 'is yours concerning it?' But Muḥammad's gathering conviction necessarily transferred the question to the world (though the verb is singular), to the dubious, the casual or the ill-disposed around him. We are then on the threshold of a steady interplay between the deepening destiny of the one and the sharpening hostilities of the many. As the incidence of revelation was the more ensured in the receptivity of its instrument it was the more insistently at hand to challenge men. The resulting events in turn evoke and express the temper of the confrontation and write themselves into the contents of the Qur'ān. In all its vicissitudes the single thread is the unfolding of prophetic identity, shaping and being shaped as it proceeds.

The event of the Qur'ān within the personality of Muḥammad is much more, however, than a *locus* of issues between him and men. As such, it is the reckoning of the divine with the human through the Prophet. The spokesmanship on behalf of God which *waḥy* confers becomes a kind of touchstone of the divine will. In having to do with Muḥammad men have to do with God's representative. There is involved here, for orthodox Islam, no metaphysical or theosophical rank. The apostolate of Muḥammad, nevertheless, comes to be conjoined in practical terms with the divine purposes. In entrusting a message, the voice that said 'Cry!' bestowed also a supreme standing. It made, in Muslim belief, the final *Rasūl*, the revealing beyond which there is no other.

Here belongs the ultimate question, both for history and for religion, respecting the *charisma* of Muḥammad. His office was free of the pretentiousness that lives with surface things. It lived above the patterns of cheap arrogance or vulgar grandeur. Its instinct for authority moved in realms more terrifying and absolute than these. It meant nothing less than the delegated directives of God. There is no understanding the Qur'ān without taking the measure of this quality, whether it be with admiration or—by criteria outside Islam—with apprehension. There are times when it seems almost to usurp the sovereignty it serves. Its epitome is the recurring phrase: 'God and . . .', 'God and His apostle', God in close bracket with a messenger or, better, a messenger always bracketed with God.

There is a hint of it in a very early Surah within the long retrospect of the orphan passage (93). The adjacent Surah 94 reads: 'Did We not enlarge your heart and lighten you of your load, the load which weighed you down? And did We not exalt your fame?' (vv. 1–4). This 'renown' or 'celebration' of Muḥammad, in the role of the apostle, emerges in a later passage as the very chorus of heaven. 'God and His angels celebrate the Prophet,' says Surah 33: 56. 'O you who believe, call down blessings on him and salute him with peace.'

The sense here of God 'praying upon' Muḥammad (as a literal translation reads) is generally taken to denote a 'calling down of blessings upon him', a sort of celestial attestation of his task and person. The verse provides the formula *Ṣallā Allāhu 'alaihi wa sallam*, which devout Islam rehearses after every mention of his name or title. That devotion, aided by Ṣūfī instinct or theological speculation, has read the saying in terms of the divine delight in the essence of truth personified in Muḥammad, and Shī'ah Islam has developed from it the varied doctrines of emanation and the theory of the Imamate in 'the light of Muḥammad'. Our concern is with the biographical study of this 'renown', with its inwardness as Muḥammad's understanding of himself.

It has been easy, and often congenial, for external critics to dismiss it as plain obsession or denounce it as gross pretention. It has been equally easy and congenial for Islam to hail and cherish it as the manifest miracle only ill-will or damnability could question. History—and, indeed religion, to be worthy of its nature—must insist on sterner and deeper criteria than these. Here is simply the inescapable Muslim form of the pride and perjury of all religion, its inherent vocation to possess and serve the absolute, and its inevitable temptation to forget that the absolute is not itself. By the first, Muḥammad's sense of Muḥammad, his surrender to apostolate as the utter authorization of himself, his total assurance in *charisma*, are profound and compelling religious realities. By the second, they are urgent question marks against themselves.

The Qur'ān does not often broach this issue. It steadily associates enmity to Muḥammad with enmity to God, disobedience to Muḥammad as disobedience to God, recognition of Muḥammad with recognition of God. Belief in neither is valid without belief in both. Just as authentic monotheism is supposedly unique to Israel, by the canons of Judaism, so here the right monotheism is unique to Islam. The Qur'ān understands Muḥammad's political campaigns and purposes as synonymous with the divine ends and the vehicle of the divine power. There is about its confidence this awesome simplicity, this untroubled directness, this lack of the interrogative, this absence of the dimension of tragedy.

It is not that the sovereignty of God is ever in doubt, but that it is never in dilemma with its instrument. It is not that the instrumentality is ever in rebellion, but that it is so seldom in question. The divine is at once so uncomplicatedly omnipotent and the prophetic so assuredly available. What the external reader has always to do is to let the authority tell against the assumptions of it, to assess the *charisma* by its own original criteria. Or, in better words, it is to live always with the first question: 'How shall we know what the night of authority is?'

In this the Qur'ān itself comes to our aid. There is a passage of large relevance to these thoughts, with which we may best leave the theme of the Prophet in his *charisma* to await it, in other forms, in the three succeeding chapters. The final verses of Surah 28 (vv. 85–8) are generally believed to be close in date to the *Hijrah*, if not revealed during it. But, whether or not at that crisis, they have the heart of the matter.

> 'He who has laid the Qur'ān upon you will indeed bring you home again. Say: "My Lord knows full well who brings the guidance and who is the one that is in evident error." You never hoped that the book would be inspired within you: it could only have been so as a mercy from your Lord. Have, then, no truck with the unbelievers. Let them not deter you from the revelations of God seeing these have been sent down to you. Summon (men) to your Lord and on no account be among the idolators. Call upon no other as God beside God. There is no god but He. Everything is perishing except His countenance. His is the judgment and back to Him you will be brought.'

Here are the characteristic notes of the whole Quranic entrustment—conflict, exile, jeopardy, assurance; attestation, the authentic confirmed and the spurious identified; the necessity of continuing struggle and fidelity, and the sense of final destiny, God being over all. And in the centre of the passage, the clear fact—the Qur'ān was never a personal ambition, an anticipated dignity, a private honour. Except as a divine mercy, it could not have been. It was 'the gift outright'.

As such it had to be possessed. In the possessing is the whole clue to Muḥammad. In the transaction of the gift was the force, the feel, of words, the thrust and momentum of policy and power. But the granting of the Scripture laid upon its instrument the strictest duty never to lend his hand against the only Lordship. If there was the divine mandate granted there was the divine prerogative withheld.

Chapter 2
A LUMINOUS ARABIC LANGUAGE

The Qur'ān is the glory of Arabic and Arabic the pride of the Qur'ān. The voice that said 'Cry!' ordained the speech in which the answer should be made. The study of the prophetic moves into the literary. 'Thus have We inspired unto you an Arabic Qur'ān . . .' says Surah 42: 4 with an emphasis reiterated in half a dozen other verses. Among them are 16: 103 and 26: 195, where Muḥammad's foes hinted that 'some mortal', some foreigner, priming him, lay behind his preaching, whereas 'this is a clear Arabic tongue', mediated by 'the faithful spirit'. *Mubīn*, the adjective here, is a very favourite Quranic expression, meaning 'evident', 'free from all obscurity', and so 'unmistakable', and 'manifest' to all. Applied to the Arabic—as distinct from the 'error', 'sorcery' and 'enmity', which it also governs—'luminous' seems the fairest translation. The language of the book illuminates the meaning: the clue is in the Arabic.

It would be possible to take this, as the sequel in Surah 42: 4 may be said to do, in simple, practical terms, equating Arabic form with intelligible intention. The Scripture was given in Arabic in order that Muḥammad might 'warn the mother of the villages', that is, the Meccan metropolis, 'and those around it', alerting them to the surely coming day of humanity's assembly to the final judgment. Meccans were Arabic-speaking: the vital message would be intelligible to them in no other tongue.

But that practical reason does not exhaust the matter. Such simple exegesis would hold without the adjective 'Arabic'. The urgency of the message would be in itself sufficient cause why warning should be given. To serve that end, it has of course to be comprehensible and the native speech fulfils that role. But that is not to say that the choice of speech is only functional, or that their being addressed thus, in their own language has no other point than utility. Arabicity (if we may coin the term) has far larger relevance. It has to be taken up into much more subtle and soulful realms than common sense, or even of 'sense' at all.

The Arabic nature of the Qur'ān belongs with its essential criteria, its revelatory status, its quality as 'miracle', and its impact in a context powerfully attuned to the thrill of language and to the poetry of words. It is in these that we must look for the deep secret of their Scripture as Muḥammad and his disciples received it. Despite the strong paradox of his insistent disavowal of the poets, it is with them that we must begin. That paradox is itself the most telling proof of how much poetry had to do with its experience, as both given and heard.

Muḥammad's deep aversion to the poets is plain and passionate in the Qur'ān. He roundly repudiated any relation between his prophetic deliverances and the versifying of professional soothsayers and singers, the *kāhins* who were so marked a feature of his contemporary society. When hostile hearers associated him with these rhymers and their uncanny facility as oracles and word-charmers, it stung more than any other accusation. 'No! he has forged it . . . he's a poet' was their verdict (21: 5). 'Shall we indeed abandon our gods', they asked, 'for a wild poet?' (37: 36). 'Therefore reiterate,' Surah 52: 29–30 directs, 'You are truly neither soothsayer nor possessed. Do they say: "He is a poet; we will wait and see how it befalls him."?' Surah 36: 69 renews the rebuttal: 'We have not taught him poetry: that is not fitting for him.' The Scripture is a reminder and 'a luminous Qur'ān', so that 'warning may be given' undiminished by literary virtuosity that might distract attention or romanticize the impact. The Qur'ān is not 'in jest', for amusement and, if only for that reason, is not to be taken on any account as an artist's indulgence in skill. Surah 69: 40 makes the same denial: 'It is not the speaking of a poet . . . or of a soothsayer.'

However, the urgency of this repeated dissociation from the poetic must not be allowed to confuse the fact that the Qur'ān, in its power and quality, is a thing of surpassing poetical worth, and that its genesis must be understood in terms of literary inspiration. The mystery of its origins cannot be fathomed without sounding the depths of language. All the disclaimers of the poets cannot conceal the eloquence of the poems. Their 'incomparability' comes, indeed, to be emphatically their first credential. The *I'jāz* of the Qur'ān, as the term goes, its 'matchlessness' as Arabic, has been almost from the beginning its great corroborative 'miracle'. This 'inimitability' of Arabic is its hallmark. 'Bring a surah like it,' the challenge ran (2: 23; 10: 38). 'Bring ten surahs like it' (11: 13). It was, of course, *Arab* sceptics who were here addressed. It would have been idle to expect non-Arabs, even had they been around, to equal or excel the native speech, and what Arab 'competitors' were invited to outdo was the artistry. Heathen idolaters could hardly be in serious rivalry with the content. The whole point of the challenge lay in the claim that here was an Arabic eloquence without compeer, a literature which, in the strict meaning of the term *I'jāz*, left all others standing, helplessly outdone.

> But Shakespeare's magic could not copied be:
> Within that circle none durst walk but he.[1]

As Dryden said in a very different context. The thought of the 'miracle' of the Qur'ān on the lips of 'the unlettered prophet'[2] has always been the proof of authenticity on which dogma has wanted to rely. As a firm conviction, it has steadily dissuaded poets through all Muslim history from associating the Qur'ān with their verses.[3]

At first view we seem to be confronted with a contradiction. How do we reconcile the strong denial of poetic origin for the Qur'ān, with a vital insistence on the marvel of language? The fact is that they explain and even require each other. Muḥammad's sense of mission was concerned, at all costs, to exclude any confusion with professional facilities of rhyme or divination. Like Amos, he repudiated the habitual, the mercenary, the induced 'prophesying', the more earnestly to safeguard and affirm the distinctive vocation and the real task. 'I was not a prophet, nor was I a prophet's son,' said the herdman from Tekoa, 'but the Lord said: "Go, prophesy..." ' (Amos 7: 14–15). The denial of the functional, or the perfunctory, belongs with the authentic, which is radically other than the hereditary habit. Certain

[1] John Dryden, 'Prologue to *The Tempest*'. 'Magic' here in the poetic sense of 'unique capacity'.

[2] The full import of this phrase will be evident in Ch. 3.

[3] Thus, for example, a Swahili poet: 'I would have the Qur'an witness to my words, but that it is denied by the bountiful God to serve as a poem. It is not as the words of poets, O ye of little faith.' Quoted from Lyndon Harries, *Swahili Poetry*, Oxford, 1962, p. 193.

outward phenomena may seem superficially parallel to the cynical, looking for convenient gibes. But the real mission knows its own distinctiveness. In this way, the denial of mere 'genius' in the genesis of the Qur'ān is elemental for Islamic recognition of a divine initiative. That Muḥammad spoke 'from God' is the believer's understanding of what meets him in the resultant Scripture. Its status is secured for him in the very exemption of its instrument from the familiar patterns of the time and place, where poetry and the poets were so ardently admired.

But, by the same token, it follows that Muḥammad's role in the Qur'ān involves the very features that tended to the categories of thought, and so of enmity, in which his contemporaries moved. We might almost say that had he not been a poet there would have been no need to deny it. We are back again with the mystery of words. The sense in which he was not a poet is the necessary prelude to the sense in which he was. We shall do justice neither to the denial, nor to the affirmation, unless we hold them in their proper tension. This, in turn, suggests some general reflections on literary inspiration at large. The risk of misunderstanding in orthodox circles is worth taking, since no prejudice is meant—much the contrary in fact—to the unique Islamic status of what we may hope thereby to elucidate.

Throughout the whole Qur'ān, as a perceptive medieval writer observed: 'No word is ever ascribed save to God conversing with Muḥammad.'[1] How, reserving the theological questions, are we to understand the actual experience? Whence the inspiration and whence the attendant circumstance of trance and surprise, of intense collectedness and concentration and yet of agonizing unpredictability? How was it that the unlettered began so powerfully to speak, being somehow seized of words beyond himself, words which yet without himself would have found no voice?

The great Jalāl al-Din Rūmi, in his *Discourses* understood *waḥy*—the revealing by inspiring as the Quranic term may best be translated—as an act of spirit possession which temporarily displaced the normal capacities of the earthly agent, while occupying him as a residence. He ended his explanation with a somewhat dangerous analogy.

[1] Quoted by Norman Daniel, *Islam and the West*, Edinburgh, 1962, p. 37. Alternatively, 'Gabriel and the servants (of God, understood).' There are indications that this singularity was also a problem, or a provocation, for Muḥammad's people. Cf. Surah 38: 8: 'Has the remembrance been sent down just upon him among us?'

> When the Prophet was transplanted out of himself he used to say: 'God says.' From the standpoint of form it was his tongue that spoke: but he was not there at all, the speaker in reality was God. Having at first perceived himself ignorant and knowing nothing of such words, now that such words are being born from him he realizes that he is not now what he was at first. This is God controlling him . . . It became realized that it was not he who was speaking: God was speaking. 'Nor speaks he out of caprice; his is nought but a revelation revealed' (53: 4–5). God is wholly free of forms and letters: His speech is beyond letters and voice. But He delivers His words by means of any letters and voice and tongue He desires. Men have fashioned upon the highways, in caravanserais and on the banks of pools, men of stone or birds of stone and out of their mouth the water comes and pours into the pool. All possessed of reason know that the water does not issue out of the mouth of a stone bird; it issues out of another place.[1]

Plumbing in masonry seems a quite lifeless and mechanical parable for a phenomenon so intense and ardent.

Plato's Dialogue, 'Ion' grapples with the nature of inspiration by the analogy of magnetism. 'There is a divinity moving you,' said Socrates replying to Ion,

> . . . like that contained in the stone which Euripides called a magnet . . . . All good poets . . . compose their beautiful poems, not by art but because they are inspired or possessed . . . . For the poet is a light and winged and holy thing, and there is no invention in him until he has been inspired and is out of his sense and the mind is no longer in him . . . . For not by art does the poet sing but by power divine. . . . God takes away the mind of poets and uses them as His ministers, as He also uses diviners and holy prophets in order that we who hear them may know them to be speaking not of themselves who utter these priceless words in a state of unconsciousness, but that God Himself is the speaker and that through them He is conversing with us . . . . For in this way God would seem to indicate to us, and not allow us to doubt, that these beautiful poems are not human or the work of man, but divine and the work of God . . . . Am I not right, Ion?[2]

The Muslims will probably answer Socrates' question with an

[1] Trans. A. J. Arberry, London, 1961, pp. 51 f.

[2] *Plato's Dialogues*: 'Ion', para. 533–4. In this borrowing we need not be deterred by the fact that the Athenian and Meccan worlds were so far apart or that philosophers can assume plurality of deities.

eager desire to safeguard the distinctive status of the Qur'ān as faith holds it. But there is evidently much in the analysis which corresponds closely with the Quranic situation. 'There is no invention in him': the Scripture does not have its source in the Prophet's will. 'The mind is no longer in him . . .': Islam has always figured an abeyance of natural powers into which a divine *afflatus* moved. 'A state of unconsciousness . . . that we who hear may know them not to be speaking of themselves' closely describes the kindling recognition of the Qur'ān by the first Muslims. 'These priceless words' are what, as fruit and token, the idea of *I'jāz* hails as enjoying unparalleled literary power. 'These beautiful poems . . . not human but divine . . .' is precisely the end result of the fact of *waḥy*.

There are, of course, areas of the Muslim apprehension of Muḥammad which must be reserved from such comparison. But the affinities, duly limited, are unmistakable. The Islamic Scripture is certainly illuminated, as a historical phenomenon, by these aspects of prophet-poetry elsewhere in the human story. As Nabakov wrote:

> . . . a sound may be truer than reason
> And a word may be stronger than man.

It may be doubted whether, in the last analysis, prophecy has ever been other than poetic and poetry, at its truest, ever other than prophetic. There *is* versification, truly, and the mere art or music of words, contrived and delectable, for their own sake, as Muḥammad saw and repudiated. Then the language is an end in itself and the poetry, if at all, is in the pen rather than the soul. There are, too, quite prosaic prophets, if we reduce the term to declamation, rhetoric or policy. Yet 'spirits are not finely touched but to fine issues'. Where prophecy is most authentic there is poetry, kindled and kindling in the heart—a poetry which is more than an artistry of words because its quality as language is enthused with a purpose and a power that require what they create. However piety cares to define it, this is what it acknowledges in treasuring the Qur'ān.

'The prophets Isaiah and Ezekiel dined with me,' wrote William Blake, 'and I asked them how they dared so roundly to assert that God spake to them.'

Isaiah answered:' . . . I was then persuaded and remained confirm'd that

> the voice of honest indignation is the voice of God, and cared not for consequences.'[1]

There was, about that intimacy, something that Blake knew himself, a muse that awoke his slumbers, tuned his spirit and governed his song. He wrote, he said, by a sort of dictation from beyond, without straining, or study, or conscious effort. 'I dare not pretend to be other than the secretary,' he declared. 'The authors are in eternity.'[2] If there was 'genius' it was a passive ability to know spontaneous inspiration, to receive 'revelation' in unpredictable, and even uncontrolled, eruption in heart and pen together, in their strange community. There was art without artistry and truth beyond intent, poetry without effort, and prophecy all unconcerted, in any event of knowing and of telling there within himself and yet, somehow also, in spite of him.

> Hear the voice of the bard
> Who present, past and future sees;
> Whose ears have heard
> The holy Word
> That walked among the ancient trees,
> Calling the lapsed soul
> And weeping in the evening dew . . .
> O Earth, O Earth, return![3]

'The cistern contains, the fountain overflows,' he said—there is no mistaking that to which his imagination corresponds.

It is precisely this inwrought mystery of content and form, of meaning and word, which meets us in the Qur'ān and underlies the Muslim view of 'verbal inspiration'. The Qur'ān is understood to say *what* it says in an inseparable identity with *how* it says it. It constitutes a what and a how in indissoluble marriage. Its eloquence is the flow of a fountain, in whose force is its purpose. Both are 'revelation'. It is not a cistern which contrivance has accumulated.

We are bound, therefore, to appreciate, and yet abandon, Jalāl al-Dīn Rūmi's metaphor of the stone channel, since what it captures in 'otherness' it forfeits in participation. Its passivity is not of the right, or the feasible, order. On the contrary, the engagement of the Prophet's

[1] *The Prophetic Writings of William Blake*, ed. D. J. Sloss and J. P. R. Wallis, vol. 1, Oxford, 1926, p. 18.
[2] *Complete Writings of William Blake*, ed. G. Keynes, New York, 1957, p. 825.
[3] *Poetical Works of William Blake*, ed. J. Sampson, Oxford, 1905, p. 106.

powers is all the more vital for their seeming abeyance. Literary inspiration, anywhere, seems always to involve this apparent paradox. Its great manifestations can never be contrived or organized. The creative thing can never be merely 'deliberated' into being. The moment has to be awaited, when the conspiracies of grace or nature, of the spirit or of heaven, come to their rendezvous.

Yet they wait upon a restlessness they provoke. They exact co-operation. They engage with expectancy and tribulation of heart and in their wake the natural propensities and skills which they themselves have sharpened are strenuously, even painstakingly, employed. It is not an evacuated self which they possess but rather a self disengaged from established assumptions and, therefore, free *from* the capitulation that normalcy supposes and *for* the new insights into meaning and wonder. These, in turn, command and accompany the words in which they are proclaimed. The two constituents of revelation cannot be separated: the surge of utterance is the lift of the fountain and the content is its stream.

Since they cannot be *willed* into being, will itself the more joyously pursues their discovered objectives and, in meditation, yearns for their renewal. By the same token, the inspiration suffers intermission. The interludes are a necessary pattern in the spontaneity. The fountain has its moments because it has its motions. The intensity achieves its fullness only because it allows its periods. Hence, again, the discernible features of its onset, the heightening of psychic power and feeling, and the spentness in the aftermath.

These evidences from the wide field of poetic experience seem to demonstrate what obtains in the 'luminous Arabic' of the Qur'ān. The force of language bears on the import of truth and the pattern of truth is in the shape of language. The meaning makes its own music, finds its own mythopoetic words, strides within its own metre, flows down the channel of its own filling, and all these, the literary qualities, take their being from its urgency. Where thought and insight are thus alive and passionate they have—if the word is not too prosaic—an architecture of their own. The sense within them becomes a living, articulate reality, by virtue of what it is to them and they to it. The event in the soul has become an event in the world. When the poet has been found by the vision, it yields the words, and in the words it is itself disclosed. Only in the saying is the knowing and only by the knowing is the saying.

To reflect in this way is not to forget the powerful other factors, yet to be explored, in the genesis of the Qu'rān. Nor is it to obscure the doctrinal formulation of the Islamic reception of their Scripture. Rather it is to care for it by an effort of apprehension congenial to the experience for which the doctrine is vigilant. To draw on the patterns of literary inspiration elsewhere does not diminish the sanction by which the Qur'ān is unique. It is to acknowledge and study the implications of the literary status Muslim faith has always attributed to its Scripture. The Arabic is what it is, not merely for the prosaic reason that the recipients were Arabs unschooled in other tongues, nor simply that poetry was much admired among them, but that eloquence, spontaneous and ardent, in their own tongue, might arouse and assure them in the disowning of their idols. 'We have sent it down an Arabic Qur'ān, perhaps you will apprehend' (Surah 12: 2).[1]

The Qur'ān's character as poetry and Muḥammad's experience as poetic go far to explain and illuminate those features of the story which have sometimes received malicious interpretation in the west or superstitious esteem in the east. The muse of literature in its finest incidence has often been accompanied by conditions resembling those of trance and ecstasy, for which physical or psychosomatic reasons have been sought. In the immediacy of great vision, beyond the frontiers and patterns of normal consciousness, there is an intensification of psychic energy. The very powers by which the familiar struggles of striving apprehension and toiling composition are transcended sometimes pass beyond the secure ordinariness of life. Yet the trance-like, dream-like condition, flowing from the kindling insight and flowing in the utterance, is not self-induced or chronic. To take it for a physical abnormality is to invert the essence of the situation. What transpires has about it a collectedness, an impulsive quality, that no mere device can generate, responding as it does to yearnings which cannot be denied, nor satisfied without it.

'The sense of the real in the immediacy of true imagination' is how such inspiration may be described. Blake saw it as a liveliness for which all things were analogies beyond themselves—'the world in a grain of sand, and eternity in an hour'—and also symbols demanding to be known, as poetry takes them, in their livingness, and never as the

[1] The word *ta'qilūn* here (not *tafhamūn*), has to do not merely with 'taking the point', but with 'realizing the significance'. It is the word frequently used also in recognition of 'the signs of God' in nature.

abstractions of, for example, Newton's 'sleepy' physics, or as the 'ordinarinesses' of everyday life. By that vivid awareness he became, in Rilke's ringing phrase, 'a deeply kneeling man'.

All parallels in this exciting sphere are treacherous, Blake's perhaps most of all. There is an insistent individuality about all such poetry/prophecy and we cannot exhaust or identify any single example in another. But it seems indisputable that the Qur'ān is properly seen in these terms and Muḥammad by these parallels. Their eloquence, in its *I'jāz*, can only be psychically understood in this sense. Here too the very interludes become corroboration of the inspiration. All the features which the Tradition relates and prizes—the physical exhaustion, the limp body, the nervous tenseness, the quickened pulse, the feeling of being overborne by something insupportable—become intelligible. The muse of prophecy has, by its very nature, a cycle of recurrence. Its interludes (the word used in 17: 106) alternate with moods of depression, of fear lest the mystery fails to recur or that the 'possession' may be deceptive, delusory or demonic.

Muḥammad plainly knew this alternation of surety and dread, of certainty and gloom. The sense of vocation was at once crushing and sublime. In assuring his hearers that he was not 'deluded' or 'possessed' —the great, oppressive apprehension of the earlier days—he protested to them that the angel of revelation was not 'miserly' (81: 22 and 24). The connection seems clear. The all important sequence of experience—only actual in proceeding—moved with, and into, a sequel of confidence and so of proven status. But the process was critical, with its alternating prostration and authority. Is not this, in all likelihood, the 'burden' of Surah 94, already noted in Chapter 1? The conclusions to which we are drawn by considerations of literary inspiration confirm those that are required by the personal awareness of prophethood. The two are aspects of a single whole.

Later development, it is true, did not sustain the pattern of these beginnings. The poetic prophecy passed into phases of argumentative and political 'prophecy', where prose was the more accordant form. Deliverances turned into directives, ordinances and documents of law and community. The biography of the Prophet continues to comprise them all within one phenomenon of *tanzīl.* Muslim faith sees an undifferentiated status of authority throughout. But the feel and fervour of the Qur'ān, by the literary criteria, are evidence enough that there is a transition, a change of key. It is clearly in the poetry, where it lives in its strength, that we must locate the essential meaning of 'an Arabic Qur'ān'. Where prose supervenes it signals the dominance of the factors to which it is suited—command, law, politics and rule. That these displaced the poetic was the token that it could never be displaced.

The literary phenomenon of the Qur'ān has an intriguing token at the head of twenty-nine of its 114 chapters, in the presence of individual letters of the Arabic language standing in isolation before the argument begins, though always following the *Bismillāh*, or invocation. At first sight, they have a curious, even enigmatic, quality and they have puzzled many a stranger. Discussion of their meaning is worthy of pursuit in its own right and falls most properly within our present context. They imply a sort of drastic reduction to essentials of the business of script and meaning. It is as if the letters say: 'Here we are—the raw material of eloquence: arrange us into literature! turn letters into "letters", the alphabet into poetry!' To modern minds that reduction may seem almost a *reductio ad absurdum*, as if consonants at random could symbolize the task of revelation or the arts of words. Yet the impatience, if such it be, needs to be checked. For there is more behind the matter than might at first appear to a mentality sophisticated, perhaps wellnigh jaded, by the spate of letterpress. The Qur'ān belonged in a society when the art of the scribe was still 'special' enough to be the theme both of surprise and of disdain. And 'letters', then, could be a real challenge.[1]

The chief letters involved are A, L, M at the head of Surahs 2, 3, 29, 30, 31 and 32, and of Surah 7 with Ṣ added and 13 with R added. Ḥ, M stand at the head of 40, 41, 43, 44, 45, and 46; Ḥ, M, ', S, Q are found opening Surah 42; A, L, R preface Surahs 10, 11, 12, 14 and 15; and Ṭ, S, M preface Surahs 26 and 28. Individual Surahs have single instance letters as follows: 19, K, H, Y, ', Ṣ; 20, Ṭ, H; 27, Ṭ, S; 36, Y, S; 38, Ṣ; 50, Q; and 68, N. It is notable that the shorter and earlier Surahs are not included in the list. In four cases, 20, 36, 38 and 50, the letters also supply the title by which the Surah is known, namely *Ṭā Hā*, *Yā Sīn*, *Ṣad* and *Qaf*.

Some western scholars, characteristically, have proposed that these letters are the initials of the scribes who penned the chapters or of the owners of the fragments on which the Qur'ān was first recorded.

[1] See Ignaz Goldziher, *Muslim Studies*, ed. S. M. Stern, trans. from the German by C. R. Barber and S. M. Stern, vol. 1, London, 1967, p. 107.

It is difficult to believe that from this utilitarian origin they could have slipped into sacrosanct company, or have appeared thus, always at the head. Initials, in any event, are a western device and initial letters are not, anyway, definitive of words, belonging as so many of them do to prefixes not to roots. It is, of course, possible that the letters could derive from *root* elements within significant terms in any particular Surah and some interesting and ingenious suggestions have been ventured in pursuit of them.

But these latter, and certainly the 'initials' notion, must be treated with considerable scepticism, in the light of the unmistakable association almost everywhere between the letters and the theme of 'Scripture'. A moment's reflection indicates how sensible such a connection is! The fact, at all events, is that every Surah having these letters, except Surah 3, follows them with immediate reference to Qur'ān, *waḥy*, *tanzīl*, or book, all terms having to do with inspiration. Surah 3 only delays to do likewise by one verse in which it rehearses a brief creed.

It is certain, then, that the letters are there to indicate in some sense the nature of language as the clue to meaning. Since the concept of revelation throughout is literal, there must be a heavenly original of the Qur'ān on earth. This is known as *Umm al-Kitāb* (lit. 'the mother of the book'), described in 43: 4 as 'before Us' (God speaking), or 'in Our presence' (cf. 13: 39; 85: 22). It is the letters Ḥ, M which preface this explanation. Are they then in some way symbols or tokens of the celestial language, intimated to men as something which becomes Arabic in its human currency? They would then become in turn the signs of the Qur'ān's inimitability as literature.

This conclusion seems justified by the very dubiety of numerous alternative suggestions associated with various traditionalists and summarized by Al-Suyūṭī,[1] the famous compendium writer of Quranic lore. God, it is suggested, may have called the attention of the Prophet by Gabriel's uttering these sounds, since many times he was occupied when the Scripture was mediated. Or, alternatively, the sounds in the letters arrested the attention of other hearers. The cabbalistic mystics and pundits read into the letters their numerical values and deduced from them various prognoses about the duration of Islam or the status of its heroes. It was noted, too, that fourteen letters of the alphabet (a half of its total) were involved, excluding

[1] *Al-Itqān fī 'Ulūm al-Qur'ān*, vol. 2, Cairo, 1941, ed., pp. 13–18.

repetition, and these required a whole gamut of pronouncing movements in the throat and mouth. *Ṣad* might be taken as the name of a sea above which the throne of God was reared, and *Qaf* a celebrated mountain. *Mīm* and *Ṣad* might indicate the sentence in which Muḥammad was addressed *a lam nashraḥ laka ṣadraka:* 'Did We not enlarge your breast?'

Other theories are that the letters stand for names of the Qur'ān, or the abbreviations for God, Gabriel and Muḥammad, as source, means and voice of the Qur'ān, or else they authorize what follows them as being by the command (*amr*) of these. The most frequent thesis, however, finds in the letters the shorthand of the divine Names, notably: *Al Raḥmān*, 'the merciful' (from A, L, R and A, L, M, Ḥ, M, N); *Al Ṣamad*, 'the self-subsistent' (from Ṣ and M); *Al-Hādī*, 'the guide' (from H); and *Al-Amīn*, 'the trustworthy', or *Al-'Azīz*, 'the mighty' (from Y and ').[1] The great historiographer Ibn Khaldūn is sceptical about all these efforts after discernible meanings, as being without strong evidences, and he concludes that the letters are essentially 'ambiguous'[2] and, therefore, challenge the hearer or the reader to reverence for the very reason that he is not diverted into ingenious or ingenuous conjecture. Al-Suyūtī, too, seems to lean in this direction, in that he begins his full reporting of the theorists by the observation that 'every book has its secret', and this matter is the Qur'ān's.[3]

Though the wealth of speculation and inventiveness here is some measure of the mentality of exegetical piety and of the sense of miracle, it seems right to assess both the question and its interpretations as basically part of the whole phenomenon we are discussing. What the alphabet is to poetry, Arabic letters are to the Qur'ān. Even the sublimest things require the lowliest means. For revelation itself, as utterance and recital, there must needs be a, b, c. Its very inflexions must be treasured. The sense enters into them by the sequence of syntax, as shape is given to the pliant clay. The vessel hardens to hold what is given. To cherish the Qur'ān is to esteem the letters of

[1] The letters involved were even arranged into a sentence with the meaning: 'Did it not shine, the text of a truth that was hated?', referring to the obduracy that rejected what the Qur'ān brought. Sprenger, in the *Journal of the Asiatic Society of Bengal*, vol. xx, p. 280, made the suggestion that K, H, Y, ', Ṣ, in Surah 19, with its Christian bearings, was to be identified with the Latin I. N. R. I.: 'Jesus of Nazareth King of the Jews.'

[2] *Al Muqaddimah*, trans. F. Rosenthal, vol. 2, London 1958, p. 59.

[3] *Op. cit.*, p. 13.

the art and the art of letters. It was this that devotion had in mind when it treated the prefatory A, L, M and the rest, whatever their exact origin may have been, as 'signs' of the book.

It is easy enough, in most cases, to transpose alphabets and transliterate words. But the ambition to savour, from language to language, the authority of the native eloquence is often an exercise in frustration. The literary quality of the Qur'ān has largely to be taken on trust by the newcomer and the stranger. A large trust it may often seem to him, repelled and baffled as he will often be by the opaqueness of his non-Arabic. Yet the large trust has to do with a large phenomenon and is, therefore, well-advised. For only by dint of it may he move towards a susceptibility comparable to that of its own possessors.

Chapter 3
SCRIPTURE FOR THE ARABS

The red in my blood has for centuries known
That all soil is not like the soil where I've grown.
But I know who I am . . .

the poet insists, linking his identity with place and home. 'I know who I am by a hill and a heath.'[1] Inhabitants have, for the most part, the name of their territory. But he could equally have said: 'I know who I am by a lilt and a language', by the bond of a tongue. The splendour of Arabic in the Qur'ān we have now appreciated. The bearing of landscape and locale will occupy Chapter 5. But either way, whether by soil or by speech, it is community which they determine. Still reflecting on Quranic experience in its incidence, we pass from the medium of the Arabic to the measure of the Arab, in its making.

They are denoted in the original by a single adjective. In the uttering and in the hearing, the Islamic Scripture was not only a literary event: it was the focal element in a corporate identity, as leadership and discipleship proceeded from and through it. There can be no doubt that the Qur'ān was a supreme sacrament of Arabness as well as of Arabicity. It could hardly have been the one without the other. The book was seen as a matchless work. It was, therefore, by the same token, a collective treasure, the cause and the symbol of the people's pride whose tongue it employed. The revelatory event held within itself not only the mystery of words but the mystique of participation. The sphere of literature merges with what, in the deepest sense, we may call the ground of the political. The Arabic Qur'ān is the Scripture of the Arabs.[2]

[1] T. H. Parry Williams, in a Welsh poem 'Affinity', trans. D. M. Lloyd.

[2] A certain inevitable, but not essentially distorting, anachronism is involved in speaking of 'Arabs' in the Qur'ān. The word *I'rāb* (pl.) is used in the plural only in 9: 90–120;

The purpose now is to review this 'Arabness' in the significance of the Qur'ān, as the corollary of its Arabic language, and to do so in respect both of the factors in its genesis and the circumstances of its climax. In each the Arab element plays a crucial part. Without it, the prophetic mission and the institutional consequence would be, as it were, historically disembodied, evacuated of their real character.

However, as with the emphasis on Arabic in the previous chapter, there is a necessary caution, the due recognition of which only strengthens the case. The sense of poetry there was properly reinforced by the insistent disclaimer of the merely poetical. Prophecy is more than artistry—so much more that artistry can be its vehicle. Similarly, the 'Arabness' of the Qur'ān is in no essential conflict with its universalism. Islam disowns particular monopolies, even those of Arab origins. Muḥammad is understood as a 'mercy to the worlds' (21: 107), and the Scripture as the final culmination of all earlier, partial ones. Surah 25: 2 seems to corroborate this and 34: 28 declares: 'We have not sent you but inclusively to (all) mankind....'[1] It is not, finally, a perquisite of the racial identity. Its Arabness, no less than its Arabicity, is seen as instrumental. Yet, in the same way, the actuality is there and, truly recognized, is indispensable. Muḥammad is 'a warner to them [the Arabs] from among them' (50: 2) and 'no messenger is ever sent save with the tongue of his own people' (14: 4). Even the universal cannot broach the historical without a local habitation and a native people. Time cannot be interpreted without the temporal, nor the worlds receive mercy except in a world. The universal range of the Qur'ān as Muslims hold it has to be inaugurated and anchored in its particular incidence, as Arabness knew and possessed it.

It is important in this context to keep in view the present tense of history as experience. The perspectives of the centuries, the hindsight of historians, are always liable to distort or obscure the immediacy of events as they were for contemporaries. Muḥammad's community came through vicissitudes and dangers into a sense of vindication

33: 20; 48: 11–16 and 49: 14, and has the sense of desert people, not townsmen—the wandering tribes or *badū* only. The word *'Arabī* (sing.) has only the language connotation. Nevertheless, in the broad sense discussed in this chapter, it is proper and timely to see Muḥammad and the Qur'ān as 'Arab' realities.

[1] There are many questions in the actual evolution of this 'intention beyond the Arabs' and scholarship differs about whether, and how far, it can be posited in the days when Muḥammad was preaching for the soul of Mecca before the *Hijrah*. There is also a debate as to what is finally meant by 'worlds' in these verses.

and external success, in the last decade of his life and after his death, for which, in their pace and range, history has few parallels. Events developed a momentum both exhilarating and strenuous which gave to that generation a quality of destiny as Arabs that has to be appreciated, not, first, in the detachment and familiarity of historical retrospect, but in the astonishing and enthusing pride of reality. We have to reckon perceptively with what might be called 'the sovereignty of *that* generation', who knew in their own mortality the stride of destiny and the corroboration of actual achievement. The Qur'ān itself belongs with this *élan*, in the vigour and assurance of its legislation and its polity. To this theme we must continually return in imagination, if we are to discern aright the rise of Islam, and perceive its psychology. If, as H. Z. Nuseibeh observes, 'Arabism owes to Islam its very existence',[1] we may equally say that to Arabism Islam owes its first definitive occasions and the psyche of its birth in history.

Muḥammad's mission was engaged on two fronts. It made a decisive, if also paradoxical, declaration of independence from the two earlier monotheisms, Judaism and Christianity. It entailed a struggle for the soul and for the hegemony of the Arab peoples. These two aspects are essentially interrelated. The message of the Qur'ān required an Arab *islām*, since its first encounter was with Arabian idolatry. But an Arab *islām*, in the event, could satisfy neither its positive nor its negative meaning—acknowledging the unity of God and dethroning the idols—without a native character, consciously distinctive and in virile dissociation from the other Semitic faiths to whose influences the impulse behind the Qur'ān owed so much.

The double *motif* of this single theme is gathered into a rare, but intriguing, phrase in the Qur'ān, whose importance as the crux of the case makes an extensive exposition vital. It is the phrase *al-nabī al-ummī*, which for the moment we may translate as 'the unlettered prophet', used of Muḥammad in Surah 7: 157 and 158. The passage runs:

'. . . Those who follow the apostle, the unlettered Prophet, whom they

[1] *Ideas of Arab Nationalism*, London, 1956, p. 20. The remark is, of course, only one side of a reciprocal fact. Nuseibeh himself notes: 'The poems, the proverbs, the traditions, the legends and mythologies expressed in spoken literature and transmitted by oral tradition . . . moulded the mind of the Arabs, fixed their character and made them morally and spiritually a nation long before Muḥammad welded the various conflicting groups into a single organism' (p. 13).

> shall find written there to hand in the law and the Gospel, who enjoins well-doing on them and forbids them what is evil. He makes lawful for them the good things and prohibits to them the things that are foul. He rids them of their burdens and of the fetters they wore. Those who believe in him, honour him and make his cause their own and who follow the light sent down with him, surely these are the ones who triumph.
>
> 'Say: "O ye people, I am the apostle of God to you, all of you. His is the kingdom of the heavens and the earth. There is no god but He, who brings to life and brings to death. Believe then in God and His works and follow Him, that you may be truly guided." '

Here are all the central elements of the preaching—Muḥammad's commission, the inclusive guidance, the sure directives as to good and evil, the call to allegiance, the sense of destiny and the doctrine of the unity.

But how are we to understand the characterization of Muḥammad as *ummī*? The word has often been taken to mean 'illiterate', in the simple sense—the Prophet who was unable to read or write. This view has then been widely linked with the miracle of the Qur'ān, which is all the more remarkable if, indeed, such eloquence came in circumstances of total literary incapacity. The surprise of the Qur'ān would then lie, not in the partly discernible if still surpassing, shape of poetic inspiration, but in entirely mechanical terms of celestial dictation operating in complete disconnection with that conscious reflection which serves, but does not explain, the double gift of language and conviction.

Despite its impressive credibility for certain types of mind, this arbitrarily miraculous view of Muḥammad's role in the Qur'ān does less than justice to the texture of the mystery. *I'jāz* is surely the less religious, if we understand it in this form—a conclusion which in itself is strong reason for suspecting it. The Qur'ān deserves an explanation more congruent with its impact. Nor is the theory in any way required by historical evidence of Muḥammad's actual illiteracy. Rather, belief in the latter has arisen from dogmatic demand. The facts on this matter must remain an open question, with a strong assumption against any complete inability.

It is true that Surah 29: 48 addresses Muḥammad with the words: 'You did not read any book before this and you do not write with your own hand', and continues: 'Had you done so, those who make nought of it would have become suspicious.' In its context, this may simply mean that had Muḥammad been a recognized scholar, a bookish person, given to much penmanship, those who belied him would have had more ground for saying it was all his own product. The two verbs here mean 'recite' or 'utter', and 'inscribe', i.e. 'be your own amanuensis'. It is well known that Muḥammad did use scribes, that the Quranic utterances were recorded from his lips or after being memorized, and that prior to the Quranic experience he had not been either orator, poet or preacher.

We have, then, to get beyond the bare issue of an ability to recognize writing or to wield a pen, to a more intelligent and searching analysis of what the phrase *al-nabī al-ummī* intends. The clue lies in the hint contained in the verse just quoted and strongly indicated by numerous other passages. It has to do with Muḥammad's *not* being a scholar. His sources were not libraries, but inspiration. His stimulus lay not in erudition but in yearning. The flow of language studied in Chapter 2 drew its power from *waḥy* not from documents. He was 'unlettered' in the sense of 'untutored', rather than 'illiterate'. The Qur'ān was not from the world of learning but from the world of Mount Ḥirā' and 'the shadow of the wing of Gabriel'.[1]

The Ṣūfī poet, Jalāl al-Dīn Rūmī, gives this meaning of the term his own elaboration in his *Discourses*, where he writes:

> Muḥammad is called *ummī*, not because he was incapable of writing and learning. He was called so because with him writing and learning and wisdom were innate, not acquired . . . What is there in the world that he does not know, seeing that all men learn from him? What thing, pray, should appertain to the partial intellect that the universal intellect does not possess . . . . Everyone who possesses a partial intellect is in need of teaching and the universal intellect is the founder of everything. It is the prophets and saints who have effected union between partial intellect and universal intellect so that they become one.[2]

Such theosophical development, however, carries us far from the immediacies of the exegetical problem. The simple sense of *ummī* is non-scholastic, in being not 'of the schools'.

Authentic as it is, this understanding of the term does not, or need not, imply the entire absence from Muḥammad's ken of *any* antecedent awareness of Scriptures or of books. On the contrary, the Prophet's

[1] A phrase much loved by the Indo/Pakistani poet, Muhammad Iqbal to denote Quranic inspiration. See the study by Annemarie Schimmel: *Gabriel's Wing*, Leiden, 1960.

[2] *Ibid.*, pp. 151–2.

whole being, before and during Quranic experience, was pervaded by the knowledge that there were 'people of the Book', communities consisting by the possession of Scriptures of their own—possessing and, in a sense, possessed—since, by their scriptuariness they had their cohesion and identity. These people, Jews and Christians, as we must presently review, had a germinal place in the prophetic vocation of Muḥammad. How, then, was he 'unlettered', if so keenly alert to the fact of divine books, even though their contents did not reach him through sustained scholarship but only through oral and intermittent contact?[1]

There is no contradiction here. That non-possessing awareness is the whole point. The final meaning of *ummī* combines the two aspects. The word is an adjective predicative of Muḥammad's mission rather than descriptive of his person. 'The unlettered Prophet' is 'the Prophet for the [as yet] unscriptured'. There were antecedent Scriptures and there were peoples whom those Scriptures had 'made'. Arabs were not among them. Nor, for profound reasons, were those existing Scriptures satisfactory or efficacious to confer Arab identity and unity. Being already possessed elsewhere those books were, we may say, preempted, essentially unavailable for the necessary *Arab* role. The scriptuarizing of the Arabs required an Arab prophecy and an Arabic speech, for, as Surah 34: 44 has it, 'We did not bring them any books which they might study, and before you We sent them to no warner'. By such logic of the heart, it would seem, Muḥammad came to the conviction that Arab/Arabic Scriptures there must be, and, thence, to the hesitant, and finally triumphant, discovery that the necessity was being met through words he found *himself* reciting.

'The Prophet of the Scriptureless' (an Arab, for Arabs, in Arabic, understood) seems, then, the sense, most adequate to what the Qur'ān decisively is, of the phrase *al-nabī al-ummī*. Some effort has been made to translate it by 'the native . . .' or 'the popular . . .' Prophet. But neither of these usages gets to the central significance from which alone they might have derivative value.[2] *Ummī*, it is also argued, can

[1] This is not meant to pre-judge, either *pro* or *con*, the several traditional ideas of Muhammad's having been given information or instruction by Christian monks or from Jewish rabbis, either in the Ḥijāz or in travels beyond. Whatever may be the case about such occasions they are comprised under this general implication of *ummī*. See, further, below.

[2] The word 'popular', in its whole range and without particular stress on *ummī* as its ground could, however, rightly fit the undoubted economic implications of Muḥammad's

be understood as a synonym for 'Meccan', since Mecca was *Umm al-Qurā*, 'the metropolis' or 'mother of villages'. *Ummī*, too, may be understood as '*ammī*, 'national', 'of the people', and with the implication of 'Gentile', as in Syriac, a language that also has *umta* for 'nation' and *umtaya* for 'Gentile'.[1]

It is surely wiser, however, to gather these possibilities into the larger relevance. We are fortified in doing so by the fact that *ummiyyūn*, in the plural 'unscriptured or unlettered ones', is used of non-Jews in contra-distinction to the Scriptural people. Thus Surah 3: 20 gives Muḥammad direction about replying to controversy and distinguishes between 'those to whom the book is given' and the *ummiyyūn*. The contrast here would seem to be between Jews and the non-scriptuary peoples, rather than between those who read and those who do not. The aptitude may well coincide with the possession of the texts which require it, and the lack of it with non-possession.[2] But that is not the primary element in the difference. Surah 62: 2 uses *ummiyyūn* to denote men without 'the book and the wisdom' and identifies Muḥammad as God's instrument from among them to make good the deprivation. Surah 3: 75 records some among the Jews as disowning all obligations towards 'the *ummiyyūn*' which suggests an attitude of supercilious depreciation of these that has to do with more than mere illiteracy. Being Scriptured and unscriptured were far more potent factors of superiority and inferiority. Arberry's consistent rendering of 'the commonplace people' has, as it were, the quality without the clue.

The evidence, then, of the occurrence of the plural term in the Qur'ān would seem to confirm its bearing on the whole development of Islam as a new departure, of consciously Arab momentum, at once related to a precedent phenomenon and sharply dissociating from it. One may observe also that literacy, in the modern sense of a print-dominated culture, is scarcely germane to the circumstances of seventh-century Arabia. Of quite central relevance, however, was the prototype and its repudiation, 'the people of the book' and another book for another

mission as a concern for the underprivileged against the wealthy and the hierarchical. It is noteworthy, for example, that *ummī* is used in 7: 157 in the context of a programme of religious direction and social emancipation.

[1] See John Bowman, 'The Debt of Islam to Monophysite Syrian Christianity', in E. C. B. MacLaurin (ed.): *Essays in Honour of G. W. Thatcher*, Sydney, 1967, pp. 191–216.

[2] It is true that in Surah 2: 78 there occurs a use of *ummiyyūn* applied to a faction among the Jews, so that the implication of 'non-Jews' as its meaning cannot be absolute. Yet the exception does not overthrow the general sense. It is not impossible that some Scriptuaries were 'illiterate' in contrast to their own pundits, with whom 2: 78 is concerned.

people. There was continuity in the Scriptural idea and discontinuity in its final incidence.

It is important, however, that *ummiyyūn* should not be translated as 'Gentiles'.[1] Such translation is both unimaginative and inexact. Except in a provocative sense, we cannot call them that which they were to cease to be. The very seeking, by Muḥammad, of scriptuary status for his people, means rejection of 'Gentile' exclusion from it. The will to independence of the Jewish *milieu* involves refusal, not imitation, of the conscious isolationism that election pursues. That which does not make Gentiles of others cannot start by acquiescing in the label for itself. The Quranic claim to *waḥy* does not entail tribal or private theories about the rest of mankind. Its Arabness does not mean the imitation of Jewish ethnic particularity. It only coveted the Scriptural condition, without minding to copy or admire the self-understanding of Jewry. Indeed its whole psychological genesis lay in the will to escape this.

By their own road, of course, the Islamic Scripture-people learned how to be supercilious and lofty. All communities tend to depreciate the world outside them and such discrimination often focuses around the divergence of language. When the Scriptural element, in the sacred sense, is present as in the assurance of Jewry and—if we are right—in the wistfulness of Muḥammad, it certainly dominates all other aspects of communal attraction and repulsion.

The Prophet, then, was *for* the unlettered and, as noted in 62: 2, he was *from* among them, the instrument whereby the ultimate Scripture was to find a people and that people were to acquire *their* Scripture. The passages earlier studied in the celebration of 'an Arabic Qur'ān' have their import fulfilled in this larger sense. It was not only that Arab men might understand, by the intelligibility to them of the language employed. It was that they might realize that they too were 'scriptured', that there had come to them this immeasurable boon of a sacralizing, by a Scripture, of their own language and so an incorporating, first potential and then actual, of their society by the privilege of a book that was theirs.

[1] As, for example, by N. Dawood, *The Koran*, London, 1956, e.g. pp. 102, 396 and 401. On p. 330 he translates *ummiyūn* as 'illiterate people'. See also John Bowman in MacLaurin, op. cit., and R. Blachère, *Le Coran*, 3 vols, Paris, 1947–50. No doubt some general sense of uncouthness goes with *ummiyyūn*, as with 'Gentiles'. Lack of Scriptures easily equates with general illiteracy. But this vaguer sense of 'Gentile' is reparable if the essential sense is repudiated.

It may be urged that we are theorizing unduly about processes in the Prophet's experience which deserve a greater caution. But, if history is read backwards, it is lived forwards. The Arabs *did* become a people, irresistibly, by virtue of a Scripture. Muḥammad's sense of prophetic calling did prove decisive in its psychic and religious momentum, as these issued into Arab community and polity. The story marches with the Qur'ān itself. Are we wrong, then, to measure the impulse in the origins by the forces in the climax? Can we not well assess what began by pondering what came to be? The initiation must surely be understood by the dimensions of the sequel as these disclosed and achieved it. On every count, and with proper safeguards, it was an Arab theme and must so be told. In the immediacy of the Qur'ān's own history an Arab generation, by an Arab leadership, turned decisively from the great historical precedents of monotheism and established its distinctive alternative in a most lively paradox of manifest indebtedness and hearty independence.

It would be wrong to insist that the reasons were wholly or simply Arab or, to use an anachronistic word, 'national'. But the diverse elements within that history had an indubitably Arab focus and inspiration rooted in geography, temperament and culture. The emergence of Islam from the previous monotheisms was the religious making of a people and the popular taking of a faith in one of history's most fascinating partnerships. The self-sufficiency it acquired is all the more impressive for the initial dependence and the constant parallelism *vis-à-vis* the Jewish and Christian precedents. How was it, then, that the existing mono theisms could not satisfy the Arab people? Why had there to be a prophet for the *ummiyyūn*? Why were there *ummiyyūn*? Given the long existence of venerable Scriptures, why were they unscriptured? How was it that their inclusion could not be accomplished in books already to hand?

The positive answer lies in the vitality and insistent distinctiveness of the Arab will. But the context in which that will found its cause—in both senses of the word—lay in the introversion and the privacy of those earlier communities. How well Muḥammad's vocation, and the tasks it involved, could have recruited and required, from the outset, the aid and comfort of the established theisms. His battle against idolatry, the yearning for the Arabian relevance of the divine unity, were surely themes of just such partnership. There are clear evidences in the Qur'ān that Muḥammad anticipated and even assumed such relationship. When it was apathetically or derisively withheld, the cult of static and secure community implicit in that stance provoked a dynamic dissociation and an assertive Muslim self-sufficiency. Islam, we might say, grew out of Judaism and Christianity because it could not grow with them or into them. Arabia was too large to be sure: there were the facts of geography. The Arab was too distinctive: there were the forces of nature and of blood. But these came into play and found their occasions because the faiths of the Torah and the Gospel had not effectively availed them. It was the Arab consciousness which registered that failure. It did so in the person of Muḥammad.

The aloofness of Jewish community is well known in history. The remoteness and uncouthness of the Arabian dispersion only accentuated it. The belief in election and covenant, the possession of the law, Moses and the prophets, gave Hebraic religion, with rare exceptions, a posture of distance, a sharp antiseptic view of human relations. Muḥammad's Jewish contacts did not effectuate any sustained community of action or even of sympathy, but only of isolated tuition, amusement or disdain. At a later point, when the die of enmity was cast, Jewish material interests were bitterly antagonized in the confiscations and campaigns which ensued from the pursuit of power. Antipathy and sharp contention were then irreversible. But the formative experience of a closed society, conditioned to covenanted, scriptured identity, wrought only a sense of contrasted unscripturedness which then required the Arab revelation. Islam is in this sense the most abiding and massive example of an identity discovered out of an antipathy.

Hence the gathering indictment of the Jews in the Qur'ān—the reproach of their 'disloyalty', the reiteration of their obduracy against their prophets, the charge of their 'invention' of fables, and the instinct to disqualify their special status with God.

> 'That the people of the book may know that they have no prescriptive right [*qadr 'alā*] to the bounty of God. Bounty is in God's hand to give wherever He will. God is the Lord of the great bounty.' (57: 29)

But all such sharp, specific antagonism has to be seen as the other side of a new, communal self-awareness, a destiny of the Arabs in Islam. The tables, as it were, are turned. There are now new heirs to the divine action, new people of the divine mercy, new custodians of the divine purpose, new associations of the divine will. 'Obey God and obey the apostle' is the call of a new identity of interests between heaven and earth. Islam has displaced Jewry, though by a different theology of history, from centrality to God's will and made that conviction its own—all of which is the measure both of its tutelage and of its independence. The vigour of its distinctiveness is the sign of the intensity with which Muḥammad believed Arab unscripturedness to have been ended. '*Not* of those with whom Thou art angry', as the opening Surah has it, in a phrase traditionally linked with Jewish supercession. So confidently had the Arab faith-community been scriptured by the Qur'ān that it could displace and disavow the very matrix of the Scriptural ideal. The original 'people of the book' had only symbolized, and then forfeited, a status finalized beyond them.

The Quranic supercession of the Christian Scriptures had the same quality in a different key. Here the onus lies not so much in exclusivism as in divisiveness. There were, it is true, Christians of Arab birth and speech in the border territories to the north of the Arabian peninsula and in the southwest. The Quranic quarrel with them concerns their alleged confusions and schisms, their involvement in contentious subtleties over the person of Jesus, as well as distracting discords of political origin. By contrast, the Qur'ān—'a book in which there is nothing dubious'—shuns and reproves such complexities and factions and turns with relief to its own forthrightness and solidarity of will.

Nor was the accessible Christianity in any posture to obviate or mitigate these impressions. Its Scriptures were not available in Arabic to Arabs. Its life and liturgy were only shadowy presences on the periphery of Muḥammad's world, both geographical and spiritual. It was this, no less than Jewish obduracy, which left the *ummī* condition virtually undisturbed, to seek and find its own solution through the genesis, within the Prophet, of the Quranic satisfaction. Christianity, like Judaism, had contributed to make the revelatory status desirable, by its own reputation in it. But by its apathies and vacuity it had effectively withheld authentic participation in its meaning and community. When the independent Scripture came, it reflected the circumstances of the Christianity of its experience and perpetuated the alienation they entailed. 'Not of those who go astray' is the way the opening Surah runs in respect, according to general exegesis, of the Christians. By contrast with that aberration, the *ummiyyūn* emerge, beyond deprivation or distortion, into the authenticity of the final revelation.

These summary paragraphs do no justice to the tangled and fascinating questions belonging behind their conclusion. But they suffice, in this context, to state the negative elements, the paradoxical attractions and repulsions characterizing Muḥammad's relation with the heirs of earlier prophets, and in those terms to indicate the Arab newness of the Qur'ān. The positive side of the story lies within the ventures and struggles of that new, scripturized independence, *vis-à-vis* Arabian paganism and Arab tradition. By engagement in a vital conflict of its own with local idolatry, it grew in steady contra-distinction from the communities which had been its mentors and might have been its allies. There its self-sufficiency was tried and vindicated.

The chronology of this story concerns Chapter 7 and aspects of its meaning occupy Chapters 9 and 10. Here it is the positive Arabness that is in view. The Scripture which comes only to a single Prophet comes only among a single people. There are, truly, patriarchs and messengers as old as Adam, exhorting a long sequence of places and peoples. But all these only illustrate and fortify the particular crisis of the one generation in the one territory. Even the *Hijrah*, a profound revolution, as we shall see, within that Arabism, is a physical and religious journey simply between two cities of the same Ḥijāz. The Scripture coming only to Muḥammad makes an Arab uniqueness in history.

The reaction is that of a sharply defensive community. Observing, pointedly, that they had no Scripture to explain their tenacity, Surah 43: 22 understands the antagonism to spring from a will to perpetuate their fathers' ways: ' "Nay!" they say. "We found our fathers [lit.] upon a community and we are guided by their footmarks." ' Ironically the Qur'ān fastens on this stance as always characteristic of the complacent (*mutrafūha*) within any society. The point, clearly borne out by many passages, is that the Prophet was an upstart, a disturber, a threat to security both of mind and wealth, a menace to be stoutly resisted in the interest of established ways. His presence and this reaction make for an Arab version of a crisis perennial to history between a new destiny and the old order.

The people of Noah's day, of Moses' time, the population at every prophetic juncture, had resented and resisted their messengers. 'They say: "Enough for us is what we found our fathers doing".' (2: 170; 5: 104; 11: 62 and 87; 14: 10). Thus 'Ād and Thamūd, thus Israel in Egypt. Meccan conservatism likewise. Muḥammad was not even some 'great one' of their number, 'some influential citizen of the two cities' (43: 31) whom they might have appropriately followed into new ways. His words anyway, they urged, had originated from foreign informants. He might speak in Arabic but he was plainly 'anti-Arab' (cf. 16: 103; 26: 198; 41: 44). By this kind of obduracy even the native speech becomes a sinister conspiracy disguising a subtle attack on its own users. Here, unmistakably plain, are the passions of 'identity crisis'. Through the long years of Muḥammad's Meccan preaching the mass of the citizens were adamant. 'Shall we abandon our gods for a poet who is mad?' (37: 36). It is only the discontented, the unprivileged, the sensitive, whose wills are accessible to meanings establishment fears and silences.

Meccan hegemony refused to yield. The idols must be defended. Lucrative pilgrimage to their shrines must be preserved. Trade, prestige and power must be sustained. There could be no truck with a disruptive preaching about the sole sovereignty of God in a society rooted in the tradition and pattern of idolatry.

Muḥammad, with no less insistence, held firmly to his iconoclastic summons. With a few notable exceptions, his community was politically insignificant and socially despised. Its membership reflected the aspirations and privations of the poor and the 'uncomplacent'. It was a movement irreducibly within, and inevitably against, an establishment. The one could not compromise, neither would the other yield.

This situation, read within Quranic terms, contained, therefore, an inner logic of political action. It could not remain an inward, spiritual struggle, a thing of exhortation and personal conviction. It required to issue into external decision, into a trial of strength, into a battle for control. The hostility of Mecca to Muḥammad, in the cause of the *status quo*, at length precipitated the train of events which turned impasse into encounter and encounter into triumph. The devotion of the Prophet required to be achieved in the resources of the ruler. The quality of the *Hijrah*, as the hinge of that story, concerns us below.

What followed it was nothing less than a massive revolution in the Arab mind, wrought by a powerful initiative within its familiar world. Consolidating his authority in the new centre, Medina, Muḥammad served notice on the feuding patterns of the old society by interpreting the faith as untrammelled by the truces in which that society had traditionally operated. Lawless as his readiness to ignore the pattern of truce months certainly was, seen within the existing structures, it none the less reached imperiously towards a new dispensation. Truces assumed endemic, permanent disunities where, as a counsel of static tradition, truce, periodically, was preferable to unbroken war. Muḥammad, by contrast, acted in the name of a conviction that 'war was better than chronic unruliness', that the cause of an ultimate pacification justified a radical rejection of the truce system. A sharp, even perfidious, defiance of the customary mitigation of a lamentable discord was arguably a fair price to pay for its effective termination. Why adhere to truces if one could achieve peace? Was a palliative really better than a cure? Might not an outrage be committed in order to expose and explode a fundamental pessimism which organized its respites only because it was reconciled to its despair or inured to its false glamour?

This, in retrospect, is the reasoning which lay behind Muḥammad's strategy in the years beyond his entrenchment in Medina. Like the *Hijrah* itself, his military ventures against Mecca, before and after the signal victory at Badr, effectuated this profound revolution in the assumptions of Arab society. The sequel was in the same vein. The astonishing success of Muslim arms and the complete capitulation of Mecca in the ninth year of the *Hijrah* vindicated Muḥammad's religious logic and demonstrated the effective authority of a religious unity. Faith in the Arab Qur'ān was on the way, at his death, to attaining a politico-religious answer to the divisiveness of the Arabian world—a divisiveness which had defied earlier efforts to subdue it. In the immediate aftermath of his passing, it weathered the danger of chronic reversion into dissession and accomplished one of history's most swift and decisive conquests in western Asia and northern Africa.

It is this historical vindication which we have in mind in describing the Qur'ān, both in preaching and polity, as a supreme Arab event. Arabness was the arena and the proving ground of its inner crisis. It was, as it were, in the stride of a people, that the Scripture was both written and fulfilled. The case that Islam made for its Muslim shape it made within the controversies, the contentions, and the constraining of that single segment of humanity. When the story passed beyond them into other territories, the Qur'ān was ended and Muḥammad gone. The revelation coincided its preaching themes and its political deeds with their history alone. Universal as the relevance of both became, their actual incidence was shared by no other territory and by no other language. The surge of pride and possession moved with their conscious identity as a unique and original participation in the ways of God. The events which had defined their faith had triumphed over their idols, subdued their factions and assured their destiny.

The secret by which Islam succeeded with the Arab peoples where other efforts after unity had failed lay in its unification of worship. The plurality of deities and powers that characterized pre-Islamic paganism only reflected and sanctioned the competitiveness of tribal life and the precariousness of natural resources. The *Jāhiliyyah*, or days of ignorance, that preceded the triumph of Islam are not rightly so designated merely, or mainly, on account of any unawareness of the reality of God, but rather to denote a social wildness, a malaise of unruliness and restless disorder that defied correction. The poets of the *Jāhiliyyah* describe a society far from deficient in courage and loyalty, but one plagued with traditions of revenge and retaliation which made compassion and conciliation a kind of treachery.

Hence, it was not manliness or native virtues that were wanting, or even the knowledge of the sovereign power, *Allāh*, whose Name figures widely in poetry, inscriptions and compounded personal names. It was rather an effective elimination, on the one hand of chronic strife, and on the other of its celestial sanction in the plurality of supernatural forces and fears. For, however idealized and even courageous were the traditions of strife, they cruelly expended the human resources in internecine warfare and by their superstitions they aggravated the business of subsistence in the nomadic condition. Only the rigorous consolidation of the instincts of worship into a single 'fear' under a sole authority, dominating in mercy all the circumstances of ecology and economy—oases, crops, flocks, marts and fortunes—could suffice to awe and control the prodigalities of tribal conflict. Only the political counterpart of such a faith, as a single and effective earthly suzerainty, leashing manly ardours and loyalties, could implement the religious sanctions of peace.

It was these which Islam under Muḥammad afforded and which the first two Caliphs maintained. And it can be fairly argued, in the context of our present interest in the Arab elements, that this was the proper remedy, the appropriate achievement of power. Historical experience in the *Jāhiliyyah* had indicated the frustration of counsels of conciliation as long as the assumptions of tribalism remained unchallenged. It was a society which by its traditions made of meekness an anti-social slackness and of peaceableness a conspiracy against duty. The poets of the *Jāhiliyyah* are full of the theme of prowess that is swift to retaliate and scornful of those who are tempted to evade or refuse combat when a common cause or a blood-bond requires. This is vile.

Thus, in the *Hamāsah*, a poet laments the action of some in the Banū al-'Ambar who held aloof from a punitive revenge against the Banū Shaibān.

> As for my people, though their number be not small
> They are good for nought against evil,
> However light it be.
> They requite with forgiveness the wrong
> Of those who do them wrong;
> And the evil deeds of the evil
> They have met with kindness and love,
> As though thy Lord had created among the tribes of men
> Themselves alone to fear Him
> And never one man more.[1]

The concluding lines have a suggestive ambiguity. Were the defaulters in a society of noble feuding bidding for immunity from the prevailing pattern by dint of some divine favour which did not expose them to trials of strength and risks of conflict? Or does it imply that they had a divine relationship allowing them a sort of spiritual arrogance that could leave the dirty, and the necessary, work to others, while they cherished a falsely exempted sanctity? Or does it, more likely, mean that they felt themselves divinely permitted to indulge their love of family and children, their desire for dear life itself, and thus to be exonerated from the pains and wastes of honourable warfare? If so, was it not a pernicious interpretation of religion? For did not the gods expect the valiant and wait upon the strong? What sort of a heaven could it be that connived with cowardice in the interests of comfort and ease?

Certainly this temptation of sweet family love, as the poets saw it, recurs frequently in their verses. Elsewhere the *Ḥamāsah* reproaches the Bakrites, holding off from the common cause because they cared for the peace of their tents and expectation of life with their wives and children.[2] It is significant that from time to time the very same reluc-

[1] See Charles A. Lyall, *Translations of Ancient Arabic Poetry*, 2nd ed., London, 1930, pp. 1–2.

[2] Ibid., no. xviii.

tance for conflict is reflected in the Qur'ān. Muslims were loath to go forth to battle for the same domestic reasons, or held victory too dear to be bought with the sacrifice of unmolested, unmolesting quietness. The ranks of the faithful had then to be held together by vigorous incitement to action and by sharp depreciation of the passive virtues (e.g. 48: 11; 57: 8–11; 60: 2–3; 63: 9–11; 64: 14–16). There were several occasions where the militancy of Islam had to bestir a constituency which might otherwise have been unready for its exactions and its battle philosophy. The peace it wrought was that which makes the sword resolute.

The clue here would seem to lie in the notion of a power uncompromising enough to sustain peace by devouring contention. The aim was to reduce to impotence the quarrels which intermittent aggression and exhaustion only perpetuated and which meekness only abetted. Unilateral conciliation, it seemed to argue, was ineffective as long as basic turbulence went unchallenged. Disorder was endemic in a situation where the immediate loyalty precluded a larger, where the family or the tribe excluded the 'nation'. The successful strategy had somehow to make the immediate and the larger loyalties identical by consolidating all causes, claims and emotions in a single obligation.

This was the achievement of Islam. It is this which the very name implied—a submission that effectuated peace, as isolated, sporadic peaceableness did not, however noble its origins or human its instincts, as long as the pattern to which it was exceptional remained. It was inherently and necessarily a solution of force, where magnanimity could only be exercised when the issue had been settled. As such, it entailed a robustness and a thoroughness justified by its criteria. It meant a capacity to ignore compassion as an idle or an ideal luxury, as a surrender to weariness or a quest for private exemption from a system which linked honour with vindictiveness. Why have the interlude of truces, if one can break out of stalemated conflict altogether? In that event, why allow a piecemeal conciliatoriness to confuse the labours of a peace-dictating purpose of total authority?

These inner motives to power within the Arab genesis of Islam—if we read them rightly—do not impugn the 'democratic' factors which many historians have discerned in Arab society at the time of Muḥammad. To reach for power in these terms within the dialectic of the tribal situation does not of itself preclude, either before or after the event, the patterns of communal 'counsel' (to use the title word of Surah 42) prevailing within the supplanted world. It simply re-orientated them around a new centre and translated them into the larger assurance and the greater idiom of the new religio-political community to which the tribes adhered. The absolutist trends in Islamic power developed markedly only with the rise of the 'Abbāsids in the eighth century. The original Arab shape of religious authority had to do with power that was total in its claim on surrender but, by that very token, was obligated to a sovereignty understood as God's alone—a sovereignty which meant the equal dignity and right of every tribal and personal accession within it.

Encounter with non-Arab peoples and with imperial states came only after the conclusion of the Scripture. The partnership between the themes of the text and the circumstances of the one people was unbroken and unshared to the end. The Arabs, uniquely and singularly, were the people of this book. Its incidence and its presuppositions were those of their world alone. It was in respect of their society, urban in Mecca and Medina, and nomadic in the great spaces of the land, that its sanctions of power, its unifying loyalty and its effective achievement were conceived and wrought.

Mecca and Medina were not Athens or Alexandria. It was expansionist, not formative, Islam which first encountered what those further cities symbolized. In its original habitat Islam was shaped to its immediate duties as Arabia required them. What this environment both demanded and received was not options of belief, nor sophisticated philosophies for admiration, but a summons into faith, a faith that could dethrone the idols and generate a state enthroning the new authority of a single worship. This was the double meaning of Islam, meeting, shaping and disciplining a people by dint of a message of divine unity and an efficacy of political unification. Its reality is rooted in God *and* His apostle. The apostolate resides both in word and in deed. It moves through both prophecy and power.

Thus to measure the Scripture of the Arabs is in no way to assert some mundane or secular appeal to 'nationality' in the modern sense.[1] To think in such terms would be totally anachronistic. Yet Islam answered, in the profoundest way, to the world of the Arabs as

[1] As noted in n. 2, p. 54 above, the Quranic allusions to 'the Arabs' (of which there are only ten occasions) concern nomad elements in the population, and the over-all implications are not complimentary. Some of the problems latent in their motives recur in Ch. 10, but the general argument here has them in view.

Muḥammad addressed and organized it. 'Thus have We sent it down an Arabic *ḥukm*,' as Surah 13: 37 has it, 'an Arab disposing', an authoritative shape of duty and of order, belonging first to its Arabian generation.

For it was that generation which lived through the great surge of achievement as historical experience and through which the tide of events flowed which amazed the centuries. To discover the native vitality that belongs with the Qur'ān is to find the thrust of its convictions, where history knew them, in the impetus which, at exhilarating speed, possessed Arabia of an unprecedented empire. Self-comprehension came in the outworking of that great impetus. The enterprise, it is true, was soon distracted and daunted by contradictions. A basic schism within the first half century broke the first enthusing rapture. But, in its pristine authority, the future seemed to promise unlimited fulfilment. And when time turned it to retrospect it was the more cherished as the sovereignty of a golden time.

When, in its closing passage, the Qur'ān 'concluded religion' (Surah 5: 3) in the finality of Islam, history was poised to give rapid proof of its meaning, in the geographical symbol of expansion and the emotional release of success. And, over large areas of place and time, history itself submitted. In that verse of ending and beginning, the Scripture addressed a single people, 'you' the Arabs, 'your religion' *al-Islām*. Yet it did not name them save, only, as 'believers'.

Chapter 4
IN THE NAME OF THE LORD

That 'every peacemaker is a fighter'[1] suggests the parallel reflection that every worshipper is an iconoclast.[2] The militant peace studied in the previous chapter was the active quality of the faith commanding it in the theological imperative that only God is God. The charismatic, poetic and political elements in the Qur'ān were all for the sake, and by the authority, of the ultimate conviction. To the Quranic sense of God all else was instrumental. The question: What happened in Muḥammad's preaching? carries us beyond eloquence in word and energy in a cause, beyond the springs of vocation, to the doctrine of God as their reality and seal.

The surest way to study this final dimension in the Qur'ān is to isolate four Surahs as the quintessence of the whole. Muslim tradition has in fact long done so. They are Surahs 1, 112, 113 and 114, the *Fātiḥah* or Opener, the Surah of Unity, and the two Surahs of Refuge, as the last pair are called. That they occupy the first page and the last page is no more than a symbol. Their twenty-two verses epitomize Islam in its genesis and history.

[1] John Oman, *Grace and Personality*, Cambridge, 1919, p. 103.

[2] In the sense that worship cannot fail to disown its contradiction. This is plainly the point of the Muslim *Shahādah*. But even Hinduism, hospitably revering all cults in a reverence for reverence itself, finds itself impatient with insistent 'unitarianism' and wills to break down what it sees as usurping arrogance and monopoly. The 'Yes!' of Hindu worship has its 'No!' like any other. T. V. French, a nineteenth-century Christian missionary in Agra, once invited a group of Hindu youths in the college to comment on the Decalogue and was nonplussed to receive a note from one of them about the third Commandment, to the effect that there was 'impropriety in reviling any God, as it was both sinful and useless' (H. Birks (ed.), *Life and Correspondence of Thomas Valpy French*, vol. 1, London, 1895, p. 58). The instinct to ask: 'Why take the Name of any God in vain?' wills to break down the worship that refuses to allow the plural forms, that the reverence within it may be properly conceived. The Islamic Yes and No of worship is, of course, the most categorical of all religions.

The opening Surah has always stood uniquely. It is not given the usual Meccan or Medinan label attaching to every other. Though it is impossible to know its position precisely in the chronology of the Qur'ān, or to say when it was first used liturgically, it is beyond all questions of timing in its inclusiveness and status.[1] It is traditionally taken to be the 'seven verses of the oft-repeated', noted in 15: 87.[2] It is the only part of the Qur'ān, outside narrative of patriarchal prayer and the like, where there is human address to God. The emphatic pronoun of such address, in v. 5, does not occur anywhere else. The *Fātiḥah* is, therefore, properly followed by 'Amen' on the lips of the reciter. It runs:

In the Name of the merciful Lord of mercy.
Praise be to God, the Lord of all being,
The merciful Lord of mercy,
Master of the Day of Judgment.
Thee alone we worship
And to Thee alone we come for aid.
Guide us in the straight path,
The path of those whom Thou hast blessed,
Not of those against whom there is displeasure,
Nor of those who go astray.

These are the words which open to us the experience of Quranic religion, as it happened, in the kindling of discipleship and the awareness of God it defines and communicates. They are, it might be said, the sacramental point at which the confession and the confessing of Islam transact their mutuality, where the meaning is given and the giving found. It is a creed, but only in the form of a cry. Its human pronouns, unlike the formal *Shahādah*, 'I bear witness that . . .', are plural. Its faith is of God and for community. Its religious emotions of praise, dependence, prayer, guidance and entrustment are the contours of the human relation to the divine greatness. Its devotion is shore to that ocean.[3]

[1] Among the chronologizers, Dawood does not attempt to place, or displace it. Noldeke has it last among the Surahs of his first of the three Meccan periods and Rodwell eighth from the beginning.

[2] Surah 15 is itself a pre-*Hijrah* Surah.

[3] Echoing Robert Frost's poem 'Devotion':
The heart can think of no devotion
Greater than being shore to the ocean.

God is at once described as *Rabb al-'ālamīn*, 'the Lord of all being', the most repeated of Islamic religious terms, enshrined in the *Bismillāh*, or invocation of God. Apart from the *Bismillāh* the word *Rabb* occurs numerous times, involving some twenty-seven columns of the concordance. It has the conclusive Semitic sense of authority, power, lordship, ownership and possession. 'Disposer supreme' might render it well. It is responsive to *'abd*, or slave, servant, chattel, and affirms both the divine sovereignty over all and the divine competence within all. In the context of the proclamation of the unity, the phrase in the genitive, '. . . of the worlds', must be understood as the exceptionlessness of the eternal authority. God is 'Lord of all spheres and realms' as 'Master of creation'. The plural *'ālamīn* is more than the dual 'time and eternity' or 'earth and heaven' and indicates the plurality of phenomena and the diversity of nature, history and the spirit, of mankind, of jinn and angels, and of things.

The root *'alima*, with which *'ālamīn* is associated, has the meaning 'to know', and 'the worlds' are thus to be apprehended as the means whereby the Creator is known. In a number of passages the word seems equivalent to 'the nations' in preference to whom the patriarchs are chosen (e.g. 3: 33; 6: 86; 45: 16) and thus has something of the Biblical sense of 'the Gentiles' (cf. 2: 122 relating to 'the children of Israel', and 7: 140 where Moses addresses his people as preferred by God to the surrounding *'ālamīn*). But this historical sense in such particular contexts is diversified and made inclusive in the scope of the Qur'ān's world. Thus Mecca (Bakkah) in its founding is described as 'a guidance to the worlds' (3: 96) and the book as the criterion, or *Furqān*, is a warner 'to the worlds' (25: 1; cf. 26: 192; 32: 2).

But foremost, as in the *Fātiḥah*, is the theme of praise and benediction: 'Blessed be God, Lord of all being' (37: 182; 39: 75; 40: 64;

However, the poet went on to reverse the possible meaning of his metaphor, making the ocean the mastered thing in the lines that followed:

> Holding the curve of one position,
> Against an endless repetition.

Could one perhaps rewrite his lines to read

> Holding the curve of one position,
> To make perpetual recognition . . .

so that the shore is seen as responsive to the tides that fill it? This might then describe in metaphor the shore-line to infinity which is the *Fātiḥah's* devotion. Acceptable or not, the adaptation does capture both the steadfastness of Muḥammad's mission and the quality of Muslim monotheism in thought and rite. For the poem see Robert Frost, *Collected Poems*, New York, 1948, p. 308.

45: 36), to whom the faithful soul is commanded to surrender. Surah 40: 66, in contemplation of the wonder, the symmetry, the plenitude, of creation, celebrates the divine power in this repeated phrase. The laws of the physical universe conform in their cosmic pattern of order and necessity, but man's has to be a willed and voluntary amenability. Every created thing is dependent on the creative principle within it (cf. 17: 44; 24: 41; 59: 24). But the soul is laid under a 'free' obligation in that its recognition of its creaturehood is moral and religious. Hence the force of the question of Abraham to his father and his folk: 'What suppose you concerning the Lord of all being?' (37: 87) or, more bluntly: 'What do you really think of God?'

Hence, too, the answering postures of the *Fātiḥah* with its insistent confession of unity and its exclusive adoration: 'Praise be to God, the Lord of all being, the merciful Lord of mercy, Sovereign of the Day of Judgement. You alone we worship, You alone we supplicate.' The pronouns here are emphatic, to mean not merely: 'We worship You . . .', but '*You* it is we worship.' The acknowledgement of an undivided Lordship would be incomplete without the practice of an undeviating reliance. The double affirmation of v. 5 has to do with the inner struggle of all monotheism for an effective, as well as a credal, end to superstition. Within the struggle for authentic *muslims* there was not merely the battle to disqualify the pseudo-gods, but to dethrone them. It takes a lesser will to assert as a proposition that 'there is no god but God' than to attain the deep habit of soul that *has* no other god but God in every vicissitude of time and temper. Even where conviction has firmly arrived, practice may still betray the pluralist. So the confession not only repudiates other worships but abandons other trust: 'To thee alone do we come for help.'

This decisiveness, close to the vital pulse of the Qur'ān and its contra-pagan purpose, turns on the will to praise and on the confidence that praise both speaks and learns. Here the appositive *Al-Raḥmān al-Raḥīm*, the descriptive of God in the *Bismillāh*, belongs in both doctrine and emotion. The two words derive from the single R Ḥ M root, with the meaning of mercy. But they are not repetitive. Their grammatical form and exegetical interpretation indicate a progression of sense, which can be seen to be very close to what was happening in the hearers' world because of the Qur'ān. The word *Raḥmān* in pre-*Hijrah* usage occurs alone as a substantive and only later pairs with *Raḥīm* in apposition to *Allāh*. Thus 25: 60: 'When it is said to them: "Worship *Al-Raḥmān*", they say: "What is *Al-Raḥmān?*" ' (cf. 67: 3, 19 and 29; 78: 38).[1] It also occurs sixteen times in the Surah of Mary (19) with its Hebraic, Christian theme and background. The identification of *Al-Raḥmān* with *Allāh* is explicitly made in 17: 110: 'Say: "Call upon God, or call upon *Al-Raḥmān*." ' *Al-Raḥīm* is always found in association with *Al-Raḥmān* or paired with these other names of God—*'azīz*, *tawwāb*, *ra'ūf*, *ghafūr*, *wadūd* and *bārr*—namely, mighty, responsive to penitence, tender, forgiving, loving and benign. Surahs 4: 29; 17: 66 and 33: 43 seem the only occasions where *Al-Raḥīm* is used alone.

The relation of the two words within the one quality of mercy is that between essence and expression, between nature and action. Since mercy is proper to God (*Al-Raḥmān*) it is present in his relationships. God proceeds in relation to men in terms of what He is Himself. This is the meaning ventured into English by the translation 'the merciful Lord of mercy', rather than by two successive English adjectives drawn from different sources, such as 'the compassionate, the merciful'.[2] Men in Islam are summoned to reckon with God and to reckon upon Him, to recognize terms which denote Him and to depend upon their authentic implications in the actual. Thus He who is the *Raḥmān* answers to that quality in being the *Raḥīm*. It could be said that at the human level the terms correspond to the transition between concept and experience.[3]

This mercy belongs with the sovereignty of the last day, the authority of final judgment, which was the fervent eschatological meaning of the doctrine of unity. Man may not anticipate any future outside that all-embracing power. The great day is not tediously argued or tentatively conjectured. It *is*—as the awesome reality, the bar of humanity at the grand assize, comprehending the entire human scene and eternalizing all its temporal issues, so that they can never be gainsaid, evaded or disowned. This vivid conviction in the preaching of the Prophet seemed to many incredulous and derisive listeners an empty and an extravagant illusion, requiring as it did the resurrection

[1] However, it gives its title to Surah 55, which is listed as Medinan, though several chronologizers transpose it.

[2] This being the most familiar English version. If one desires to keep the single root in translation then 'the Lord of mercy' translates *Al-Raḥmān*, and *Al-Raḥīm*, which is always adjectival, becomes 'merciful' which precedes in English.

[3] See F. Schuon, *Understanding Islam*, trans. from the French by D. M. Matheson, London, 1963, p. 63, for an illuminating and extensive paraphrase of this clause.

of departed men. But to Muḥammad's community of belief and fear it was the ever-present sanction of Islam and dying truly *muslim* their only ground of hope.

Hence the inclusive prayer with which the *Fātiḥah* concludes, when it passes from praise and affirmation into petition: 'Guide us in the straight path,' the path which does not deviate, whose people, by their treading it, are divinely 'graced' and so stand in clear distinction from those whom wrath and wandering define. The sense of that double contrast with the right and the favoured has been variously interpreted. It is, however, the solemn contrast which matters, pervading the whole temper of Islamic religion. Yet the sense of the favour is always dependent and petitionary and can properly strike no postures of assurance or of pride: 'Guide us *in* . . .' rather than 'into . . .' The revelation, in its cumulative authority, gives the path of the divine pleasure and delineates the true religion. The believer's aspiration is that he may never stray and fail or falter and thus be overtaken by the divine displeasure.

It remains to ponder the word *Allāh* itself, which has in its own import all the *Fātiḥah* intends: 'In the Name of God . . .', 'praise be to God . . .' (*Al-Ḥamdu li-llāhi*). Some western writers unwisely prefer not to translate this Arabic term but to adopt it into English, on the plea that there is something about the divine in Islam which only Arabic can say, or that they need to immunize from wider religion the essential, Islamic apprehension of the transcendent.

But to do this is to privatize that which Islam, properly understood, must universally affirm. It is precisely the reality of *Allāh* in every human speech which the Qur'ānic conviction of sovereignty declares. The term exactly connotes what English achieves by the absence of the definite article, where the 'the' of specificity is absorbed, with all it can truly possess, into the very statement of transcendent Being: *Allāh*, God, *Dieu*, *Gott*, *Akongo*, *Olodumari*, *Onyame*.[1] It is true that varieties of belief diverge endlessly and perilously, in what they desire to say predicatively about the single theme of God. Those diversities, as with all predicates, enter inevitably into the awareness of the subject.

[1] 'The', of course, does not necessarily delimit, though there are many ambiguous occasions of its doing so. To speak of 'the God of truth', 'the God of Abraham' or 'the God of the Qur'ān' might in some contexts be intended 'selectively', 'the god of war' or 'the god of winter' obviously so. The usage *God*, like *Allāh*, excludes all confusion, multiplicity or partiality.

But God as the one, only subject of all these apprehensions is what *Allāh* means and, meaning, cannot require to be reserved to any single language as if there were some private idiosyncrasy about 'the Lord of all being' which could only be secured by an untranslatable word, gathering the occult and the esoteric to its usage. For this would be to deny its inclusive reach and claim. The proclamation of Islam in the Quranic event is none other, no less, than the reality of the God of all being, the awakening of men to the total, inalienable, indivisible Lordship over heaven and earth.

Yet that inclusive sovereignty was also the local summons. 'Let them serve the Lord of this house' (106: 3) was Muḥammad's early call to his fellow citizens. The Lord of all being had truly sanctioned and preserved the immediate city, as the context indicates, assuring the occasions of its vital commerce and abiding in the forms of its cultic life. These it was the purpose of Muḥammad in the Qur'ān to purify and fulfil. His own father had borne the name 'Abd Allāh and from the root of praise his own name had been given. Thus the anti-idolatry of the Meccan years of mission was no campaign for an alien or an absentee divinity but simply for the ousting of the pseudo and the plural pretenders. It was not a demand to recognize a new supremacy but to refuse and banish its distortions. The Prophet did not call to the worship of *Allāh* but for the worship of none else.

The whole post-*Hijrah* history with its Mecca-ward intentions and achievements confirms this local incidence of the universal meaning. The policies reviewed in Chapter 3 have their place within the fact of the Qur'ān only because the heart of that event makes Mecca the test case of its cause. The Prophet of *Allāh* must succeed in Mecca as surely as the Prophet Jesus must suffer in Jerusalem. For in either case the particular is where the inclusive turns.

Thus the faith within the *Fātiḥah* had the strength of both the ultimate and the immediate. Its 'We and Thou' was at once intimate, historical, present in the here and now, yet also total, universal, for every time and place. It reached from creation to judgement and asked the guidance that joined the given truth with the daily jeopardy of wandering and wrath. It lived by a personal fervour, sharply alive to the contrasts of history and its retributions.

It is this intense awareness of God which Surah 112, with its title of 'Sincerity', expresses in the tersest of dogmatic phrases and with a most articulate devotion.

In the Name of the merciful Lord of mercy.
Say: 'He is God the One,
God the self-sufficient,
Never bearing, never being born,
None is equal to Him.'

The central word here is *Al-Ṣamad* in v. 2, meaning the self-sufficient, or the all-adequate.[1] It may be taken in apposition both to the attribution of unity in the preceding clause and the statement of non-contingency in the succeeding clause. For *Al-Ṣamad* means one whose resources are wholly his so that his being is neither derived nor given. He is not in the chain of contingency and of flux, which characterizes all humankind, where fathers beget their sons and were themselves begotten, having their being only by dependence and in earthly non-perpetuity. There may be historical relevance to this phrase in particular directions of Quranic controversy. But its essential and abiding thrust lies outside monotheism in the contra-pagan contentions of Islamic witness. For the contingency of deities, in their hierarchies or in their whims, is precisely the belief and the blight of paganism. Conversely, the meaning of unity is not some bare arithmetical unit, but the sole ground of trust, the inclusive locus of power and of sovereignty. The final verse states the same truth in the negative, making all else, all other, subordinate, dependent, tributary.

If Surahs 1 and 112 in this way epitomize what the Qur'ān meant and means, with and through its quality as a profound charismatic and political event, the question follows as to the spiritual temper it generated and sustained as an event in the souls of men, in the prayers and yearnings of disciples. We cannot better find the answer from the first precarious and vital years than in the two closing Surahs of the book. These have always been linked by their common theme and called 'The Two Refugees' or 'The Two Refuge-Seekers'. They breathe intensely the atmosphere of personal religion, proceeding through the years of Quranic history as men followed it in their inner piety and response.

In the Name of the merciful Lord of mercy.
Say: 'I take refuge with the Lord of the daybreak,

[1] The word is unique to this Surah. Rodwell, Dawood and 'Abdul Latīf, among others, translate it as 'the Eternal' and Arberry as 'the everlasting Refuge'. Pickthall has: 'the eternally besought of all', Muḥammad 'Alī: 'He upon whom all depend', and Yūsuf 'Ali: 'the Eternal absolute'.

From the evil of what He has created,
And from the evil of the enveloping darkness,
And from the evil of those who bind their spells.
And from the evil of the envier and his envy.'

(Surah 113)

In the Name of the merciful Lord of mercy.
Say: 'I take refuge with the Lord of men,
The King of men,
The God of men,
From the evil of the whispering insinuator
Who whispers in the hearts of men,
From jinn and men.'

(Surah 114)

Refuge is a well-nigh universal element in religion, joining, as it does, the sense of finitude with the sense of transcendent power. *Taʿwīdh* in Islam is the Muslim dimension of this response of human wistfulness to divine capacity. The theme runs throughout the Qur'ān, though these two last Surahs are its fullest and perhaps earliest expression. Thus, for example, 23: 97–8:

'And say: "My Lord, I take refuge with Thee from the evil promptings of the Satans/and I take refuge with Thee, O my Lord, from their attentions." '

We find the phrase on the lips of Noah (11: 17), Joseph (12: 23), his brethren (12: 79), Moses (40: 27), Mary (19: 18), and frequently in the narratives of Muḥammad himself in encounter with controversy (e.g. 40: 56), in recitation of the Scripture (e.g. 16: 98), and in counsel to Muslims (e.g. 7: 200; 41: 36).

In these latter verses there attaches to the phrase, both in the imperative and the indicative, the sense of an appeal as to a referee, against falsities and calumnies. Seeking refuge is then a response to the menaces and distortions of contentious folk and an assertion of the divine care for truth over all that threatens it. It is then an emotion appropriate to times and places of special crisis, whether in utterance or in conflict.

But in the final Surahs this deepens and broadens into perpetual and perennial aspects of human frailty *per se*, into the steady enmity of evil outwards and inwards to the imagination and the soul. Here it is a reaching for those securities that, in all Quranic thinking, are exemplified and corroborated in the processes of nature. Thus 113: 1 and 3,

> When creeping murmur and the pouring dark
> Fill the wide vessel of the universe . . . [1]

celebrate and invoke 'the Lord of the daybreak', the Lord of the explosive dawn, the *falaq*. The word, according to Al-Baiḍāwī, includes all that can be understood within the meaning of 'bursting forth'.

> For He to whom be praise has cleaved the darkness of nothingness with the light of being, especially what comes from some source or other like fountains, rainfall, plants and children, with the specially recognized sense of the morning. The meaning has to do especially with the transformation of the state of things, the exchanging of the apprehensions of darkness for the delightsomeness of light, and it is a parable of the day of resurrection, with the sense in the reader that He who is competent to dispel the darkness of night from this world is competent also to dispel the fears of the one who seeks refuge with Him.

The imperious sun symbolizes all erupting energies—seed and bud, womb and child, word and will. The morning pledges and pictures the competence to which every fear of evil may repair, even as these are told and shadowed in the rare eclipse or in the nightly pall of darkness.

Many are the ills of creaturehood, the physical and the circumstantial factors making for dismay and terror, and so for refuge. Fire and plague, poison, sudden death are ills in the creation. More sinister are the voluntary evils that stem from human malice and ill-will. Human associations conceal the mischief and the threat of destructive appetites and passions, the jealousies and imprecations of the envious. The sense of 113: 4 (lit. 'women blowing on knots') has to do with curses and spells, which, like the resolves they expect to effectuate, bind and bedevil the world of persons in relation. The final verse makes explicit the meaning in envy.

[1] William Shakespeare, *Henry V*, IV, Prologue, ll. 2–3. This captures exactly the sense of *ghāsiqin idhā waqab*, of darkness descending, shrouding, haunting, with the fearing of the proverb, *al-lail li-l-wail* ('night is for woe' or, better, 'dark gets at the heart').

From all these God is man's refuge, against all these his strength, and in all these his 'present help', for He is (in 114: 1–3) 'Lord and King and God of men'. The three nouns here, say the commentators, are intended to describe the whole reality of God in relation to mankind, as the One who originates, rules and transcends. To the *Rabb* men are servants, to the *Malik* they are subjects and to the *Ilāh* they are worshippers. The use of *Ilāh* here, in construct, denoting *Allāh*, is very rare indeed.[1] The comfort of 'the refugee' is the knowledge of that sovereignty and mercy through and beyond all that men do. There was also for Islam the truth conversely that men who can be thus related to God are therefore to be themselves acknowledged consistently with that relationship. To see them under God, as the realm of his power and praise, is to know them hallowed into mutual duty and common standing. This theocratic world answers the fears of men in that it proportions all their ends and subdues their pretensions. Since God is infinitely greater, why be awed by men or how be long presumptuous against them?

Such theocratic logic, however, only avails when the imagination, with all its baffled and distraught anxieties, lives with it in steady recourse to the God of whom it speaks. It is this that 'the refuge-seekers' do, yearning to feel, rather than merely to argue, the case. They are alive to all the conspiracies of life, the machinations of perversity, the evils that insinuate themselves into human counsels, inward and outward, personal and social. The *khannās* of 114: 4 is 'he who slinks or steals away' when the divine Name is mentioned, who contrives his evils in concerted evasion of God and the subtle deception of men.

Here in simple directness is the popular world of the Qur'ān's first audience and the authentic sense within it of the divine reality Muḥammad proclaimed—a sense of power and defence, of reliance and urgency, as to men walking in the midst of perils, warily and anxiously, but yet befriended and secured. Here is the intimidation of superstition, a universe of demons and dangers, of occult practices and haunted minds, with all the attendant psychology, yet reaching towards a unifying of its fears in a single authority open to its cry and adequate for its peace. Here is the God to end gods, in the fear that ends fears, in the power against the powers. The invoking of the

[1] It is the (in English) non-capitalized word in the *Shahādah* following the absolute negation: 'There is no *god* but . . .' This in the Qur'ān is the altogether preponderant usage.

One against the many enters thus into the emotions of the fearful because it is the steady, enheartening burden of the Prophet's words. It is to just such a world that his task relates. In responding, 'the refuge-seekers' also discover something of themselves, in pitting their resolve against every adversary with the pronoun 'I'. It was in such personal liberation, however many fears remained, that men could measure responsively the meaning of *islām* and number themselves with it against the tyrannies of dread and unbelief.

The modern reader is well-advised not to turn away in sophistication from what he may be tempted to consider a primitive and naive polydaemonism, from which he is exempt by skills and sciences. For it was from exactly such elemental human things, as these in Surahs 113 and 114, that the authority of Islam emerged. It was from just such crucial emancipations, as pagans knew them, that the religious victories over subtler evils of spiritual pride itself could develop, once the categories of evil were taken inward to the conscience and the criteria of refuging in God were also deepened. The Quranic principle that to fear God is not to fear (cf. 9: 18 'He who fears nought but God') was enlarged, by the very virtue of these beginnings, into the whole range of temptation and its defeat. That same principle of the unfearing fear taught the necessity of the final reverence which alone sufficiently subordinates all man's other loyalties. That nothing can rightly absolutize itself is the meaning of the rule of God and its invocation. When that truth is defied there is no escape from the entail of frustration and tyranny except in returning to the only rightly ultimate sovereignty. Only the Name of God allows men safely to revolt in repudiation of evil. But only the Name of God saves that repudiation from new and usurping tyrannies of its own. There are more 'whisperings in the breasts of men' than these closing Surahs intend. But there are none for which the refuge they ask does not urgently avail.

Four Surahs, representative as they are, may not be equated with the whole. There are all the accents of repetition, the sequences of narrative, the crescendo of action and the slow pace of law. But, given these, the *Fātiḥah*, the Unity and the Refuge-Seekers are our proper clues to what, in the farthest reaches of the question, was happening in the Qur'ān. It belongs to chapters that follow to set the whole event of the Scripture in its immediate environment of scene and strife, in order to discover its parables, move with its story and stand in its enterprise of word and will. Both that purpose, and the retrospect we have now gained, are dominated by the figure of Muḥammad as spokesman for God. In the transition we may recall the poem of Alexander Pushkin, 'The Prophet'. For it conveys, even in translation and with uncanny force of detail, the Muslim dimension of the human in the Quranic.

I dragged my steps across a desert bare,
My spirit parched with heat,
And lo, a seraph with six wings was there:
He stood where two roads meet.

Soft as the coming of a dream at night
His fingers touched my head:
He raised the lids of my prophetic sight,
An eagle's wide with dread.

He touched my ears, they filled with sound and song.
I heard the heaven's motion,
The flight of angels, and the reptile throng
That moves beneath the ocean.

I heard the soundless growth of plant and tree.
Then, stooping to my face,
With his right hand he tore my tongue from me,
Vain, sinful tongue and base.

A serpent's fiery fang he thrust instead,
Through my faint lips apart:
He slit my breast, and with a sword stained red,
Hewed out my quaking heart.

A coal of living fire his fingers placed
Deep in my gasping side.
Dead, as I lay upon the desert waste,
I heard God's voice that cried.

Arise! O prophet, having seen and heard:
Strong in my spirit, span
The universal earth, and make my word
Burn in the heart of man.[1]

[1] From F. M. Cornford and E. P. Salaman (trans.), *Poems from the Russian*, London, 1943, pp. 20–1.

Chapter 5
THE LANDSCAPE OF THE ḤIJĀZ

'Nay! I swear by this land, the land of your belonging, by father and fathered. Truly in trouble have We created man' (Surah 90: 1–3).[1] The invocations of the early Qur'ān return repeatedly to the immensities of nature and the mysteries of birth. Physical features both of land and people recur through its poetry. The dominating sense is of harshness in the landscape and hardship in the human lot, relieved by the gentler temper of the oases with their groves and gardens and by the brittle luxuries of city dwelling. The geography of the Qur'ān embraces both the nomadic and the urban, the tribal spaces and the cultic metropolis, the precipitous escarpments of dry ravines or the wastes of shifting sand, and the precarious, caravan-borne merchandise of streets and fairs. The aim of this and the following chapter is to focus in turn on these two aspects of Quranic locale, from which almost all its metaphors and parables are drawn. The topography of Muḥammad's native land has a lively relation to the book which is its greatest pride.

'Who will give you to apprehend the steep ascent', continues Surah 90, to know the '*aqabah*, the rocky defile that winds its toilsome way among the boulders and across the rugged screes towards the summit. For this is how 'the freeing of the slave and the feeding of the hungry' tell against the grain of human indolence and self-regard. Moral man is nothing if not a mountaineer.

So it is from generation to generation, the fathers and the fathered, man created in troublous kind. Not, for the Ḥijāzī, those local benedictions of Arabia Felix to the south, of which Milton sang, with only approximate geography and wilder romance, in *Paradise Lost*.

[1] 'The land of your belonging' translates a phrase where some versions use 'resident', 'lodger' or 'indweller', and the next clause is, lit., 'by a begetter and what he begot.'

As when to them who sail
Beyond the Cape of Hope, and now are past
Mozambic, off at sea north-east windes blow
Sabean odours from the spicie shoare
Of Arabie the blest, with such delay
Well-pleased, they slacke their course and many a league,
Cheered with the grateful smell, old ocean smiles.[1]

Rather, as Charles Doughty wrote in his *Arabia Deserta:*

> Here is a dead land, whence, if a man die not, he shall bring home nothing but a perpetual weariness in his bones.[2]

The Ḥijāz, it is true, gained from the trade of those fragrant spices and incense passing by and through it from the South Arabian shore to the tables and the altars of eastern Christendom. The trade routes lay along the Red Sea and through the chain of oases, Mudawara, Tabūk, Al-'Alā' and Yathrib (or Medina), on the easier, eastern flank of the Madā'in, or mountain spine, which runs parallel with the narrow, coastal plain, or Tihāmah, on the eastern shore of the Red Sea, and slopes on its inland side towards the plateaux of Najd. The range increases in height as it merges, southward, into the high lands of 'Asīr and the Yemen. The Ḥijāz itself has the scantiest rainfall and retains little of what it receives, save in isolated areas of clay soil where, as in Al-Ṭā'if, gardens of dates, wheat and barley become possible.

The country has no perennial rivers reaching the Red Sea and though the Meccan region and the port of Jiddah derived some commercial advantage from their position at the waist of the Red Sea, with closest Arabian access to Ethiopia, the shore for the most part is coral-strewn, humid with damp breezes, arid and inhospitable. The western and eastern aspects of the mountains abound in dry wadis, subject to rare but violent sudden floods, when torrential rains occur. There are also on the eastern side, great volcanic *harrat*, lava-strewn beds of rock, sometimes as large as thirty miles in width and a hundred miles in length, where the landscape is punctuated with extinct craters.

Beyond is the forbidding country of Najd, the high land and, as

[1] John Milton, *Paradise Lost*, iv, 159–65.
[2] Charles M. Doughty, *Travels in Arabia Deserta*, vol. 1, p. 56.

its name may also mean 'the exhausted land'. God 'guides men', says Surah 90: 10, to 'the two Najds' by the merciful gift of keen sight and urgent voice—those indispensable resources of the traveller. The terrain becomes a parable of the good and the evil, the alternatives where the ways part into the unknown. Here as everywhere in the Qur'ān topography underwrites the ethical.

We find the landscape of the Ḥijāz, and the human meaning of its features, grim and grand, dominating the imagery and the homilies of the Scripture. The day of retribution will be like the shifting mountains of sand (73: 14)—those wind-borne disruptions of the contours, or like the treacherous cliffs that detach themselves and pour into the valleys. The evil man is as one 'who sets his house on the edge of a crumbling precipice that crashes down with him into the infernal fire' (9: 110). The believer who parades his bounty, or compromises it with injury, is like a smooth rock, whose narrow shelf of soil is swept away by a torrent and only barrenness remains (2: 264), in contrast with the irrigated garden where the flash flood is harnessed productively and there is dew when it fails (2: 265).

Arabian history was awed by the recollection of whole prosperous communities which had disintegrated and passed away through the collapse, sudden or cumulative, of their earthworks and irrigation systems, most noteworthy of all the catastrophic end of the Ma'ārib dam and the irreparable loss of the precious oversoil by uncontrolled erosion. The dark spectre of such tragedy haunts the water courses. If these should disappear in the night, how shall the day survive? Thus Surah 67: 30: 'Say: "Bethink you! If in the morning your water should disappear into the ground, who then would bring you running water?".' The parable of the devastated garden in 68: 17–32 turns such fearful conjecture into fact. Its owners, anticipating the morrow's harvest, failed to bethink themselves of God and put out their fellows from their minds, to find, in the morning light, a blighted and ruined waste.

These images of parched and barren earth suggest the 'careworn faces' of eternity, with 'only the cactus thorn' for food (88: 3 and 6). The cruel sirocco, 'withering wind' (51: 41), figures in the story of the tribe of 'Ād, a strong and ancient people of Quranic retrospect. In its path everything turns to 'wan-ness' (30: 51)—plants and fruits and faces—until decaying vegetation lays a dark pall upon the wadi valleys (87: 5).

But the precarious tillage of the Ḥijāz springs also into sudden vigour by the quickening rains. 'By the heaven of returning rain'—the rain that brings 'returns'—runs the invocation of 86: 11—'and by the earth bursting with growth: the word is verily decisive: it is no idle pleasantry'. Repeatedly the Qur'ān makes the reader visualize the glad, incredible wonder of renewing vegetation, not in the steady, predictable sequences of the temperate zones, but in the arbitrary, unheralded, emphatic interventions of tropical downpour, saturating the earth almost before the darkening clouds have roused it for the onslaught.

> We poured down the copious rain,
> Cleaving the ground like fissures
> And making grain
> And grapes and vegetation,
> Olives and dates
> And laden orchards,
> Fruits and pastures
> All to grow, delightsome for you and for your flocks.
>
> (80: 25–32)

The dead land, thus quickened, is a sign from God (36: 33–5). (See also: 22: 5; 32: 27; 35: 10; 43: 10; 50: 9–11; 57: 16; 78: 14–15; 79: 27–33.) The very ground 'quivers' or pulsates and swells with the new life which the fructifying waters bring to birth out of the rainless dearth and death (41: 38–9). But the benediction cannot be assumed perpetual: the shadow of withering drought is always waiting to threaten again. The colour fades from the landscape: the greens and reds of leaf and fruit give way to grey, to brown, to dry decay. 'They languish and you see them turning yellow and He makes them like broken shards' (39: 21). The land is strewn, as it were, with the débris of desertion, with the relics of a departed fertility (cf. 56: 65; 57: 20).

The clouds that give sign of rainfall are a lordly feature of the Quranic sky. 'He spreads them in the heaven as He will' (30: 48). 'Do you not see', asks 24: 43, 'how God drives the clouds, folds them into themselves, banks them into great soaring heights? And then you see the drops teeming out of them and the hail following in their train . . . with flashing lightning of a blinding brilliance.'

The arts of agriculture, turning thus on the vagaries of rain and the narrow confines of oases and irrigated gardens share the Qur'ān's vistas with the nomad. Its most graphic metaphor is that of the mocking mirage (24: 39).

> 'Those who disbelieve, their works are like a mirage on a vast plain, where a man in thirst thinks he sees water, but when he comes up to it, there is nothing there. There indeed he finds God, and the reckoning he has to pay.'

Or, in the briefer misery of 13: 14, prayer to the false gods is 'as a man reaching out his two hands to water, but he does not grasp it to bring it to his mouth'. The nomad is schooled to know the shadows and the light: he is inured to torrid heat and skilled for shade (35: 20–1). He sees the mystery and the solidity of the mountains 'like pegs for the cradle of the earth' (78: 6–7). He notes the colours of the hill strata, white and red and black (35: 27), whether from a 'rose-red city' of legend or by the evidence of a quick discerning eye along the track. Are the strata perhaps the physical counterpart of 'the stairways', 'the ascents', of Surah 70, by which the angels and the Spirit ascend into the far heavens, even as Jacob, the nomad, slept at Bethel and saw the hillside like a ladder taking his vision by steps into the divine presence? (Genesis 28: 10–19).

The lofty places are a perpetual reminder of the modest lowliness of the human condition (17: 37), the finitude and frailty of man, who was not party to their tremendous genesis (88: 19–20). Nevertheless, he threads the ravines with his caravans and flocks. They have been made the highways of his passage, the arena of his skill in discerning direction and guiding his charges (21: 31). Need we doubt that the ruling concern of the Qur'ān with 'guidance' and 'the right path' is illuminated by the crucial urgencies and choices of the nomadic life, where landmarks are vital and where wild beasts may be prowling in the way? Evil-doers, says 74: 51, are 'like startled asses fleeing from a lion'.

The night sky too is alive in that world. 'By the heaven and the night star', cries Surah 86: 1, invoking the nightly *ṭāriq*, visitor of piercing radiance[1] and attendant on Muḥammad's vigil. The heavens are a very mansion of stars, a panorama of constellations (85: 1–2) receding into vast anonymity at the breaking of the dawn: 'Tell the

[1] Some take it to mean 'a meteor', while Pickthall has 'the morning star', the name *ṭāriq*, via a famous Muslim general, passes into *Jabal Ṭāriq*, anglicized into Gibraltar.

praise of your Lord in the night and at the declining, or retreating, of the stars' (52: 49). Neither day nor night outstrip each other. Sun and moon rule decisively in their fixed circuits and dominion (36: 37–9). The stark contrasts of night and day, with no intervening twilight to mediate their swift transitions, are intensely vibrant in the Qu'rān.

'I take refuge', says Surah 113, in a context we have explored more fully in Chapter 4, 'with the Lord of the daybreak', the Lord of the erupting, exploding sunlight, which breaks majestically from the eastern horizon into the immediate sovereignty of day. The dawn is sung in the invocation of Surah 91: 'By the sun and his morning radiance and the moon that follows after: by the day telling his splendour and the night that hides him away', and the high noon again in 93: 1. Almost a fifth of Surah titles are linked with natural phenomena, with sun and darkness, stars and winds and sands.

Transitory in this unfailing rhythm of night and light are the shifting haunts and fleeting passage of the badū (the bedouin). 'When will the promise come?' Muḥammad is asked by the incredulous. Promptly comes the answer in a caravan metaphor: 'It may be that already what you would expedite is riding there behind you' (27: 71–2), as if a man in the van were to dispute what is in the same column with him in the pilgrim convoy or the merchants' camel train. 'Stage after stage you will surely ride,' observes 84: 19. Pharaoh's councillors in 11: 98 are likened to a flock led down to a watering place which proves only a deceptive trap. The mustering of evil-doers to the judgment is like a crowd of hobbled camels (19: 72). By contrast—in one of the Qur'ān's most quoted sayings—'whoever submits his face to God in well-doing, he has truly laid hold of the firm rope and God's is the issue of all things' (31: 22; cf. 2: 256).

The '*urwah al-wuthqā* here has a rich nucleus of meanings.[1] It is 'that by which anything is held fast', such as the rope on a saddle harness or the loop on a pack. But it denotes other dependables also, in the nomad's world—a group of trees that abide in drought and at which one can maintain subsistence, and thence, by association, the environs of a place possessing such verdure. It can mean also a company of men from whom, or with whom, there is profit, and it is a synonym for the lion. Exegetes later took 31: 22 to mean 'There is

[1] Arberry has 'handle', Dawood 'firmest ground', Pickthall 'hand hold', and Rodwell 'sure handle'.

no god but God', since there is nothing firmer on which one can depend than that saying. But, however we read this wealth of implication, its background is with the traveller in his goings and his means. It may be right, then, to link with it the summons of 3: 103: 'Take firm hold all of you on the rope of God (*ḥabil Allāh*) and do not be divided,' a most fitting word for nomads and wayfarers. They know that isolation is death.

The caravans of Mecca, with their winter and summer sequence in Surah 106, become almost synonymous with the well-being of the city. Their 'organizing' (*ilāf*), in the sense probably of their gathering and equipping, sustains the population and so epitomizes the very will to be a city. With only a fifth of its denizens viable by local husbandry, overland traffic and communications were critical. 'Having neither seed produce nor udders', Mecca had to live by negotiated security.[1] So 'the convoying/conveying of the Quraish' (106: 1) may be seen to stand for the will to order amid the vulnerability of life, for the idea of civilization by the 'safe conducting' of relationships. These, in turn, properly conduce to worship and thanksgiving. For the inviolability they intend can only abide in the mercy of God and the trust of men. The whole Surah has an eloquent simplicity, mirroring at once the hopes and jeopardies of men in their ecology and the caravan as the crux of both.

In the adjacent Surah 100, with its well-nigh untranslatable fervour, we find the landscape erupting into violence by the brutality of men who pervert the fine strength of nature's noblest creatures and blaspheme the dawn with the din of the *ghazwah*. The mounted raiders on their snorting horses, trailing dust clouds behind their hoofs, attack the sleeping camp and scythe through the tents with ruthless speed. 'Surely man is graceless before his Lord.'

There are happier scenes offshore. As a land based literature, dwelling with sands and cities, the Qur'ān has place, too, for the fascination of ships, and, that, not only in the narrative of Noah.

[1] The figure of one-fifth is from current statistics. Some read *īlāf* for *ilāf*. The basic sense is 'to gather', 'to make up the number of' (even, 'to make up a thousand'). Arberry has 'composing' which seems a trifle literary! Pickthall has 'taming', and Dawood 'protection'. There is the further sense of 'safe conduct' negotiated by treaty for the security of the sacred territory and its people. R. B. Serjeant suggests that the winter caravan went down to South Arabia for the trade fleet from India, and the summer one took merchandise north to Syria. See A. J. Arberry (ed.), *Religion in the Middle East*, vol. 2, Cambridge, 1939, p. 6. See also Lane's *Lexicon*, vol. 1, p. 79. 'Quraish' has no 'the' in Arabic but it is well to supply this in English.

The Ḥijāz has a long coastline, though the ports are few indeed. From the mountains behind the coastal reefs of coral and the dank lowlands, the ships of the Red Sea passed in view like 'landmarks' (42: 32; cf. 55: 24), cleaving the waves with their prows and trading in the bounty of God.[1] One vivid passage takes a storm over the waters as a parable of the lostness of the *kāfirūn*, the rejectors, 'like shadows on the heaving sea, where billows heap upon each other and clouds pour over the tumult of the waters and in the horrid darkness a man can hardly see his own hand' (24: 40). In its benign moods, however, the sea yields food and ornament, fish and pearls, shells (35: 12) and coral (55: 22). There is beneficence, too, for the Qur'ān in that 'bar' between 'the two seas', the ban that forbids the salt to invade the fresh and separates the tides from the wells and streams (25: 53; 55: 19–20). This is the *barzakh*, or strand, that pre-figures also the great divide of death (23: 100), that guards the shores of mortality from the dwellers in

> . . . that undiscovered country
> From whose bourn no traveller returns . . .

This sense of the sea and of the long land trail northwards and southwards, brings the contrasts and affinities of near and distant territories into the landscape of the Ḥijāz. The awareness of the other, by report or token in merchandise, by the reputed abundance of what the native land yields rarely, by rumour and by stranger, deepens the possession of one's own. The invocation of Surah 95, 'By this land secure', echoing that of Surah 90, is preceded by 'the fig and the olive and Mount Sinai'. There can be no doubt about the third, its fame alive through scattered Jewish settlements within the Ḥijāz, living by Moses, or through Christian stories of its famous monastery. There are strong traditions, through Abū Hurairah and others, that 'the fig' stands for Damascus and 'the olive' for Jerusalem.[2] While, thanks to

[1] Charles Doughty relished the sight as he descended towards Jiddah in 1876 at the end of his epic journey: 'I beheld then the white sea, indeed gleaming far under the sun, and tall ships riding and minarets of the town. My company looked that I should make jubilee' (op. cit., vol. 2, p. 539). Islam of course brought the minarets and Doughty had his own good reasons for delight. But the thrill is perennial.

[2] The Tradition runs: 'Among cities, God has chosen four: Mecca, the city of excellence; Medina of the date palm; Jerusalem the olive; and Damascus the fig.' Surah: 23: 20, however, salutes 'a tree that springs forth from Mount Sinai, yielding oil and relish for all who eat'. See Guy L'Estrange, *Palestine under the Moslems*, London, 1890, p. 73.

its monks of St Catherine, Sinai was celebrated for its olives, it seems likelier that Jerusalem, with its Mount of Olives, is intended.

It is Sinai, though, in all likelihood, which recurs in the opening verse of Surah 52, to which also it gives a title Al-Ṭūr, the mountain of the book of Moses, here conjoined with the sacred house at Mecca and both, in turn, embraced by the invocation of the arching heaven ('the uplifted firmament') and the flowing tide.

This feel for the fame and sanctity of other haunts of history in the ways of God gives, we may say, a neighbourhood to the topography of the Ḥijāz. The landscape, too, bore some physical traces of the presence of the historic monotheists. Had not God used human struggle to drive back idolaters, runs the logic of 22: 40, 'truly cloisters and churches and prayer houses and mosques' would have been destroyed. The great Surah of Light passage (24: 35 ff.) speaks of 'houses' God has willed to be reared in his name for prayer and rite, for the abiding of men who have forsaken all commerce for the unbroken remembrance of God. These shrines of worship had their place in Muḥammad's perspective from travels beyond the Ḥijāz, we may conjecture, rather than from any local prominence. But, either way, they certainly belong with the locale of the Qur'ān, as also do the remains of the legendary pagan past, the ruins of Al-Ḥijr, for example, in Surah 15: 80 ff. 'Journey through the land and see,' for transience is the common feature of all human habitations.

Even more fundamental yet, to the topography of the book, is the sense of nature as itself an awesome reverence perpetually offered to the power beyond itself. This theme will concern us again in Chapter 10. But Surah 52, quoted before the preceding paragraph, anticipates it in joining the sanctuaries of religion with the vault of the sky and the swelling sea, in one solemnity. The conscious worship in the human prayer is kindred to the universal obeisance of the natural order. Man is not unique in worship, though he worships uniquely in the responsive awareness of reason, emotion, and discipline. But

> Have you not seen that God it is to whom everything in the heavens and on the earth gives praise and the birds on the wing. He knows the prayer of each, the praise of each. (24: 41)

There is a valuable discussion of all the Quranic passages relating to the olive, its oil and lamps, in Clermont Ganneau, 'La Lampe el l'Olivier dans le Coran', *Revue de l'Histoire des Religions*, vol. 81, 1920, pp. 213–50. Note p. 228.

Crawling things, no less than angels, have their anthem (16: 49). 'Those in His Presence are not too proud to do Him service and they grow not weary therein. Night and day unfailingly they praise Him' (21: 19–20).

But there is also the other side of the coin—nature as the sufferer from the iniquities of men. 'Corruption is evident on land and sea in consequence of what men's hands have wrought' (30: 41).[1] *Fasād*, the noun here, is a very frequent word and has to do with the distortion of the works of nature by the patterns of human self-will, by the idol-shaping propensities of men who defile the natural in disowning the divine. The judgment of the Last Day will ask the infant buried alive for what sin she was murdered (81: 8–9).

Perhaps this, in the final sense, is the context in which to set the intriguing references of the Qur'ān to 'easts' and 'wests' (plural) and to 'the two easts and the two wests'. (See 37: 5; 43: 38; 55: 17 and 70: 40. 73: 8 uses the singular 'Lord of the east and west'.) We noted earlier 'the two Najds' or highlands of Surah 90: 10, where there is a poetic dual, rhyming with eyes and lips. Commenting on 43: 38, the great Al-Baiḍāwī writes of 'the distance the east is from the west and the west from the east'. But in 37: 5, he observes that there are 'the easts of the stars' and 'the easts of the sun', adding that the sun rises every day in a specific place and there is a corresponding arc of sunsets in the west, as the point moves within the solstices. The two easts would then be the distance between the furthest points on the arc of the horizon in the 'side stepping' sunrises of the year. Al-Baiḍāwī on 55: 17 confirms this by his reference to the winter and the summer 'easts and wests', pointing out 'how many benefits there are which cannot be numbered' in this cycle, 'such as the tempering of the air, the change of the seasons and the things that happen fittingly in each'.

The east-west alignment, so to speak, of the Arabian world is so instinctive that, surprisingly, the Qur'ān uses no words for 'north' and 'south'. Or, rather, the words for them are pre-empted to denote 'left' and 'right', their directions, that is, as one faces east towards the *Ka'bah* in Mecca. It is in this sense that the words *shimāl* and

[1] Some speak here of 'drought', but this seems difficult in view of what follows about the hands of men, unless we are to understand the dust-bowl and the criminal ill-use of natural resources.

yamīn occur in the book.[1] The main commercial lines in the Ḥijāz were north and south, but the natural 'orientation' by authority of the rising and the setting sun was eastwards across Arabia and westwards to Africa. These two directions having to serve the whole 180 degrees of the compass, could we conjecture that we have 'easts' and 'wests' when the semi-circle is bifurcated, either leftwards or rightwards, to give north degrees of east, or south degrees?

This conjecture—it can be no more—is illuminated by the otherwise cryptic reference in Surah 24: 35 f. to the oil of the olive in the lamp of the house of prayer, in the great parable of light. It is said to be 'an olive neither of the east nor of the west'. Setting aside much possible mystical exegesis here, there seems a clear reminiscence of Zechariah 4: 12 in the Old Testament, where two olive trees poured their oil into the bowl that fed the seven lamps. One tree stood to the right and the other to the left, that is, in Quranic senses, 'south and north'.[2] The Qur'ān speaks of only one olive tree, 'neither of the east nor of the west'. However the association may be interpreted, the divine light is universal, the light of 'the Lord of easts and wests', whose servants need not build temples, as the pagans might, with a careful axis eastward that only one day's sunrise would perfectly endorse. Of that Lordship all directions speak and of the crucial tests of man their polarity may tell.

The pre-Islamic poets, in the main, used nature as a foil by which to tell the prowess of their heroes in odds surmounted and trials overcome. There was little personal relation to nature in itself, little cosmic passion in their verses.[3] Nature was a quarry for heroics and for love panegyrics, but scarcely a responsive witness to the very soul of man. With the Qur'ān it is different. There comes a new religious awareness of the world around, and its language is imperious. How is it that men kindle a fire so that all around glows in its beams, yet somehow they cannot see? People can contrive to walk by the momentary glare of the lightning flashing on their tracks, but are in grosser darkness when the storm has passed, though all their natural faculties remain (2: 17–20).

[1] Thus the country south of Ḥijāz, and of 'Asīr (Milton's 'Arabie the blest'), is the Yemen, the land to the right; while *Al-Shām*, to the left, is the familiar name for Syria and the north country, or for Damascus, its natural capital.

[2] See Clermont Ganneau, loc. cit.

[3] See G. E. von Grunebaum, 'The Response to Nature in Arabic Poetry', *Journal of Near Eastern Studies*, vol. iv, 3, 1945, pp. 137–51.

Every landscape then, all ecology, all occupancy of the good earth by the tenant man, ends in awesome accountability implicit, for the creature, in the very energies of the creation in which he finds his empire. Those energies are celebrated in the enigmatic yet vibrant invocation of Surah 51: 1–6:

> By the winnowing winds,
> The rain-laden clouds,
> By the swift running courses,
> By all that disposes,
> Faithful is all that you are pledged.
> The judgment will indeed befall.

There are participles only here, for which in plainer languages nouns must be supplied, so that the parts of nature may be left to imagination and the commentators. Winds, waves, clouds, rains, sands and storms, are all 'scatterers', while 'the burden-bearers' may be mothers in pregnancy as well as laden clouds or camel-trains, or even angels. 'The coursing things' likewise are streams and fountains, tempests, birds on the wing or fleet-footed animals, and 'the disposers', the agencies that divide, distribute and determine. But all these, in their endless, tireless or relentless sway, move and labour, pass and return, by 'the command' or *amr*, of their Lord. His is the ordinance, within the cycles, the chemistry, the sequences of things, the planets in their circuits, the measure of time and season, the factors by which events, commodities and potencies are conditioned and decided.

However we search or conjecture its details, the passage, in its graphic intensity, sets man and the physical world of his habitation in the perspective by which the Qur'ān teaches and judges. If the artist would paint Muḥammad's Ḥijāz this must be his mood. By 'the tracks in the trackless heaven' let men abandon the contradictions in their souls (vv. 7–8).

Chapter 6
MARKETS OF THE CITY

There were two cities in the making of Islam. There is only one, decisive and supreme, in the metaphors of the Qur'ān. Though Yathrib, when it became Medina, by the *Hijrah*, had its vital role in the external evolution of the Prophet's mission, Mecca remained the essential mould of his mind and his affections. His birthplace was the constant haunt of his thoughts. Its genius for trade and high finance dominates the imagery of the Scripture. The physical emigration of AD 622 made no difference to the undisputed sway of the Meccan scene over the imagination and the language by which Islamic theology was nourished. The city proudly described as *umm al-qurā*, the mother metropolis, was equally *umm al-arā'*, the matrix of the vivid terms into which the preaching of Muḥammad cast the living themes of God and man, of death and eternity.

They came, overwhelmingly, from the market and the counting house, from the investments and mercantile instincts of Mecca and the Quraish. Though, strangely, the word *tājir* (merchant) does not figure in the Qur'ān, and *tijārah* (merchandise) only on nine occasions, commerce is the central theme in the life it mirrors and in the vocabulary by which it speaks. Everywhere, in simile, allusion and assumption, the merchant in his merchandise bestrides the stage. There were no doubt numerous artisans and craftsmen in the city—coppersmiths certainly, rope-makers, saddlers, chandlers, labourers and carpenters, but we do not hear of them. Only the lowly potter has a mention in the Scripture (55: 12) and then only in the context of the 'clay' of the creation of man. Not even the celebrated perfumers of Mecca come into the text, although the traditionalists are frequent witness to their arts in the entourage of Muḥammad.[1] For Doughty, they were the

[1] See H. Lammens, 'La Mecque à La Veille de l'Hégire', in *Mélanges de l'Université Saint-Joseph*, tome ix, fasc. 3, Beyrouth, 1924, esp. pp. 201–3—a mine of careful research into the background of Muḥammad's Mecca.

sweetest impression of the city his faith barred to him eleven centuries later. His delighted account of them is perhaps a gentle prelude to our present purpose in the sterner, soberer reaches of the city's banks and the columns of its ledgers.

> Long trains of loaded camels . . . descended before us to the Holy City. The most of these carried sacks. O blissful sweetness in the pure night air of rose blossoms, whose precious odours are distilled by the Indian apothecaries of Mecca. This is the *'aṭr* which is dispersed by the multitude of pilgrims through the Muhammadan world. . . . The crackling of the sweet smelling watch fire made a pleasant bower of light about us . . . the heaven was a deep blue, all glistering with stars
>
> '. . . that smiled to see
> The rich attendance on our poverty.'
>
> We were the guests of the night and of the vast wilderness.[1]

The crafts and skills which related to what Surah 106 calls the *ilāf* of the Quraish do not come into the pages of the book. Its whole context of idiom and similitude, in the urban sphere, is with the accountants and the bankers.

The compulsion to commerce, as we have seen in Chapter 5, lay in the facts of geography. The site of the city, called the 'hollow of Mecca' in 48: 24, is hailed in 3: 97 as

> '. . . the first house appointed for mankind . . . that at Bakkah, a blessed place and a guidance to the worlds. There the signs are, the signs that are clear, and the standing of Abraham. Whoever enters there, he is secure.'[2]

But the security meant here was that of spiritual sanctuary, not natural endowment. When Abraham prayed for provender and preservation

[1] Charles Doughty, *Travels in Arabia Deserta*, vol. 2, p. 527. Perhaps it may be right to wonder here when non-Muslims may be free to visit Mecca. Surely the time is ripe to end the ban.

[2] It is remotely possible that the form *Bakkah* here, instead of *Makkah* (Mecca) belongs with this forbidingness or straitness of the city's situation. The change from 'm' to 'b' is usually explained as a common, consonantal variation without significance. But the suggestion has been made that it echoes 'the valley of Baka' theme of Psalm 84: 7, where there are similar associations of hardship, uninviting terrain, and also sudden rains to inundate the place, and the presence of pilgrims. But the intriguing idea is highly conjectural. Mecca (thus) is only mentioned elsewhere in the 48: 24 passage, the background of which is the Treaty of Al-Ḥudaibiyyah between Muḥammad and the Quraish. *Bakkah* is sometimes explained as meaning 'the shrine', while *Makkah* is the whole city. Or it *may* have to do with 'crowding' or 'breaking'.

on behalf of those of his seed whom he caused to inhabit the valley of Mecca, he spoke of it as 'a valley where no sown land is' (14: 37). The barrenness of the locale was likewise much in the anxieties of the Quraish when they weighed the import of Muḥammad's preaching. 'If we were to follow the guidance you have,' they told him, 'we would be torn from our land' (28: 57). In reply the Qur'ān reiterates to them the sanctuary-security of their city and adds the reassurance of the broad movement of goods and victuals.

> 'Have We not secured them a sure sanctuary, an emporium of every kind of produce brought thither in yield as our provision?'

Both parties read those vital life-lines clearly enough. The great controversy had to do with the faith, not with the vigilance, of their custodians.

The religious stature of Mecca, through all its passionate issues, presupposed the economic ways and means, and these were always critically dependent on energy and expertise. The markets of Byzantium, through Gaza and Damascus, were a far cry from the coasts of Ḥaḍramaut. The cross trade likewise, from Ethiopia to Basrah, meant long months and lengthy risks. The hazards of marauding tribes were only partially surmounted by diplomacy. The size of the convoys made them easy quarry. Goods brought from one extremity were many moons from their sale in the other. They were theft-prone, loss-prone, decay-prone, seizure-prone. Camels and cameleers had to be recruited and hired from elusive or suspicious bedouin.

The situation might almost be told in the musings of Shylock, pondering a loan to 'the merchant of Venice', if we turn his nautical language to suit a mainly landborne commerce.

> To have you understand that he is sufficient. Yet his means are in supposition . . . ventures he hath abroad: but ships are but boards, sailors but men: there be land-rats and water-rats, water-thieves and land-thieves . . . and then there is the peril of waters, winds and rocks . . . the man is, notwithstanding, sufficient.[1]

'In supposition' the Quraish also were, their sagacity always pitted against factors which, their resourcefulness apart, could at any time

[1] William Shakespeare, *The Merchant of Venice*, I, iii, 14 ff.

deliver them to ruin. Their 'sufficiency' was always in constant engagement with their jeopardy. They made it good by their native competence and their instinctive trading sense. The impressive organization of the Ummayyad Caliphate at Damascus after AD 661, under Mu'āwiyā, owed much to the training of Abū Safyān, his father, in the management of Mecca's intricate economy in the immediate period of Muḥammad's mission. As a city-born community, Islam was heir to the words minted in this milieu and all of them current in the local speech, and spontaneous to the general mind.

The strength of Quraishī business enterprise lay first in its rigorous book-keeping. Caravan power, both of men and beasts, was carefully noted in documents of hiring and lading. Sums and figures, meticulously registered by their officers, served an oversight not to be fooled or cheated. These omniscient ledgers baulked the forgetfulness or the deliberate chicanery that might otherwise have been tempted into dispute. The range and the time-lag of the caravans required collective expenditures and borrowing against distant results.

This structure of the Mecca economy leaves its traces on almost every page of the Qur'ān. Migration to the more agricultural setting of Medina did not greatly modify the commercial terminology. The themes of destiny and faith are dominated by the thought of profit and loss, gain and bankruptcy, and human and divine computing. Accordantly with those unerring records of the business house, the world and every personal existence in it are meticulously ledgered. Each soul has its tally. The days and the years, in the most literal sense, have their toll. 'Verily with Us is the accounting of them', says Surah 88: 26. The word here is *ḥisāb*, the common term for reckoning, which occurs in one of the titles of the Day of Judgement (*Yaum al-Ḥisāb*) in 14: 22; 38: 16, 26 and 39; and 40: 28. *Al-Ḥasīb*, 'the accounter', is one of the divine Names. Surah 33: 39 observes: 'God is the sufficient reckoner,' and 4: 88: 'God is watching over all things as a reckoner.'

This divine reckoning underlies the idea of the *Kitāb* of every man, not—in this usage—the 'book' of revelation and *Kitāb* as a synonym for the Qur'ān itself, but the dossier, or file almost, of the individual's existence, where his balance-sheet of good and ill is set down. The fact of this single word as a term both for revelation and reckoning has gone far to shape and confuse Muslim popular theology. We shall notice a corresponding double sense in the word *qadr* in Chapter 9.

The 'books' of the Quraish, with their tell-tale columns, those recordings the nomad cameleers could neither emulate nor elude, were a constant source of impotent surprise.

'This is Our Book', runs 45: 28, 'which utters the truth against you. We have made a complete register of your transactions.' The *ḥisāb* of every client is individually recorded and the 'book' is handed to him in the Judgment, into the right hand or the left hand, according to whether the contents are worthy or unworthy (69: 19–26). God who raises the dead writes down all they 'send forward' and all their entail, assessed and enumerated. The word here, from the root *aḥṣā*, to number, is used for example in 19: 94 and 72: 28 and in conjuction with *Kitāb* in 18: 47 and 78: 29, where it means exactly a 'book-keeping' from which nothing, however minute, is omitted. The eternal issues are settled with indisputable precision. There is no gainsaying the omniscient ledger. Do we hear the futile protests of disputatious bedouin across the bank grilles of Mecca in the querulous words of the condemned:

> 'The book will be set down and you will see how apprehensive of what is in it the evil-doers are, how they say: "Woe to us! What is it about this book that nothing escapes it, big or little, all is reckoned there?". They find all their transactions down in it: your Lord is impartial to all.'
> (18: 49)

The stringent accounts of Mecca were both exact and efficient. The reckoning of the Judgment Day is likewise *sarī'a al-ḥisāb* (2: 198; 14: 51; 40: 17), just as those in the course of human history—where the word is also used—are condign and conclusive (e.g. 65: 8). Souls are requited strictly according to what they have earned. Tradition has it that God can complete the accounting with the whole creation in about half a day.

The finances of Mecca echo through the Qur'ān also in respect of loans and rewards. There were clearly economic implications in the very preaching of Muḥammad and reassurances, in several respects, that the menace of iconoclasm to the city's standing and prosperity would be more than countered by the compensations in true faith. Muḥammad's contemporaries knew as well as Abraham the paucity of non-mercantile resources. Hence the words in the declaration of Mecca's immunity from pagan pilgrim obligations in Surah 9: 28:

'If you are apprehensive of privation, God will enrich you of His bounty, as He willls.' God, according to 3: 171, does not allow the wage of the believer to waste. 'With Him in truth is a great wage' (64: 15; cf. 73: 20), and 'if you lend a goodly loan to God He will repay it twofold' (64: 17). The wages of goodness always exceed what is earned (6: 161; 10: 27; 39: 36). God never cheats, wrongs or defrauds and thus the believer and the devout are also the wise and the blessed. The verbs *kasaba*, to gain, *jazā*, to pay or requite, and *ajara*, to give wages, with *thāba*, to reward (in a good sense), are frequent in this context. There are passages which think of the believers as 'sold to God', receiving eternal bliss in exchange for their surrender. 'God has purchased from the believers their selves and their possessions in exchange for paradise' (9: 112). Likewise 2: 102; 4: 76 and 14: 33 commend those 'who sell this life for the life to come' in reference to the readiness of early Muslims to risk, to fight and to die, for Islam, rather than plead domestic satisfaction and immunities. For, in that sense, as 64: 14 insists, children and goods may be a danger and a snare, a *fitnah* or cause of inward 'sedition' (the developed political sense of a growing term) in the soul against the claims of faith. By contrast, 'excellent is the wage of the doers' (29: 58; 39: 74).

In all these ways the commercial habits of thought and speech in Mecca served and moulded the notions of religion. Unbelievers, by their false reckonings, 'sell themselves' cheap and treat the signs of God as a paltry commodity. Or 'they buy this life at the price of the life to come' (2: 80). 'Do not sell our revelations for a poor price' is the warning (to Jews) of 2: 38—a metaphor that recurs in 2: 73; 3: 71; 5: 48; and elsewhere.

Alertness to gaining and losing and the making or fumbling of bargains is a steady idiom in the Quranic world. The operative word here is *khasira* and its derivatives, notably the participle *khāsirūn*. These are found some sixty-three times, almost invariably in metaphorical context. It is one of the readiest terms for the unbeliever, denoting ill-judgment, folly, and bankruptcy. It implies both scorn and condemnation. 'To decry the signs of God' and to give the lie to revelation is to have a bad bargain on the Day of Judgment. Surah 10: 95 warns: 'Take very good care not to be among the sign-rejectors of God, for so to be is to rank among the losers.' Refusal of Islam as religion, according to 3: 85, is to opt for loss.

But not finally to lose requires tenacity and constancy. The intrusion into this Meccan world of *islām* itself constituted the largest test of discernment and of staying power. For it *seemed* to run counter to the instinctive securities of the Quraish, while holding within itself the unrecognized promise of great gains. That inclusive stake apart, the ordinary exchanges of commerce have their ups and downs, their graph of varying fortunes. So the ill has to be taken with the good. Is it then in financial guise that we may read the poetic refrain of 94: 5–6, *Inna ma'al 'usri yusran* ('with the hardship comes the ease' or 'gain after strain' or 'with the bitter there's the better')? Could this be a merchant's comment also, a sort of Latin *opportune importune* ('when seasons serve and when they disserve')? The phrase recurs in 65: 7 in a setting which suggests this:

> 'Let the man of ample resources expend them and the man whose means are limited spend according to what God has given him. God does not lay obligations on any one beyond what He has bestowed on him, and God has made it that after *'usr* comes *yusr*, the bad and the glad in their sequence.'

In a context about usury too—the theme of a later paragraph—we have the comment:

> 'If anyone is in difficulty [*'usr*] let it go, pending an easier situation: but it will be better all round if you waive (the debt) as a voluntary almsgiving, did you but realize it.'

There is no occasion, of course, to limit 'hardship' and 'ease' to this monetary realm, but it seems clear that the contrasts often started, and sometimes stayed, precisely there. For Mecca's sensitivities were nothing if not first financial.

'O you who believe,' runs Surah 61: 10, 'shall I point you to a commerce that will deliver you from the pains of hell?' The Quraish were hardly minded to understand it so and were more concerned with the immediate realities of trade and their more obvious present perils. Their natural propensities made them sceptical of a message which threatened their traditional pursuits. The impending day, said 36: 50, would rudely terminate their ability to go on making testaments, investments or commissions. There would be no trading on the Day of Judgment and no 'befriending' (14: 36). Its stark authority would cut across the familiar world of joint stock and collective finance and leave every soul in solitary unaidedness before the divine justice. 'No shuffling there.' The claim of the grand assize upon every separate soul, sundering as it did all bonds of kin and kind, could not be blunted by the feebler bonds of the cash nexus.

In one sense, then, the commercial parables availed only negatively. They were eloquent only because the eternal transactions so completely overwhelmed their logic. Yet the urge towards them in the Prophet's inspiration was inseparable from the *argumenta ad homines* of the Qur'ān. The criteria of successful business were employed as similitudes to challenge and overthrow its pagan suppositions and its compact with gods many and lords many. Muḥammad attacked the merchandisers in their own idiom. He broached their salvation in the meanings of their economy. 'He sent no messenger before you who did not eat and go about in the market places,' Surah 25: 20 told him. Perhaps the emphasis here is simply on the humanity of the apostolate, a down-to-earth-ness about prophets and their ways. But perhaps, as Ibn Ḥanbal suggests, 'the evil of the lands is in their market-places'.[1] The preacher of the divine will has, therefore, no option but to move and have his being where his hearers are, both in their physical occupations and their mental engrossments—the Qur'ān on Main Street.

It is here that the theme of usury presents itself (2: 275–9; 3: 130). There is some mystery about the Quranic prohibition, which did not emerge explicitly until the Medinan period and the juncture at which Muḥammad was in direct military confrontation with the Quraish, for whom, of course, it was second nature. 'Usury', they said, 'is the same as trade.' Certainly, as we have seen, the equipping of the caravans, the payment of scouts, the care of safe conducts, the wastage of commodities and indemnities against other risks, as well as the distances covered and the long duration of the ventures, necessitated the use of capital and justified, in their view, the payment of interest. Money, without which commerce in such forms (and there were no others) would have been impossible, was thus a commodity more valuable than material goods and deserving of reward for its expenditure at risk. Nor was it feasible in the Meccan situation to require immediate contact between the money-owner, or gainer, and his return, such as the shop-keeper represents, or the labourer by the day. Geography, not to mention rapacity, forbade that simplicity. The bedouin too, as the Qur'ān itself indicates, were evasive and trouble-

[1] *Musnad*, iv, 81, quoted in Lammens, op. cit., p. 245.

some. Those who made their camels and instinctive skills rewarding had some ground to claim securities against their trickery. These, in part, were practical arguments behind the exacting of oaths and the built-in guarantees that usury involved and against which Muḥammad set his face.

It is probable that we cannot rightly gauge the issues over usury, without reference to the Islamic transference of militancy from the arena of the tribal to that of the religious, where it could be mastered for a single cause. This aspect, pondered in Chapter 3, may be taken to explain the antipathy of the Qur'ān to the Quraishī traditions of usurious self-seeking. From one angle, it could be claimed that usury was at least a peaceful way of constraining the property of others into one's own enterprises. It was in that way more just than the *ghazwah*, the raid and the ambush. It did not crudely confiscate or openly purloin. It offered fair returns for the resources it employed and did not violently dispossess their owners.

But, by the same token, we are involved here in the very modern contention over 'orderly' exploitations and the whole problem of oppressive, or potentially oppressive, structures which, superficially considered, show a reasonable face. The Quraish, in practising usury, were innocent of *ghazwah* belligerence. Indeed, their whole philosophy sided with arranged securities, with safe-conducts and commercial 'law and order'. In defying this traditionalism, as Muḥammad did, to the point of contravening months of truce and systems of safe-passage, in what cannot be denied to be aggressive means, Islam was issuing a challenge to the supremacy of the Meccan system, including usury, as perpetuating a *status quo* inimical to the kind of unity Muḥammad sought.

There seems little doubt that the Medina veto on usury was a crucial factor in the final showdown with Mecca, calling into radical question, as it did, the whole pattern of Mecca's power. Its popularity with the tribes was evident, at least by short-range considerations. Entrenched as they were, the Meccan financiers were certainly avaricious exploiters and profiteers, doubling and redoubling (3: 130) to the point, according to 2: 275, of madness, deluded by Satan. The claims of *Zakāt*, of alms, and the demands of the Muslim campaign for *islām*, were the more likely to be met if the acquisitive instinct and its central institution were radically denounced. This is reinforced by the comment of 30: 38, a Meccan Surah:

'What you derive from usury, gaining from men's capital, does not gain with God. What you bring in alms, seeking God's face—those are the ones who have the increase.'

The prohibition of usury, leaving as it does a complicated legacy for exegesis in a different age, seems *in situ* an integral element in Islam's drive for a unitary society and for a religious authority, as well as an important tactical factor in the reduction of Mecca.

Commerce, usury apart, remains legitimate and proper. Those who became Muslims, in withdrawing from usury, were to require and to receive their capital (2: 279), but without the addition of interest. The transition to non-interest was to be eased in cases where it involved special hardship (2: 280). The legists and jurists have long debated the implications here and the feasibility of a commerce, ancient or modern, which restricts profit to the immediacy of transactions and requires money to be always and only within the personal supervision and operation of its actual owners. They are also abidingly occupied with the institutional control of human cupidity.

All the Quranic metaphors of commerce move within this implicit but fundamental interrogation of the commercial at the bar of the human. The man within the commerce, his faith and his destiny, are the vital 'business'. Compared with this crucial, religious seriousness of existence, all other canons of prosperity or poverty pale and fall away. Yet the religious and the human, in their priority, fit all too readily into the commercial criteria. The robust assurance of the metaphors is never in doubt nor their fitness for the issues. It is this, perhaps, more than any other consideration, which measures how deeply the ethos of Mecca penetrated the Islamic word. Trade remains a worthy parable of the eternal gains of faith. Men may 'send on before them', as the frequent phrase runs, their good deeds and know that they will not fail of reward. Morality itself may be seen as a transaction in profit. To serve God is to make a sure loan. 'Whatever good you expend, it will be repaid to you and you will not be wronged' (2: 272). Unbelief is the bad bargain.

Prosperity is the *falāḥ* of the Qur'ān, 'the good' to which the *adhān* summons the believer within the call to prayer. The participle akin to the noun is *mufliḥūn* (pl.) 'the prosperers', which occurs, with the verb, some forty times. 'Indeed, the believers are prosperous,' says the opening verse of Surah 23 (cf. 31: 5 and 87: 14 with 91: 9). These are 'the party of God' (58: 22). The root verb has associations with husbandry and the plough, but comes, in the urban context, to imply success and well-being. Its use, e.g. in 23: 1, may be seen as a kind of Quranic 'beatitude', 'happy are they who believe', and the sequence there sets this benediction in conditions of devotion, humility and rectitude. Surahs 59: 9 and 64: 16 take the commercial bearings of the metaphor far beyond themselves into the deeper reaches of self-awareness: 'Whoever is on guard against the avarice within—they are the ones who prosper.' The immediate context is the generosity of the Medinan hosts to the Meccan Muslims on the morrow of the *Hijrah.* The 'good loan to God' (64: 17) here is the self-transcendence of which the circumstances of commercial aid are the test and the occasion.

By contrast is the reproach of the miser, the man in the counting house in Surah 104, gloating over his wealth as if it had made him immortal, or the avaricious figure in 92: 8, whose whole horizon is his money. This is the sense of the significant word *istaghnā*: the man finds all his wealth in wealth, with the implication of an utterly false sufficiency, an independence which the Qur'ān reproaches elsewhere (64: 6; 80: 5; 96: 7) as a virtual repudiation of human community and a fearful insolence against God. Surah 92: 7 and 10 make a satirical play on words with the *'usr yusr* theme: 'We will ease him of his ease, or 'We will ease him to his knees.'[1] Men have to understand that they do not own the treasures of the world. For the treasuries of the earth are God's alone (15: 21–2).

Or there are the 'stinters', the sharp fellows of Surah 83, who demand full measure in their own case, but falsify the scales for others, weighing them or selling them short. As befits the context, the scales of merchandising are a recurring metaphor. 'We shall set up the just balances for the day of resurrection' and they will not err even to the weight of a mustard seed (28: 47). Surah 55: 8–9 enjoins the same exactitude in exchanges among men that belongs with the 'balance' of the world and of the planets. The *qisṭ* of the external cycles and orders of life requires to be fulfilled also in the social orbits of men (4: 135; 5: 8; 6: 152; 7: 29; etc.). The truth of the former is one with the integrity of the Scripture itself to which it is conjoined (57: 25). So Shu'aib to his community:

'Fill the measure and do not deceive, and weigh with honest scales

[1] In the sense of utter, abject reversal of fortune.

[*qisṭās*] and do not diminish people's goods and do not behave falsely in the earth, corrupting it.' (26: 181–3)

Surah 101 grimly, tersely, joins the scales of judgment with the nemesis of the fire.

All these are metaphorical corollaries of the life of Mecca, the imagery of the message of the Qur'ān as a mirror of its urban place. But glimpses of the *sūqs* and haunts themselves are rare in the extreme. We do not know from the text what nationalities might have been encountered in the streets. Mecca, says 22: 25, has been appointed equally for all men, resident or nomad, as a sanctuary. But the 'stranger in the gates' we cannot identify, whether Indian, Syrian, Ethiopian or Egyptian. In view of the tight Quraishi control it seems unlikely that foreign traders did more than make brief business visits, without establishing firms or depots independent of the local aegis.[1]

Nor can we readily list from Quranic reference the commodities in the caravans or the bazaars. Descriptions of paradise make note of bracelets of gold (18: 31; 22: 23; 35: 33) and silver (76: 21), and of silks and green brocades (*sunuds*) (in the same passage and in 44: 52). All such surmisable local colour is incidental in the undeviating religious purpose of the whole. For the rest, there is the woman bowing under her load of firewood, fastened by a rope of palm fibre—a common enough city sight but yielding, in Surah 111, a bitter imprecation against one of Muḥammad's earliest and most implacable foes.[2] Or the vagrant dog wandering around in the streets with his lolling tongue, indifferent alike whether you spurn or ignore it—parable of the unbeliever (7: 176). Or the much maligned donkey who brings at least a touch of humour to the otherwise unbroken seriousness of the business of life in the Qur'ān. 'Those who have been loaded with the Torah and then have not gone along with it are like a donkey laden with books' (62: 5)—recalcitrant and unaware of what they carry, mere vehicles and obstinate at that! The donkey appears again in 31: 18, to no better advantage. 'Be modest in your ways and speak quietly: truly the most raucous of voices is the braying of the donkey.' Eastern markets know the sound well.

But the most vital element in the Meccan scene, the well of Zamzam itself, finds no mention by name in the Qur'ān. The water which,

[1] Cf. Lammens, op. cit., p. 246.
[2] One would expect the rope to be across her brow.

according to Tradition, saved the infant Ishmael, and drew the folk of Abraham to the valley, shared with the sacred stone and the edicule in the pilgrim veneration. Like the fountain *Salsabīl* which figures in the picture of paradise (76: 17, cf. v. 5), Zamzam meant both life and legend for the city, its one natural asset, the custody of which was one of the prized prerogatives of the Quraish.

But the waters themselves were no human prerogative.[1] They were dependable only by the divine mercy. On that revocable circumstance, which nature afforded but only God ensured, the whole structure of the city depended and the long, far reach of its rulers' will to organize and their expertise. Hence the mingled urgency and confidence of the parables it yielded for Islam, *sub specie civitatis et aeternitatis.*

[1] Cf. 18: 39 and 67: 30 for vital waters that failed.

Chapter 7
THE POINT OF TIME

> A hundred new worlds lie in its verses:
> Whole centuries are involved in its moments,

wrote Muḥammad Iqbāl in his lyrical *Javid Nama*,[1] saluting the perpetuity of the Qur'ān. But it is the moments that must be taken before the centuries. Our first duty is with the point of time, with the Muslim Scripture in its immediate incidence and its particular chronology. The time factor is narrower, calendar wise, than that of any other religious document. Yet the significance for time in general of that calendar measure has always been a matter difficult of definition. A variety of problems, both practical and dogmatic, attach to the duty of relating the world of Mecca and Medina and of prophetic biography to the setting of later times and other places.

The reader has an early intimation of questions of time in what we can only call the presence and absence of chronology in the book itself. It is not arranged in chronological order, as every stranger finds when he takes up its perusal and is bewildered by sequences which seem to show no sequence. Yet its chapters are assigned, by its own authority, to two distinctive periods, divided by a central event, the *Hijrah* from Mecca to Medina. Chapters are identified as those that precede the departure from the one capital of Islam to the other, and those that follow it. But this concession to the calendar, basic as it is, does not dictate a physical division of the whole accordingly. The Surahs or chapters are identified, on either side this watershed, only by a note at the head of each, which has no power to control their position in the book. Their location is determined by the completely non-chronological factor of approximate length, beginning from the longest (Surah 2) and proceeding to the shortest at the end. Thus even

[1] Trans. A. J. Arberry, London, 1967, ll. 1133–4.

the crucial pre- and post-*Hijrah* consideration is a central division which does not divide. It reads like a strong hint that the calendar is very significant. But the hint is one which the book itself refuses to take.

It can, no doubt, be said that this is the deliberate isolation of one event as pivotal, so that all chronological relevance may be compressed into one emphasis. Hence the special study we have purposely made of the *Hijrah* in Chapter 8. But to concede this inclusive import by a singular insistence on a point in time, seen as a great divide, and reinforced by the derivation from it of a new calendar, is surely also to require a relevance in the forward logic of events from it and the momentum of factors towards it. We cannot sense a culmination without a *chronology* of 'after' and 'before'. Nevertheless, the arrangement of the Qur'ān diffuses and disperses these, ignoring its own pivot. The pages themselves, we may say, do not turn on their own hinge.

This presence and absence of chronology deepens into other problems. There can be no doubt that the Scripture is 'situational', involved, that is, in times, places and occasions. Of necessity, it has a narrative as the locale of its meaning. The contexts immediate to the incidence of the contents are inseparable from their interpretation and their import. This is freely and fully recognized as inescapable. Even the eternal cannot enter into time without a time when it enters. Revelation to history cannot occur outside it. A prophet cannot arise except in a generation and a native land. Directives from heaven cannot impinge upon an earthly vacuum. The Qur'ān, for Prophet and hearers, in the seventh century, was a 'here and now'. In that historical sense, we in the twentieth century start from the fact that it was 'there and then'. And, within itself, it comprised some twenty-three years—years which, in their concurrence with it, necessarily succeeded one another and, in their succession, contained the co-incidental events with which the words and meanings of the Scripture were associated.

That temporal presence and relation, however, which chronology merely traces and fixes, reverence and the theologians have somehow always suspected and discounted Having the revelation in possession, they sought to detach it from all circumstances and connections and to save it from ever being 'dated' by making it 'dateless', as if innocent chronology was in some way an offensive conspirator against authority and sanctity. In many circles, the non-chronological form of the Qur'ān as it stands, however we account for it, becomes in this way a virtue in disguise or, rather, a proper parable of the necessary transcendence of mere point and circumstance which the believer should attain. God had not allowed the Qur'ān to be arranged in sequence, in order to preclude notions of the time factor and of calendar time itself, seen as embarrassments to its celestial status.

True, the Surahs, especially the longer ones, are composite within themselves as well as irregular in time, so that the continuous reader oscillates bewilderingly across the years and has, indeed, a better chance of being in historical step if he starts at Surah 114 and reads back to Surah 2, than is he lets the paging guide him. But no matter—the way the Qur'ān is canonically must be seen as providential. The nature of the providence is easy to assume. Chronology could not fail to have been applied to its canonization if the Prophet had ever indicated so, or if God has so willed. The way it is the querulous must find salutary, even as the faithful find it welcome. We are being properly, divinely, discouraged and frustrated if we mistakenly endeavour to 'incidentalize' Quranic meaning, to link *what* it is with *when* and *where*. We must needs follow, in memorizing, reciting, perusing or expounding, the sequence of Surahs, serial and inward, as they stand in the dissonance of dates, that we may better apprehend the music of their truth.

But this 'orthodox' satisfaction with non-chronology in the arrangement of revelation cannot for a moment dispute the necessarily chronological experience of revelation, on the part of Muḥammad. The Qu'rān clearly enjoins an understanding of itself which makes 'contextuality' central and fundamental, both to its existence and its relevance. By its own evidence and character it is a 'gathered' book, a successive Scripture, an accumulating whole. *Waḥy* occurs *seriatim*. Whatever may be true of the numbered Surahs, they were a number in succession. This fact is of so crucial a significance that it deserves to be fully expounded from within the Qur'ān.

The historical experiences of Muḥammad in what may be called the episodic recipience of the book, as already studied, belonged with poetic eloquence, Arab leadership and religious mission, all with their precise and particular qualities, passions and burdens. The initial revelation, earlier pondered in Chapter 1, was, plainly, a highly 'singular' event. At the point of its occurrence there was no certainty that it would not also be a solitary event. The assurance of revelations following each other dependably was only gradually and painfully achieved and proved.[1] The Prophet seems to have been anxious for his integrity and for his sanity, if the vision failed of corroboration, and for its continuance once a 'series' had become actual.

In both respects, the Qur'ān, as prophetic and psychic event or history in itself, was essentially cumulative. Its steady sequences, as they proved to be, naturally moved with, and related to, a parallel setting of external circumstances, awaiting, reflecting and illuminating those deliverances. Muḥammad preached as he heard and he heard as he preached. He received as he mediated and mediated as he received. He ruled as he was directed and directed as he was ruled. He was throughout an apostle in a context, a protagonist in the field, a spokesman with an audience, a man with a mission.

This quality of history in the Qur'ān, of the Qur'ān as history, would seem so obvious and incontrovertible as to be superfluous to emphasize, were it not for the sustained reluctance of classical theology to allow the contextuality its full implications. To insist that there were 'occasions' of, and for, the Qur'ān is not to mean or imply that these were also the 'causes' of it, which is what doctrine-makers have feared. Nor is it to suggest or desire any sort of equation framed to say: '*To* that time argues *only* to that time.' This, again, is what orthodoxy has feared. In its anxiety to preclude an antiquarian Qur'ān it has failed fully to possess a historical one. The end of this timorous logic is precisely to incur the antiquarianism one fears and resists. For one cannot proceed *to* the abidingness of the Qur'ān, in word and meaning, unless one intelligently proceeds *from* its historical ground and circumstance. The very irrelevance that belongs with relegation to pure past is exactly the nemesis that awaits any will to escape it by ignoring the quality of the real past. To have the book immune from history is to make its own history irrelevant.

Happily this conviction emerges indisputably from the Quranic text itself. There are several important passages which underline the necessarily periodic and contextual nature of its contents. An early Surah, 75: 16, directs Muḥammad not to precipitate the Qur'ān impatiently, not to urge it on more rapidly by getting his tongue moving

[1] A. Draz (*Initiation au Coran*, Paris, 1951) believes that the interval may have been as long as three years. He makes the return of *waḥy*, not its first onset, to mark Muḥammad's passage from *nabī*, or 'prophet' to *rasūl*, or 'apostle'.

with it, and the next verse goes on: 'Ours [God speaking] it is to bring it together [or 'gather' it] and to utter it. So when We recite it, you follow the recital of it and then Ours, too, is the explaining.' The word here translated 'recital' (*qur'ānahu*) is an action, not a thing, the Qur'ān, as it were, in process, a recital which, coming from God, engaged the Prophet in repeating the syllables and, as the grammarians say, 'moving the vowels'. He is not to be 'in a hurry' with this. For what is involved is by its nature a process, the continuing and completing of which is in God's care. The Prophet needs to be a patient auditor if he would be a loyal utterer. Attractive as the idea might seem, the living Qur'ān could not be had all at once.[1]

This impossibility is referred to in clearer terms elsewhere. Surah 20: 114 warns Muḥammad: 'Do not be impatient for the Qur'ān before its revelation [*waḥy*] is completed for you. Say: "Lord, let me increase in knowledge."' In 17: 106 it is explicitly called 'a Qur'ān which We have given *seriatim* [lit. "separated out"] in order that you may recite it to the people at intervals and We have caused it to come down successively [lit. "We have sent it down sending down']". In this same connection, Surah 6: 7 observes: 'If We had sent it down a (whole) book on parchment they could touch and handle, those who disbelieve would have said: "This is nothing but plain sorcery."' Surah 25: 32 records the unbelievers tauntingly wanting it that way: 'Why has the Qur'ān not been vouchsafed to him in one single whole?', and the answer: 'that your heart (Muḥammad) may be strengthened, We have chanted it as We have chanted it,' that is, gradually.

This gradualism, spread over twenty-three years, means that the chapters and verses of the Qur'ān impinge upon a succession of temporal events, known in a technical phrase as *asbāb al-nuzūl*, 'the occasions of the descent'. It is this fact which underlies the description of every verse as an *āyah* or 'sign'. The word which we have seen applied to phenomena in nature denotes also the sentences of the book. For these also disclose a meaning 'signed' in a situation, discernible in

[1] This passage has been understood as relating to the manner of recital of the existing (or partially existing) book, as being, that is, a regulation for the community. But it seems to be directed expressly to Muḥammad himself and only the meaning suggested above does justice to the phrase about 'gathering it'. Over-hasty reciters could hardly be ensuring a yet incompleted revelation, but an over-zealous preacher might think he was. Or was it the impatience of his followers, improperly pressing on his composure? Or the verse may refer to Muḥammad's patience within each several occasion, rather than to an eagerness about the ensuring of the whole. But, in all events, the periodicity for which we are arguing is plain.

an event. Content and context must be seen together; for the one possesses the other. The 114 Surahs of the Qur'ān belong with the 300 months of Muḥammad's career as *Rasūl-Allah*. His vocation initiates the earthly Qur'ān and his death closes it. Through the sequences of his career—yearning, vision, utterance, pertinacity, controversy, endurance, rejection, emigration, militancy and triumph—the accumulation of the Qur'ān moves in parallel relation, fusing meaning with mission, and truth with setting. It is as events unfold that the whole grows into entirety.

It may be useful to summarize here the main calendar, as it were, of the book, the engagement of its themes with time and circumstance. The genesis of the Scripture in the inaugural experience we have already pondered, with the attendant factors of Arabic joy of language, Jewish and Christian associations and Arab sense of destiny—all in their several ways waiting upon the religious urge. That mission soon came to grips with pagan obduracy and passed into a long and painful struggle against unyielding 'establishment', employing every device of dissuasion, threat, cajolery, and persecution to forestall it. Verbal controversy fills the middle and later Surahs of the Meccan period with a lively running exchange between the Prophet and the main body of his fellow citizens. Here the content of the Qur'ān engages with the charges, gibes and incredulities of the people. The reports of these ('They say . . .') become a steady refrain with the countering directive to Muḥammad ('Say thou . . .'). The themes are idols, death, resurrection, judgment, authority, Scripture, status, poverty and motive. Here comes the reinforcement to Muḥammad's cause of the precedents of the patriarch/prophets whose generations showed the same stubbornness and folly.

The utter incompatibility of the 'sides' in this encounter is passionately declared in Surah 109.

> Say: 'O you who deny (this faith),
> I do not worship what you worship;
> Nor do you worship what I worship.
> Never shall I be a worshipper of what you have worshipped.
> Never will you be worshippers of what I worship.
> Your religion is yours, and mine is mine.'

Muḥammad has only a staunch negative for any suggestions of compromise or abeyance of witness.[1] He is fortified by the assurance that lies in the very sequences of the Quranic recipience itself, once these had come to be dependable and habitual. Surah 93: 3–4 no doubt reflect an early apprehension before this settledness of experience.

> Your Lord has not abandoned you, nor does He disown you.
> Truly what is yet to be is better than the beginning.

That everything had come out of orphanhood and poverty, as the Surah goes on to recall, only made the reassurance the more telling. Muḥammad had, as it were, a powerful 'Ebenezer, hitherto has the Lord helped'.

Steadily, therefore, the crisis sharpened as the impasse became more evident between an unaccommodating messenger and an unyielding constituency. The *Hijrah*, studied elsewhere, in the detail it deserves, as the watershed of the entire narrative, was the logical climax. The preaching career of Muḥammad in what the Qur'ān calls *al-balāgh*, the proclaiming, moved into the political sequel, into the claims and the vicissitudes of power and arms. Nascent Islam broke out of the Meccan constriction and developed, in parallel progression, a cultic definition, an effective policy and a legal framework of its own—all in the new context of Medinan opportunity and danger.

There followed a growing dissociation from Jewish norms and links, which had played their part in Muslim origins, but now fell more and more away, through the gathering self-sufficiency of Islam and the increasing disfavour of Jewish elements—factors which the *Hijrah* accelerated and brought into the open. In the pre-*Hijrah* pressures of search and anticipation, Muḥammad underwent the experience traditionally known as 'the night journey' to Jerusalem (Surah 17: 1). Early in the post-*Hijrah* story, however, Jerusalem was displaced by Mecca as the direction of Muslim prayer (Surah 2: 144) and Mecca's repossession emerged as the central logic in the whole 'argument' of Medinan Islam.

The Battles of Badr and Uḥud as the primary physical crises of that story, have conspicuous place in the Qur'ān, the former especially in Surah 8: 1–19 and the latter in Surah 3: 102–75. These passages deal with the circumstances of the engagements, the attack on the caravans,

[1] The issues sometimes raised to the contrary, especially in respect of Surah 58: 19–30, will be dealt with in Ch. 9 below.

the hesitancies of some Muslims, the over zealousness of others, the disposition of booty, the lessons of the fields themselves and reflections on their meaning. Badr, as the first and signal victory of Muslim arms, is described as 'the day of the criterion' (v. 29)—the encounter in which vindication had been manifested and the 'salvation' of the cause decided. These are among the clearest narrative pieces of the Qur'ān in their extensive and detailed reference to events. Surah 59 seems directly connected with the expulsion of the Jewish Banū Naḍīr from their territory in requital for their breach with Muḥammad. Through all this period, culminating in the conquest of Mecca, there are frequent references to the *munāfiqūn*, the dubious or hypocritical people around the Prophet, who were calculating the pros and cons of a still fluid issue, playing for their own ends with the uncertain stakes of time-serving and subterfuge. Muḥammad's alertness to their duplicity or their hollow allegiance only tended to make their cunning the more subtle and elaborate. This atmosphere of intrigue is part of the political price exacted by the invocation of force.

The treaty of Al-Ḥudaibiyyah, in AH 5, by which Muḥammad gained substantially in negotiation with Mecca, is the general topic of Surah 48. Having been barred from an intended pilgrimage that year, he secured the right to make one the year following, of three days' duration, unarmed. More importantly, a ten-year truce between himself and the Quraish allowed either camp to receive whatever tribal accessions they could gain, though Muḥammad made the seemingly unequal concession that Meccan deserters to his side would be returned though Muslim fugitives to Mecca would not. Events, he hoped, would nullify this and meanwhile he had acquired the prestige of negotiating as an equal. The Surah seems intended in part to allay the fears of loyal disciples who mistook the truce, with the extradition compact, for weakness and did not appreciate its potential for the final cause.

The ultimate capture of Mecca is celebrated in 17: 81: 'Say: "The truth has come and falsehood is routed: truly the false was meant for extinction."' Occasions in the period after victory at Mecca are noted in Surah 9—the victory at Ḥunain against the Hawāzin and the Thaqīf (v. 25 f.) and the expedition to Tabūk (v. 81 f.)—where there are questions of spoils and of readiness for combat and queries of sincerity. In the ninth year after the *Hijrah*, in the 'Release' proclamation, Muḥammad declared the end of the immunity for pagan pilgrimage and the termination, after four months, of all obligations to pagans except in the case of specific treaties, which would be allowed to run their course. Surah 9: 1–24 records the text of the proclamation. Muḥammad's farewell pilgrimage to Mecca is understood to have been the setting of Surah 5: 5, the verse which declares the perfection of religion, the ultimate realization of *al-Islam*. Within a few weeks, Muḥammad died in the fulness of victory and the Qur'ān was complete.

These, in barest outline, are the most conspicuous biographical revelational junctures of the Qur'ān, the salient occasions within its chronology. Call, encounter, *Hijrah*, consolidation, triumph are the five main sequences of the narrative. The inner logic is from vision to word, from word to controversy, from controversy to crisis, from crisis to statehood, from statehood to arms, from arms to success, from success to unification. But each progression in the history must be seen as carrying along with it the dialectic of the whole, the impetus of the factor prior to it, making the series a developing drama where each element, by Islamic logic, is loyally itself in the process. Other criteria might at every point dispute or disown the sequence, but not the Islamic. The mission in the initial vocation, by Islamic counsel, could not stay with preaching, nor live with impasse, nor shrink from force, nor bear with tragedy, nor rest without decision, nor be satisfied without success. The chronology of the Qur'ān, then, is a calendar of vindication in time, and of time as vindication, by dint of the energies of action within it.

With the stream of these events went, no doubt, a manifold of obscurer details, not now explicitly recoverable from the allusions of the book, or not even reflected at all in its pages. But the main current is unmistakable and leaves the student in no uncertainty as to the broad circumstantial setting of the *asbāb al-nuzūl*. Before asking the questions for which we are now ready about 'the point of time', it will be right to linger in one area of Quranic incident—the one that has to do with what we may call the inner, or the private, Muḥammad.

It is striking that the personal name occurs only in the title of one Surah and in four isolated verses. It is as the *rasūl* that he is designated and addressed. The office in the Qur'ān always governs and dominates the 'Muḥammadan'—in the strict and only proper sense of that adjective (which does not occur in the Scripture) as pertaining to the man as man. The Surah is 47, where, in v. 2, we have the clause: '... those who believe in what is sent down to Muḥammad'. Surah

3: 144 emphasizes that 'Muḥammad is only a messenger (*rasūl*)' and that 'messengers before him have passed away'. He is a mortal among mortals and his death would be no signal for cowardice and no occasion for superstitious surprise. Surah 48: 29 renews the simple attestation of apostolate and enjoins on his followers mercy towards each other and severity against their foes. Only 33: 40 has, as it were, a wholly personal import in observing, with a clear pathos, that 'Muḥammad is not the father of any man among you.'[1] Yet this grievous heirlessness was far from being a merely personal tragedy.[2] For it profoundly affected the expectations for the future and it undoubtedly underlay the several diplomatic marriages which Muḥammad undertook in the political days beyond the death of Khadījah and the *Hijrah*. Like any other builder of power and of a new régime, the Prophet was vitally concerned for the succession—though the general context of Surah 33 has to do with an episode that cannot altogether be explained in these terms.

These explicit references to Muḥammad by name do not, of course, exhaust the personal incidents, marital and domestic, which occur in the Qur'ān, and which here we do not stay over.[3] For our present purposes they may be seen as simply underlining, in their down-to-earth character and their sharp, individual quality, the honest particularity of the Qur'ān. It is a book within a society, with a mores and culture of its own, a book *via* a personality with impulses and concerns, as well as *charisma*, of a vigorously human sort.

One of the most revealing of these personal incidents is that which gives its title to Surah 80, 'He Frowned'. According to the related tradition, Muḥammad was in converse with certain Meccan notables, whose accession he anticipated, when the interview was interrupted by a blind man seeking instruction. The Prophet apparently showed some annoyance and the passage firmly rebukes his implied preference

[1] There is also the passage in 61: 6 in which Jesus is said to foretell the coming of a prophet after him 'whose name is *aḥmad*' (or 'Ahmad'). If we take the (capitalized) proper name, it is a synonym for Muḥammad and is then to be taken as a precise foretelling of him. The other (non-capitalized) sense would mean a 'more excellent, or praiseworthy' prophet. Arabic has no distinction to indicate the reading we should prefer. In either case it is Muḥammad who is meant in the comparison and the expectation.

[2] The same circumstance is the point of the ridicule in Surah 108: 3, 'the one cut off' (*al-abtar*). Like an animal with a docked tail so is a man without progeny. The Surah measures something of the intensity of the animosity against him.

[3] Notably Surah 33: 37–40 about the marriage with Zaynab and Surah 66: 1–5 having to do with marital questions in the household.

for the influential converts and his impatience with the eager, but disabled, intruder. The very presence of the story in the texture of the Surah would seem the clearest proof of its authenticity and in its honesty and utterly human quality it provides an eloquent witness to the actualities of the real history. In no other verses do we come quite so close to Muḥammad as a living person in the very *sūqs* of Mecca or to Islam as a faith in the making.

Leaving other 'incidentalisms', as they might be called, within this general impression of realism and environmental there-and-then-ness, it remains to try to isolate the main implications of the time context of the Qur'ān from which the continuing meaning must be transposed and identified for succeeding and changing centuries. What is implicit, in the seventh century encounter of a prophet with his world, for the ongoing community of the book which derives from that history? What is their relevance for humanity beyond them? What, out of its environment, does it say outside it? Or, in short, what is the point of its time?

The answer is both served and disserved by the mass of Islamic Tradition or *Ḥadīth*, relating to Muḥammad's person and mission. By its very existence as a definitive element in Islam's sources and criteria, this great body of material, memorializing and invoking the historical Muḥammad, confirms the central role of context and time and place, as we have argued it. For the business of Tradition is to perpetuate the Prophet as the present contemporary of every successive generation, guiding its ways and directing its values. It means the meticulous conservation of the one point in time as the ruling authority for all time. As such it speaks an emphatic conviction about the locale truth has in history. By virtue of Tradition a particular retrospect becomes the vital principle of Islamic existence. The *asbāb al nuzūl* become, as it were, *abwāb al-tārīkh:* occasions of revelation are the doors of history. The 'incidentalism' of the days of the Qur'ān becomes, so to speak, the 'fundamentalism' of the centuries. This is the service of Tradition to an age-long concern with Muḥammad as he was.

Yet there is a disservice at its heart. For the temper of Islamic traditionalism has been instinctively deferential, even servile, towards the time factor. Its dominant attitude was to return to the seventh century criterion in Muḥammad as if time, then and after, had a static quality. Reports, sayings, occasions, of and around the Prophet were devoutly loved, collected and repeated. They were treasured as necessary to the meaning and reading of the Qur'ān. They illuminated and amplified the *asbāb al-nuzūl*. They made good much which the Qur'ān itself had left to silence and they vastly implemented and enlarged the scope of Qur'ān-originated law. The centrality of Tradition is thus the most eloquent witness to the crucial quality of the local history.

But, in this passion for contemporaneity of Muḥammad through capacious and retentive recollection, the traditionalists quite failed to reckon with moving time. There was the critical fact of the 'date' but no critical factor of 'datedness' in their cognizance. They returned to a past without allowing that the present need do more than recall it dependably. Thus the science of *Ḥadīth* criticism or collection turned squarely on the idea of *isnād*, or support. A chain of corroboration had to go back unbroken from the latest reporter to a 'companion', or eye-witness, or ear-auditor, of the Prophet. Each adjacent pair of links in the human chain had to be proved contemporary as evidence that the one had indeed communicated with the other. Biographies of 'companions' and narrators were studiously compiled with this intent and 'dossiers' also on the character and credibility of the persons involved. Where links were proven and reliability, in these personal terms, attested, Traditions could be said to be 'sound' and the science of criticism satisfied. For these were its only anxieties. No internal criticism was allowed to intrude. The question should not be: Was Muḥammad likely to have said this in his situation? or: How did the circumstances in Mecca/Medina bear on this occasion? or: Is this reported action truly in character? Instead the Tradition was content, and being content was decisive, if the matter had a sound 'chain' of human reporting, A to B to C to D to E, etc., all honest men.

In this way the powerful 'retrospect' of Tradition nevertheless excluded the significance of the time. It revered *what* Muḥammad had done and said *when* he did and said it, without venturing responsible decisions about *how* the when affected the what, or how a different when should imitate it in the the kind of loyalty that cannot be attained without internal criticism. The critical conditions, as noted, bore only on those who had related the Traditions and left no room or need for creative weighing of the guidance discernible. It was a loyal retrospect which cherished time by ignoring its passage.

There are many fascinating aspects of Tradition which do not bear upon our present case, but none that require us to alter it. The great labours of the canonical editors of the third Muslim century, pruning its by then voluminous proportions, vitally served the needs of lawyers and of the faithful, but without revising, in any essential way, the confidence in retrospect *per se.* Even its yeoman work in disowning manifest abuses proceeded on a static criterion of what abuses are.

Traditional Tradition, then (the phrase has real point), supposes a passive role for ongoing time in its obedience to the paragon time, a care for strict memory not for creative repossession. Even so, it remains the plainest argument for taking the Qur'ān historically. Legal opinion (*ra'y*) and consensus (*ijmā'*) and initiative (*ijtihād*) in turn proceed from it as means to the *Sharī'ah*, or sacred law. So the Qur'ān is definitive but not exclusive, final but not total, in the realization of Islam. These enlarging sources of reference are required because the book is positioned in time and subsequent times demand direction. They are possible because the time of the book is understood to be a proper quarry of precedent, with the Prophet as its treasure. Such direction, thus both available and necessary, is always under the veto of 'repugnancy' to the Qur'ān but develops at the same time beyond it. As Muḥammad Rasjidi remarks:

> The Qur'ān was revealed almost fourteen centuries ago and the Traditions concerning the Prophet who lived that long ago, exclusively in a desert society, cannot serve as explicit guides for every situation which might arise centuries later and especially in the complex societies of the present day.[1]

If, then, the implicit guidance has to be drawn out by a creative and responsible quality of response, there is all the more crucial place for Quranic history. The present and the future of loyalty, we may say, turn on a right sense of the past, of Quranic situations as the source of both explicit Tradition and implicit wisdom. 'Nothing', observes Dr Fazlur Rahman, 'can give coherence to the Quranic teaching except the actual life of the Prophet and the environment in which he moved.'[2] He goes on to insist that Tradition should not be seen simply as helping to fill the void left by the demise of Muḥammad, but as vital also for the days of his Quranic role itself. He could be the referee

[1] In Kenneth W. Morgan, *Islam, the Straight Path*, New York, 1958, p. 406. This work is an edited anthology of Muslim contributions in self-expression. Dr Rasjidi is Indonesian.

[2] See 'Concepts of *Sunnah*, *Ijmā'* and *Ijtihād* in the Early Period', *Islamic Studies*, vol. 1, 1962, Karachi, p. 10; reprinted in *Islamic Methodology in History*, Karachi, 1965.

to whom recourse was proper for elucidation of the text in exegesis, only because he stood at the centre of the experiences within which its contents reached him. Either way, then, the biographical milieu is fundamental. There could be no clearer token that the Qur'ān is meant to be contextually understood than this vast wealth of Tradition.

It is feared in some circles that this statement of the case jeopardizes, or even violates, belief in the Qur'ān as miraculously mediated and consigns the Prophet's experience to historical relativity. That fear, explicable as a yearning for the inviolate which all religions exhibit, is none the less unworthy of the concept of revelation itself, and would disqualify Tradition also in its instinct to take history as the source of authority. The valid distinction between the Quranic/prophetic and the biographical/exemplary in Muḥammad cannot rightly be invoked against this conclusion. For while it is proper to distinguish between *waḥy*, or experience issuing into Quranic words, and *ilhām*, or general *charisma*, leadership and authority, the first merges imperceptibly into the second in its historic incidence and its context. It means a distinction in status within revelation, not of context within time. Muḥammad cannot *begin* to possess a personal relevance to truth only in posthumous terms. We cannot sustain a theory of the Qur'ān and the fact of Tradition on a hypothesis which would disqualify their co-existence in the same time and place. To make either immune from 'circumstantiality' and from biography would mean that while Tradition could never authentically emerge, revelation itself, intelligently seen, would also have become impossible.

We return from these implications of Tradition, for the understanding of the place of history, to our broad questions about the point of the time. What are the areas in which the Qur'ān—to phrase it this way—gives its immediacy into its perpetuity? There would seem to be two elements in the answer. There is a deep 'struggle to mean', a battle for language, the labour to communicate through the vexing medium of words. This fascinating semantic issue occupies Chapter 9. There is secondly the theme of *effective* monotheism in Chapter 10—the struggle to actualize *islām* in 'the making of Muslims', to conform the moral and social patterns of the first generation to the new order of Islam. Both are the measure of the *Jihād* about the *Jāhiliyyah*.

The political and power structures already noted in Chapter 3 are presupposed. But state and rule are only, if also indispensably, conditions of a more ultimate task. The twin duties of witness and life, of *balāgh* and *da'wah*, of surely affirming and rightly achieving *islām*, embody in their essential character the ultimate point of the time of the Qur'ān.

Meanwhile the fulcrum of that history in the *Hijrah* merits a separate study in justice to its decisive quality, both for Muḥammad's mission and Muslim existence, as well as for the inauguration of the Islamic calendar.

Chapter 8
THE CRISIS OF EMIGRATION

'Depart from them a fair departing,' Surah 73: 10 directs (in literal rendering), enjoining on 'the enmantled' Prophet in the earliest days the duty of patience and courtesy in the face of accusation and resistance. The pattern held sway for thirteen long and weary years until the crucial *Hijrah*, or 'departing', which drew the whole community of Muslim faith from its natal city to a new centre, turning it almost overnight from a religious minority under duress into a potential statehood and a political reality. The geographical element in the transition was both the symbol and the crux of the decision by which Islam achieved its Meccan cause and inaugurated its Medinan form. The two cities are the poles of the one crisis. The *Hijrah* is at once both the departure and the arrival of Islam.

'The fact that the Prophet prospered and died in a place not his birthplace is perhaps a mystic hint,' Muḥammad Iqbāl once wrote in an early notebook.[1] Hint or not for the mystic, it is the most solid and eloquent of realities for the historian and the expositor. By the *Hijrah* neutrality became impossible. Islam was finally out from under the Meccan impasse of casual or malevolent indecision, and into the irrevocable shape of its new political destiny. Community in faith had now taken precedence over blood relationship. By an act of self-imposed exile, Muslims had foreshadowed the inclusive character of Islam. Against the foes of their own household they were finding a new one.

For an event so vital and formative, the Qur'ān surprisingly has little direct to say. The *Hijrah*, though it starts the calendar, does not

[1] As reported by his son, Javid Iqbal. The immediate point he had in view was a concern against the 'idolatry' of nationalism—a point to which Iqbal often returned in his desire to utilize national ardour, for its counter-imperialist value, without the compromise he feared of a right Islamic universalism, for which crude nationalism was 'the worship of Baal'.

entitle any surah. The Surah of Exile (59) uses another word *Al-Ḥashr* and refers to a mustering outside Medina, some time after the Muslim arrival there, of elements in the city hostile to the influx of Meccans and to Muḥammad's growing identification of the city with his own interests and to their resultant embroilment with the Quraish. The Surah of the Cave (18) does not celebrate the cavern where Muḥammad lay concealed with Abū Bakr during the *Hijrah*, as Tradition relates with vivid detail, but rather the long hideout of the legendary Seven Sleepers of Ephesus. Nor does the Surah of the Spider (29) have to do with the traditional story of how the two fugitives were saved from Quraishī detection and capture because a spider's web hung across the cave's mouth and dissuaded the pursuers from exploring it. Surah 29 is concerned only with the general parable of human fragility (v. 40 f.) and the vanity of an idolatrous trust.

According to exegetical assumption in many quarters, there *is* a circumstantial reference to the *Hijrah* in the enigmatic opening of Surah 36, where v. 9 says that 'We have covered them over so that they do not see'—a reference which commentators take to mean the inability of Meccan conspiracy or antagonism to vent its wrath successfully against Muḥammad, before, during or beyond the *Hijrah*.[1] Whether or not this is the intended sense, the Qur'ān is plainly, and significantly, indifferent to precise details. It does not share or serve the speculative curiosity of later biographers but holds its concern to crucial issues and the overall sense of the divine authority and destiny. Echoes of surrounding verses in Surah 36 are heard in other passages and they could well refer to more inclusive themes of mortality and judgment and the groping darkness of death.

The only explicit passage about the *Hijrah* would seem to be that in Surah 9:40–1, with its use of the Hebraic word *Shechīnah* and its clear allusion to the two in the cave.

> 'When the unbelievers drove him out with his closest associate, and he and his "second" were together in the cave, he assured him: "Sorrow not: God is with us." And God caused His peace (*Sākīnah*) to come over him and aided him with legions unseen. Thus did He utterly humble the counsel of the unbelievers and exalt the divine word to supremacy . . .'
>
> (9:40)

[1] The most frequent explanation of the possible allusion here is to the occasion when four conspirators were sent to murder Muḥammad, each from a different tribe, to 'divide' the onus. He cast dust on their heads and this foiled them.

Whatever help friends withhold out of fear or the love of ease, the divine succour does not fail. The passage concludes with an obvious reference to the material 'lightening' that all exiles sustain: 'Go forth, light and heavy and strive with your possessions and yourselves in the way of God. Did you not know it, you could want no better thing.'

Below in this same Surah and elsewhere, there are other references to the expanding of property and the bearing of loss in the behalf of faith. It is not always clear to which precise occasions, often post-*Hijrah*, they relate in the successive encounters with antagonism. But the *Hijrah*, clearly, is the focus and symbol of them all. It was the single event which dramatized and entailed all other expressions of the same logic in adventure, sacrifice and duty. To forsake and to repossess—those two poles of all effective migration—became the recurring claim and vindication of all Muslim action. It was with these, in their double import and demand, that the divine *Shechīnah* was seen to belong as a heavenly presence whose tranquillity corroborated the initiative it rewarded.

For individual Muslims, abandoning Mecca and people, city and family, the *Hijrah* meant a crisis of personal independence. These who threw in their lot with Muḥammad were crossing their own Rubicon as well as his. Emigration meant an end to ambiguity of allegiance. The sanction it gave to loyalty was far less revocable than a verbal confession or even a doctrinal and devotional assent. To revert to Mecca from Medina, though not impossible (as we see from the Treaty of Al-Ḥudaibiyyah), was a far less feasible step than a mere abandonment of prayer or credence. The craven-hearted could not now merely slink away into obscurity or subterfuge, while craven-heartedness, in the very committedness of their fortunes, was now less likely to beset them. *Hijrah* itself has somehow stiffened the sinews it had exercised and toughened the fibres it had energized.

It differed also, decisively, from the earlier migrations of Muḥammad's first disciples to Ethiopia. Those had merely sought sanctuary and refuge, while the main brunt of Quraishī opposition continued to be borne in residence at Mecca with all the handicaps and exposures it entailed. The 622 migration was of a completely different order. It left no unwilling hostages behind and it did not shelter in a merely beneficent haven it had no mind to usurp. On the contrary, in the definitive first year of the *Hijrah*, Muslim–Quraishī tensions opened into military conflict and unambiguous political challenge. Medina was never merely a refuge, but always in intention a base and a structure of power. Adherence, on either side, sharpened, therefore into a political and military either/or. Muslims graduated, so to speak, by the *Hijrah*, from a group into an army, from a community of faith to an order of authority. A long and patient endurance of minority status was transformed into a determination for political determination.[1]

The old historians, as well as the Qur'ān, are very clear about Muḥammad's understanding of a divine permission for this development and by emigration his followers *ipso facto* shared and served it. The second pledge of 'Aqabah, which immediately preceded the *Hijrah* had pledged the contracting parties, the Prophet and his Medinan sympathizers, to mutual identity of cause and of enemy. Establishment in the new city could only ensue on such a basis. The *Hijrah* was thus, in concept and by prelude, a decision for active military measures against Quraishī recalcitrance and, in that form, a definitive conclusion to the long and strenuous 'open question' of prophetic vocation as long as it lived, in Mecca, with its tribulations. The migration was the end of passive suffering and enduring patience: it was the beginning of vigorous self-assertion and political activism. It was a movement from the fortitude of Mecca to the forts of Medina.

It is from this point that apostasy emerges in the Qur'ān as a critical dimension in Islamic reckoning. It could not exist before the *Hijrah*, when frailty or indecision had only 'religious' implication. The *Hijrah*, in its sequel, meant that emigrants were now committed to Islam by physical rupture with the past, as well as by spiritual conviction. Those would-be emigrants also, who, through intimidation or ruse of their foes, had failed, at least initially, to make their exit from Mecca, found themselves in a different kind of ambiguity from that of earlier credal hesitancy. Surah 39: 53 f. are generally understood in such a context, as being a reassurance to some impeded emigrants that there was no irremediable 'apostasy' in their delay, provided they made good the deed.

It is well then to recognize the costliness in personal terms of action in *Hijrah*. There was a real material forfeiture of security and of estate and, more importantly, there was a crucial transaction in relationships, with faith taking precedence over family and religion over blood. Muḥammad 'Azīz Lahbābī has called this 'the autonomy of the person'

[1] The play on the single word here, in its two senses, exactly fits the situation.

and 'a search for personal authenticity',[1] in place of simple tribalism. The same author claims that in the rise of Islam, with the *Hijrah* as its primary crisis, 'we are witnessing a complete transformation in Arab mentality'.[2] The personal loyalty of the Muslim now becomes, in his view, a sort of promethean challenge by the individual ranging himself against the tribal pantheon. By the aggregate of those self-emancipating persons, Islam itself comes into critical identity as an *Ummah* or people, with whom the book and the prophethood are thus affirmed in voluntary exile and courageous adventure.

The Abrahamic would be a surer and a more fitting realm of metaphor here than the promethean, were it not for the fact that Abraham's double repudiation of gods and of people was made in single loneliness and without assurances of a Medina such as the pledges of 'Aqabah had allowed to Muḥammad. Abraham was a *muhājir* without *anṣār*, an emigrant without helpers in an exile beyond guarantees. Even so, the decisions implicit in the *Hijrah*, both for the goers-forth and the takers-in, the Meccan émigrés and the Yathribite hosts, were both strenuous and definitive. They achieved the logic of the past and settled the shape of the future. The migration was not just one more episode in the narrative of a cause and a career. It was their crux and climax. It has to be read as the accumulated, yet specific, rejection by Islam of the tribal prestige, the vested self-interest, the idolatrous hegemony and the religious traditionalism of Mecca.

It is clear in retrospect that such purposive exile was latent from the outset in the meaning and the challenge Muḥammad brought to his native city. In the early call to 'the one in the mantle', Surah 74: 5 had given the simple imperative: 'Flee abomination.' The initial vocation to be apart from idolatry and its works had ripened and broadened into a total defiance of the hierarchy and the populace with whom the idols stood. 'The fair departing' (73: 10) by which the preacher had first registered his case against his people in their superstitions had grown into an entire repudiation of the establishment that ruled them.

Once made, the decision set the future as firmly as it crowned the past. It begat the two inter-acting elements in the Muslim community, 'those who went forth' and those who received them in. The emigrants

[1] In *Le Personnalisme Musulman*, Paris, 1964, p. 4. The terms here have too much of a modern ring to relate strictly to the seventh century and the Arabian setting. But there is a sort of proleptic truth about them.

[2] Ibid., p. 17. Muḥammad did have some blood relationships in Medina, through his great-grandmother, Ṣalmā, wife of Hāshim.

from Mecca became the immigrants into Medina and, as such, gave enlarging occasion for Islamic community simply by needing it. The *anṣār* or 'helpers unto victory' (to conflate the double import of the root word) were the necessary counterpart of the *Hijrah* and by their hospitality enabled the emigrants to make good their exile by replacing their abandoned resources. In that very process bonds were forged on both sides, in the psychological rehabilitation of the one and the committed recruitment of the other a—recruitment that became avowed precisely in that its cause was indigent. The very weakness became an occasion of strength. Being necessitous on the part of the émigrés made the *anṣār* the more necessary. The resulting partnership turned a critical situation into mutual benefit of spirit.

It was thus that the *Hijrah* was saved from being a mere exodus of protest and emerged into active measures against Mecca, in pursuance of the pledges of 'Aqabah that had preceded it. The frequent Quranic phrase *hājarū wa jāhadū*, 'they went out in emigration and they went forth in struggle', now comes into prominence (e.g. 2: 218; 8: 72; 74, 75; 16: 110) with the familiar expression *fī sabīl Illāh*. 'in the way of God' (e.g. 22: 58) as the path of Muslim duty, whether of émigrés or helpers. The concluding section of Surah 8 is careful to explain that the identity of interest between the two groups was to be flexible and dynamic.

By the same token the *Hijrah* meant no respite for Meccan adherence to idols because the ardent iconoclasts had departed. On the contrary, it had to become the prelude, not to geographical co-existence, but to a steady attrition of manpower and of confidence among the Quraish. Muḥammad was careful to insist, until the treaty of Al-Ḥudaibiyyah, that new adhesions to Islam from the forsaken city were to be readily received. The interests or prejudices of existing believers, whether over spoils, clannishness or priorities of rank, should not impede the numerical enlargement of Islam. The *Hijrah* might have required a moral élite: it was not to create a preserve of privilege. As long as over-riding circumstances admitted, *hijrah* had to remain an open duty of new believers to fulfil and of old believers to aid, until the original city had been successfully incorporated into Islam. For only thus could there be an Islamic end to the need for purposive exile.

The counting of the years by the Muslim calendar from the point of the *Hijrah* is, then, a proper symbol and a sure instinct. The event which more than any other defines Islam is critical both for what it concludes and what it inaugurates. It has to be seen as the epic of a religion requiring by its inner quality to become political. It discloses in retrospect the inherently self-ordering nature of the Islamic society, its impulse, in the words of 'Azzām Pasha, 'to engender . . . a state'.[1] It signalizes a religious repudiation of idolatry which finds its only feasible sequel in separate political autonomy and in victorious physical mastery.

The logic of this power-concern of original Islam has been pondered in the discussion of Chapter 3. Our only duty here is to see it Quranically at the juncture of the *Hijrah* itself. There is no doubt that the fact of the exodus was seen as both the ground and the occasion of the new militancy: 'Leave is given them to fight because they were wronged . . . and were unjustly expelled from their habitations for the reason only that they say: "Our Lord is God"' (Surah 22: 39–40). The same passage continues with the assurance that God will indeed aid those who aid Him, give victory to those who make Him victorious, and corroborates its conviction with the view that this is the general principle of religious survival and security by which all faiths have had their institutions preserved: 'Had it not been for the fact that God defends men, some by others, truly cloisters and churches, synagogues and mosques, where His Name is the steady theme of praise, would have been utterly destroyed' (22: 40). It is this vital sense of policy which makes the actual *Hijrah* as it eventuated in Muslim origins, the *hajran jamīlan*, 'the fair departing' of 73: 10.[2] It is the ultimate climax of the early command in 74: 5–6: 'Flee defilement.'

How right then to let the ultimate issues of the *Hijrah* arise from the same original context of Islam and to set them within the scope of the further command of 74: 6: 'In giving do not have aggrandizement in view.' For it is where the preaching first encountered the idolaters, in its spontaneous urge to separate from their transcendental compromise, that we must find the frame of reference for the political *Hijrah*. The latter was the climactic circumstance and service of the former. Without 'the mantle' of Surahs 73 and 74, there need have been

[1] In *The Eternal Message of Islam*, trans. C. E. Farah, New York, 1964, p. 41.

[2] The phrase is variously rendered :'Leave their company without recrimination' (Dawood); 'forsake them graciously' (Arberry); 'depart from them with a decorous departure' (Rodwell); 'part with them in a decent manner' (Qadianī Aḥmadī); 'leave them with noble dignity' (Yūsuf 'Alī) ;and 'avoid them with a becoming avoidance' (Lahore Aḥmadī).

no exile. There, at his investiture, if we may so describe it, his 'robing' as a prophet, Muḥammad is directed not to turn vocation to advantage, not to employ what comes to him *qua* prophethood as a means to self-inflation. The words in 74: 6, 'in giving, do not have aggrandizement in view', are not of unambiguous interpretation in their first context and we are, with deliberate intention, projecting them into the later situation. But they certainly refer to 'wishing, willing or bestowing', anent what vocation brings and thus relate, at least prospectively, to the large 'empowerment' which the *Hijrah* finally attained. That which is acquired through the exercise of the prophetic gift and all that ensues from it are to transcend the personal equation. The mission calls for scrupulous service—no less, no more, naught else. Prophecy is not a perquisite from which to gain, nor is discipleship an occasion for masterly increase. To serve the only cause is to have no personal cause to serve, since God must be all in all, and patience (74: 7) is the only condition of the servant.

Including the ultimate in the initial, this reading of the Surah of 'The Mantled One' brings us to the final criteria within the *Hijrah* and its sequel. Even in the repudiation of idolatry there will be things to repudiate. Every vocation is beset with the temptations of its own purposes. *Hajr* has to be *jamīl.* The very search for authority must be submissive to criteria beyond itself. *Hijrah* is plainly not a self-defining term. It is rather the place for an answer. Deliberate exile in the Name of God is the geographical symbol of obligation from which there is no departing.

Throughout the pre-*Hijrah* Qur'ān there is an insistent distinction between *balāgh* and *ḥisāb*, between preaching or 'communication' and 'reckoning' or verdict (3: 20; 5: 99; 13: 40; 16: 35; 24: 54; 29: 18; etc.). The *ḥisāb*, or 'accounting', here is certainly eschatological in its primary sense and has to do with the divine judgment of recalcitrant humanity. But that ultimate vindication of the truth in the total discomfiture of the false is in some measure presumed and demonstrated in the anticipatory and external defeat of the idolaters, for which *Hijrah* is the necessary preparation and prelude. Or, if the sense of the divine reckoning is so wholly projected to the eternal sphere that *ḥisāb* cannot be rightly seen at all in post-*Hijrah* events, there is certainly a departure from *balāgh* alone in the new shape of destiny as the *Hijrah* fashioned it. It is in fact the very essence of the Medinan situation that Muḥammad is no longer merely preacher and that he no longer waits on the wills of men for a response to words. Rather, in the interests of the words, he moves to constrain their persons to his power. He terminates a passive or patient sufferance of their contumely in bidding for an effective subjugation of their resistance. Where Islam is potentially universalized in *Hijrah* it is inherently politicized in *Jihād*. The move *out* of Mecca *with* the faith presages the move *against* Mecca *for* the faith. In that transition, not only is the *Hijrah* implemented in its prospective relevance, but Islam is defined in its essential character. In both transactions there is implicit the most fundamental question of all religion, namely the relation and the relevance of power to truth.

For an issue so crucial the Qur'ān has no explicit discussion. Its confidence that truth approves power and power suits truth is as implicit and assured as its conviction about the reality and sovereignty of God. Indeed the two confidences belong together.

There is, however, one passage which a 'foreign' reader might linger over and be tempted, by a private exegesis, to extend into reflections the Qur'ān does not apparently intend and for which traditional Islamic reading would have other, and quite inwardly persuasive, interpretation. It occurs in Surah 3: 79–80:

> 'It is not right for any man to whom God has given the Book and authority and prophethood and to turn and say to men: "Be servants to me rather than to God." Rather he should say: "Be God's men, in that you know the Scriptures and are students of them." He would never direct you to take angels and prophets for your masters. How could he direct you into unbelief, *muslims* as you are?'[1]

Here, whatever the minutiae of exegesis, is a clear affirmation of the divine sovereignty in the very sphere where the greatest temptation

[1] There are here some important questions of translation. It is possible to take *'ibādan li* (here translated: 'Be servants to me') in the sense of 'Be worshippers of me'. Likewise *kūnū rabbāniyyīn* ('Be God's men') may be held singly to the realm of worship. The passage then would be simply a repudiation of 'deification' of the prophets, whether with or against their will. But this undoubted import of the verses does not exclude the more political significance here understood. There are many historical precedents associating 'divinization' with political absolutisms and the human servitude the latter demand is no less heinous, when required and given, than the former. The words *'ibādan* (which might be rendered 'servitors') and *rabbāniyyūn* certainly have a connotation which must include allegiance as well as worship. Arberry, incidentally, takes the second as meaning 'masters' in the sense of experts in the Scriptures ('Be masters in that you know the Book . . .'). But 'God's men' seems on all counts a sounder rendering and makes a more intelligible contrast after 'instead' or 'rather'.

can occur to compromise it, namely the sphere where it most aggressively and consciously asserted and served, the sphere of the trust of revelation and the discharge of prophetic calling. Where prophecy claims a political obedience in the pursuit of its spiritual mission, there must be the more intolerant jealousy for the sole Lordship of the God who calls. Prophecy and Caesarism are utterly incompatible. The service of God cannot be dominated by human masteries. Where these arise they must be themselves submissive. The subordination to God of all causes must include most of all the cause that espouses the inclusive surrender. Divine mission and human autocracy cannot co-operate.

Only by the true fear of God, then, only by a sole worship, are men liberated from the improper claims of lesser authorities, There is plainly something reciprocal in this truth. Improperly to invoke power in the interests even of God's truth is to jeopardize that truth itself. For it is then betrayed by its own allegiance. Prophethood, and all that goes with it in the Qur'ān, are categorically within a divine sovereignty which, therefore, conditions and controls all its claims upon men. It is precisely when prophethood passes over from a minority message to a mission state that the crisis here present becomes most acute.

Was it for this reason that Muḥammad Iqbāl, for example, saw in the *Hijrah* the sure veto of Islam on the political idols of race, state and patria?[1] This was the repudiation, as it were, to epitomize repudiation, the parable event in which Islam proved the positive of its negations and symbolized, in distinctiveness, its will to truth? Was the *Hijrah* then the great defiance, the chosen identity affirmed in refusal of the false? If so, it becomes by its own nature a dynamic thing. There has to be *Hijrah* within *Hijrah*, the critical achievement of the end within and sometimes against the means.

For there is, within us all, the Mecca which we cannot leave. To rebel truly means an interminable tension. The 'fair departing' is not simply geographical. And there are evils from which no exile can be found because we carry them in our hearts. And there are evils which exile cannot cure except by the quality of its return. *Hijrah*, then, is only the end of the beginning, enlarging the tasks for which it liberates the spirit and taxing them with its own temptations.

There is, in this light, no conclusion more apposite than the words

[1] In *The Reconstruction of Religious Thught in Islam*, Lahore, 1931, where he argued for the 'temporary' quality of nationalism within the abiding shape of a universal Islam.

of Surah 9: 118. The passage has to do with the emigrants and the 'helpers' and uses the familiar words by which they are described in the *Hijrah*. But, according to Tradition, it refers to a much later occasion in the mutual endeavours of the Muslim partners when a trio of men 'were left behind'[1] and were so overcome with remorse or self-accusation that the vast world seemed to 'close in upon them', corroborating the strictures of their own hearts. Then it was, the verse declares, that they 'realized how there is no refuge from God except in Him'. God turned to them in mercy, it adds, enabling their repentance.

Whoever, precisely, these defaulters were and whatever the circumstances of their delinquency, they confessed a universal principle. All the inner *hijrahs* of our hearts are 'from Him and unto Him'. The realization of judgment upon us is the only context of mercy for us. The idols we repudiate as meriting the divine anger cannot be truly renounced save by the workings of grace. It is only in condemnation recognized and acknowledged that salvation is begun. It is a condemnation which cannot be simply externalized against the culprit Meccas of our denunciation. For it stays, to reprove, as well as justify, the mission that it kindles. To 'perceive that there is no shelter from God except in Him' is to find by forsaking and so to become by receiving. They are the two sides of a perpetual 'emigration'.

[1] The instance, which in precise form is relatively unimportant, may have to do with three Medinans who failed in some way as *anṣār* or 'aiders'. The reader has also to conjecture in what sense they were constrained to, and by, repentance, What matters is the larger reach of the phrase that summarizes the inner experience.

Chapter 9
THE STRUGGLE TO MEAN

'The beginning of education', said Epictetus, 'is the sense of words' and the beginning also of its tribulations. There are few serious themes which do not suffer from the opaqueness of language in league, no doubt, with the obtuseness of minds. The two hindrances so often abet each other.

The Quranic 'education' of the *Jāhiliyyah* was by no means immune from this situation. The perceptive reader of the Qur'ān learns to appreciate Muḥammad's verbal burdens and to take the measure of the conflicts his message entailed. With the place and time of the book there belongs a profound, yet also perennial, problem of semantics, of the relation of language to meaning and the toils of meaning in language. This sphere of Quranic study may well be counted among the most fascinating.

'A book in which there is no doubt' or 'whereof there is no dubeity' (Surah 2: 2), is the ready assurance of the Qur'ān about itself. The phrase attributes to it the sort of certainty attending the Last Judgment of which the same phrase is repeatedly used. Both are 'indubitable' things. But within that certitude as to the status and the content of the Scripture, there goes, nevertheless, an extensive area of dispute between preacher and pagan, between prophet and precinct. The very forthrightness employed a vocabulary of contention. Muḥammad could not have accomplished his mission without provoking the antagonism it involved and between the two there necessarily intervened the common ground of a contested ambiguity of words. With, and within, the familiar tensions arising from vested interests and privilege and pride and the *status quo*, there were matters verbal and conceptual relating to genuinely religious perplexity and confusion. Not all the controversies against Muḥammad are to be seen as politically reactionary. There were, in lower key, perhaps, but even deeper import, the struggles of apprehensive, puzzled and even wistful minds. The very meaning of his preaching, especially in the earlier years, must be seen as proceeding within the bewilderments and pitfalls of common speech.

'Common speech', for all its eloquence, means the Arabic Qur'ān. There has been an admirable enterprise in western Islamics to investigate the 'foreign' words in the Qur'ān,[1] in order to throw light on the background of Muḥammad's relationships and to explore the contemporary meaning of his usages. Such study serves to elucidate the interchange between the Ḥijāz and adjacent territories in and before the Prophet's generation. Many of these loan words from Aramaic, Hebrew, Persian, Greek and Ethiopic, enter into the semantic problems we have here in view.

We need not stay, in this context, to note orthodox reluctance, since about the tenth century, to allow that such borrowings occurred. There has been a strong will to believe that the words are native Ḥijāzī Arabic. The present point is simply that there are words in the Qur'ān, borrowed or native, alien or popular, which must be regarded as the arena of urgent semantic issues. These, in their currency, and in their potential both for isolating and conjoining meanings, were the pivotal points, language-wise, of Muḥammad's apostolate. This 'crucial vocabulary of the Qur'ān' and chiefly its Arabic elements, are a study no less relevant than that of 'foreign vocabulary' alone. In the religious conflict ensuing from the Prophet's vocation, statements in sound, current Arabic words were 'foreign' indeed to the ears and the susceptibilities of his pagan hearers, or became so when his intent and their import were fully clear.

Our aim in this chapter relates only to certain salient examples to illustrate a much larger field and it is hoped, in the process, to suggest an alternative way of interpreting the Quranic topics of Satanic distortion and of abrogation, which would appear to make much more sense in this light than in the arbitrary shape that controversy has hitherto given them.

The readiest way into the matter is perhaps to ask simply whether divinities exist, whether idols are realities. If God is One and One is God, the answer would seem to be in the negative: 'There is no god

[1] Notably the pioneer study of Arthur Jeffery, *Foreign Vocabulary of the Qur'ān*, Baroda, 1938. See also D. S. Margoliouth, 'Some Additions to Jeffery's *Foreign Vocabulary* etc.', *Journal of the Royal Asiatic Society*, vol. 90, 1939, pp. 53–61.

but God'. But, in that event, the statement is unnecessary. Non-entities do not need to be denied. One cannot negate what has never existed. Yet the very denial, being as it is urgent and imperative, seems by its very anxiety to suggest there is, indeed, some reality in the subject it denies. There is in Islam a vehemence against idols which, on this reckoning, hardly squares with their non-existence.

The point, of course, is that idols *do* exist in the belief, or the perversity, of idolaters. The imperious negation means to cancel the fictitious entity in the mind, by asserting the non-entity in the real. It invites, or commands, the intelligence and the will to register the illusion-quality of the idol and only when this happens does the truth of its non-entity prevail. Until then the illusory character of the conviction gives a pseudo-being to its content, as far as the idolater is concerned. His idols exist as illusions and as such are powerful, tenacious, distressful, facts of belief. And facts of belief are facts of the situation—all the more desperately facts because they are not facts. The plural phenomena of the sense world, too, of nature and of personal human life, where idol illusions arise, and return, are irreducibly factual and present.

The apologist, Tertullian, in the second Christian century, knew well this paradox of militancy against the non-existent. For him all pagan life was at once illusory and deadly. The idols in which he did not believe were for that very reason to be 'recognized' on every street corner and in every market. Non-existent as they were, they effectively sealed every profession, in his view, to Christian participation. Crafts, teaching, letters, soldiering and public office, had all to be foregone since they could not be pursued without some apparent admission, if only in a courtesy or an allusion, that idols, being spoken of, were being 'meant', and being 'meant' were given being. Even if a beggar were to bless you by his gods for your gift, you were false to Christ. Even reproach could not undo your having played into the hands of his delusion. One could scarcely live in the same world with idolaters. Yet how, otherwise, could you save the world from idolatry?[1]

This theme has to be seen as a living and developing struggle within the career of Muḥammad as a preacher. It is a struggle turning, in measure, on the sense of words, the range of convictions and the reach of denial. Beliefs cannot be challenged or changed without continuing vocabulary. No revolutionary ideas or attitudes can clothe

[1] *De Idolatria*, xxii.

themselves in wholly new terminology. For it is the currency of existing words and usages that they require to convert. One can never educate or emancipate except by beginning with the given world, with the existing notions and their verbal dwelling places. The reformer moves with this common discourse if ever he is to move beyond it. His battle is for the meaning of the speech that avails.

It turns also on the capacity to provide truly for the emotions that are liable to be left stranded by the disqualifying of the old familiarities of word. For these are also haunts of feeling and of psychic 'security'. In its steady accent on the 'signs' of God in the external world, the Qur'ān retrieves for the imagination within *tauḥīd*, or unity, just those aspects of phenomena which of old led men to idolatrous assumptions. Paganism in its own way was warm and pragmatic. Idol-veneration was the other side of crucial anxieties of heart about protection, aid, favour, access, efficacy and the like. The question may rather be: 'Is their intercession assured?', not: 'Do they exist?'. They are 'guardians' before they are 'beings', living by human necessities rather than human abstraction. In a pagan society the names of plural divinities abound in greetings, festivals, functions of commerce, hospitality and every kind of social exchange, and in family and place names. Allegiance ramifies into every realm of collective existence, is jealous for the prestige of shrines, the hegemony of tribes, the prowess of arms and the rivalries of trade. To question their existence, therefore, is much more than to deny a proposition. It is rather to precipitate a crisis in which the whole soul and ethos of a community are at stake. It is nothing less than a conspiracy to disrupt the world. To succeed it must achieve a conversion of conversation itself.

These general observations, scant and evident as they are, prepare us to consider a symptomatic event in Muḥammad's early mission around which much unnecessary and improbable contention has centred. It makes an excellent first example here of the semantic problem and so merits exposition at some length.

In Surah 53: 19–30, there occurs one of the familiar exchanges between the Prophet and the Meccans, which probably belongs to the third or fourth year of his preaching. It is not entirely clear at what point in these early days the anathema against idols became explicit, either in Muḥammad's words or—the more critical question here—in his listeners' apprehension. The great interdependent themes of his mission we have already explored. But there is clearly some room for progression of emphasis in the encounter and even a certain flux of issues, impossible of precise recovery by historians. At what point did utter incompatibility emerge between Muḥammad and the Quraish, either in respect of his witness to their beliefs or their reaction to his words, fraught as these were by complicating factors of kinship, policy, priorities and fears? When did their rejection become total, after its advance through amusement, irritation, calculation, threat, hesitancy and hatred? When was his sense of *all* the implications steeled to a final option for repudiation, exile and warfare? Where did both decisions develop and turn through incidents in their sequence and words in their import?

It is sufficient only to raise these queries to introduce what, by any reckoning, must be one of these incidents, and that a crucial one. The passage in 53: 19–30 opens with the question: 'Have you considered Allāt, al-'Uzzā and Manāt, the third the other one?' (lit. 'Have you seen . . .?' with the sense of 'having an opinion of'), surely a semantic question about these three pagan goddesses. It continues: 'Do you have males and Him (God) females?', certainly a taunting and polemical enquiry. Has God only daughters when men produce sons? 'What an odd arrangement' ('an unfair fate') that God, the all-disposer, should have this contingency handed out to Him! The satirical tone continues in the factual declaration:

> 'They are nothing but names in your usage [which you have named]—you and your fathers. God has revealed no authority for them. They [men] are following nothing but a supposition of their own fancy. Truly is the guidance now come to them from their Lord. Does man's fancying make things so? Truly to God belongs the last and the first.' (53: 23–5)

Taken as it stands, this piece of living 'evangelism' of the unity against idolatry belongs unmistakably with the struggle to persuade and condemn. It demonstrates the armoury of the Prophet—jest, anger, argument and passion. It is verbal iconoclasm at its best, fearless and resourceful.

Early Islamic historians, however, have complicated, though in my view also corroborated, this picture by recording a tradition alleging that, between the words 'that were an unfair fate [for God]' and the phrase 'they are nothing but names', Muḥammad inserted what they interpret as a concessionary clause: 'These [the goddesses] are the females exalted, whose intercession is to be hoped for.' Al-

Wāqidī, Al-Ṭabarī and others report this as a concession and it is supposed that Muḥammad either wavered in his conviction about the unity or was ready for some sort of compromise about the goddesses. They go on to say that, on the basis of these words, all or most of the Quraish prostrated with Muḥammad. It is further suggested that the *modus vivendi* with the pagans was durable enough for news of it to reach the Muslims whom Muḥammad had sent for safety into Ethiopia. By this narrative, the statement of v. 24: 'They are merely names . . .', becomes a retraction of the compromise on Muḥammad's part when, either the agreement had broken down anyway on other grounds, or he had realized his lapse and corrected it. The interlude during which, allegedly, it stood, was of undetermined length.[1]

It is important to keep in mind that this story is not a calumny from without, but a report embedded in Muslim Tradition itself. Its content requires us to hold that, being so apparently compromising, it could not have been fabricated. Traditional Islamic interpretation relies on the explanation of Satanic distortion of the words in prophetic speech, and to this we will come presently. Modern, liberal commentary either rejects the whole story, despite the difficulty of so doing, or else prefers to emphasize, as it very well may, the incontrovertible 'recovery' and the firm, final trend of Muḥammad's mission into total enmity to idols and undeviating faith in the unity of God. Western critics who have accepted the narrative have sometimes used it provocatively, without probing, as we must, the whole setting, seen, not so much as extenuation, but as encounter.

Before that, however, we need to evaluate the Satanic disruption theory, since this, in an odd way, witnesses also to the real problem. It is based, in part, on Surah 22: 52, which some claim was revealed to reassure Muḥammad after the (alleged) mistake and his reversal. It runs:

> 'No apostle or prophet We have sent before you, but experienced (how) Satan interjected into what he imported (or intended) when he spoke. Then God cancelled what Satan interjected and thus God makes His signs authoritative. For God is all-knowing and all-wise.'

[1] Some (e.g. W. Montgomery Watt, *Muhammad at Mecca*, Oxford, 1953, p. 104) take the words: 'They are merely names . . .' to be in fact a Medinan verse. But this is to argue on grounds which, on the hypothesis to be considered here, have no validity. The words can be intelligently seen within the same, single, Meccan context.

The sense here is that Satan sought to disrupt or distort the meaning of the Scripture, as it was given, by (lit.) 'casting in' other words, either by causing the speaking prophet to stumble over the right text, or by actually adding extraneous and deceptive material. This is said to be the experience of all messengers and Muḥammad need not be surprised that he is no exception.[1]

God saves the situation and frustrates Satan by annulling or abrogating what got surreptitiously into the text and making clear what is the right reading. It is this phenomenon which is thought to be referred to in Surah 17: 74: 'Had We not strengthened you, you might well have inclined somewhat towards them' (i.e. in compromise)—though these words are more intelligible if we presuppose a spiritual and living tension over language and intent, rather than an arbitrary sort of *Satanus ex machina* countered by *Deus ex machina.*

It is exactly this that we propose to do with the whole passage in Surah 53 and with the interjection idea of Surah 22. Can we not plainly find in both the circumstances of a struggle *in via* to affirm and establish a meaning in the face of prevarication and confusion?

The Arabic words *idhā tamannā* in 22: 52 and *mā tamannā* in 53: 24 are crucial: 'if he intended' or 'wished' in the first case (referring to an apostle), and 'what he wished' in the second (referring to the idolater). The derived verb *tamannā* means 'to desire' or 'to wish', but, applied to statements or texts, can mean 'to read' or 'to intend.' It points to the desired import of a usage, the premeditation of a mind in a phrase. It is akin to the *qadara* root, meaning 'to evaluate' or 'to think worthily of'.[2] 'If he reads' is thus a proper translation, in the sense of the 'reading' or the 'meaning' he desires to convey.

The Satanic distortion, then, need not be seen as an externalized, arbitrary, merely mischievous, trickery, but the inherent pitfalls of meaning in the setting of tension, intrigue, interests and relationship. Sense is never in a vacuum of discourse, but in a context of serious circumstance and engagement. So there is always jeopardy in a prophet's effort to mean things (22: 52). Satan—evil, prejudice—lie in wait in the saying and the hearing. Only God, over all, is mighty and wise.

Likewise in 53: 24 the idolater's notions do not confer reality on

[1] Some translators prefer 'Satan cast suggestions into his longing', making an urge to be well-received or ingratiating on a prophet's part the nub of the matter.

[2] Cf. *Mā qadarū Allāha haqqa qadrihi* in 6: 91; 22: 74 and 39: 67–99. 'They did not esteem God a true esteeming,' or 'They did not have the right idea about God.'

what he talks of: 'Does man's fancying make things so?' His conceptual, or wistful, intentions do not correspond with reality.[1] What he talks about are 'mere names', and even his passionate credence gives them no objective reality. Nevertheless, when the preacher, disturbing his illusions, vehemently disqualifies his notions, he uses the same names and is referring to the same things. Is it not possible that his satire may be misunderstood or his very emphasis misconstrued? There is a wistfulness about some superstition that does not want to be undeceived. There are vested interests which stubbornly cling to discredited things. Even nugatory use of the names may fall on unreceiving ears. In a situation so charged, in any event, with ambiguity will the theory of deliberate, almost negotiated, compromise, made and withdrawn, be the only or the likeliest hypothesis? Did the Quraish *think* Muḥammad was still negotiable? Was he not himself realizing and achieving the nature of his mission in parallel progression with his gradual discovery of its implications?

As for the recorded prostration, is it inconceivable that Muḥammad was prostrating to 'the Lord of the worlds', whose 'signs' were present in the phenomena that pagans divinized, while the Quraish were prostrating to an 'Allāh' they genuinely recognized at the summit of divinity, without renouncing his endless subordinates and 'daughters'? It would not have been the first time that worship was at once common and contrasted. Certainly in the sequel the struggle continued, with Muḥammad resolute and paganism stubborn.

We conclude, then, that the heart of the matter has to do with a semantic struggle to mean and convey. Tradition about an actual compromise has simply formalized or fossilized a point in that ongoing tension, while the idea of Satanic interjection has given the highly charged ambiguities of real encounter a simplistic shape that conceals a more subtle travail.

This understanding of the issue is corroborated by the pragmatic factors at which we have already hinted. Deities mean shrines and shrines mean markets and markets mean prestige and profits, and collective pride. Allāt was the goddess, it seems, of Al-Ṭā'if some distance to the south and east of Mecca, Al-'Uzzā of Nakhlah near Mecca itself,

[1] This rendering fits the passage better than to translate the phrase as 'what he coveteth' (Pickthall) or 'the whims of their souls' (Dawood), since these phrases could hardly apply to divinities who, for pagans, are already real. The idolater is deceived in giving substance to empty terms, before he is misguided in hanging wishes on that emptiness.

and Manāt, primarily, a worship of Medina, though her centre was midway between the two cities. Was Muḥammad inviting 'consideration' (53: 19) of divinities external to the Meccan *ka'bah* itself? Were the Quraish yet fully challenged in their own dearest sanctuary of all? Were the deities here more those of outsiders than (saving, it seems Al-'Uzzā) their own? However so, the existential question seems to have been intercession rather than dogma. In the verses that follow, the intercession of angels in heaven is rhetorically, but not categorically, disallowed and 'female angels' are said to be the fantasy of unbelievers. From this idle surmise, the wise man will turn in rejection, even as the deceived turn away from the Qur'ān. God is well aware of both.

There is, plainly, here a choice and a crisis, the crux of which concerns the true and the false, the sure and the suppositious, and of these language used, heard, misheard, unheard, is the vehicle. It is notable that the 'inserted' phrase in Surah 53, according to Al-Ṭabarī, was: 'They [the goddesses] are high-fliers (*gharāniqah* or *gharānīq*) whose intercession is to be hoped for.' The word 'high-fliers', sometimes translated 'swans' or 'cranes', indicates birds remarkable for sudden, soaring flight, on account of which they could stand for intercessors, who must rise up to God. It has also the connotation of 'beauties', perfect and without defect, used, possibly, in both the congratulatory and the defamatory double sense of the English. Could Muḥammad's allowance of their intercession have been satirical and taken for explicit? Did he mean that their invocation was popularly, but deludedly, practised?

The question then returns to whether divinities exist, how their protègés are disabused of the illusion, and how the sole Lordship of God is to be known and relied upon. It is relevant, in this connection, to observe that the words for 'idol', 'image', etc. (*asnām*, *tamāthil*, *suwar*, *anṣāb* etc., pl.) are strangely rare in the Qur'ān.[1] The general usage is derivatives of the root *sharaka*, to 'associate' with God, where the emphasis is on some active 'alienation' of the divine prerogative of worship, trust, awe, knowledge and the rest to some fictitious deity or power. Thus the concern always focuses on the *practice* of idolatry and there, too, rather than in the merely notional, retrieval must begin. In that conflict there are many vicissitudes before the assurance, 'they are no more than names', becomes an effective emancipation for minds

[1] See, further, Kenneth Cragg, *The Dome and the Rock*, London, 1964, p. 127.

and spirits with whom even 'names' are reals, for folk who have yet to pass from the fictitiously real to the really fictitious and on to the really real in God—the journey which, with the baffling aid of words, it was the Prophet's task to teach them to accomplish. Surah 53 would seem to have been one of the stages, no more, no less.

We have to be diffident about this conclusion, since the melodramatic version has so firm a place in tradition and conditions the usual approach. It is well, therefore, to be confirmed by other aspects. The matter of abrogation is one of them. The theme recurs in 2: 106: 'We do not abrogate any verse or cause it to be forgotten, without bringing a better or a like one. Do you not know that God has power over all things?' Much literature has gathered around this whole topic[1] and medieval scholarship in Islam developed more than a score of ways of relating 'abrogated' and 'abrogating' things. If and when the relevance is legal or administrative, one may readily see how circumstances would make early directives obsolete and new ones imperative,[2] though there remains the problem of the 'eternity' of the whole. Recent study of abrogation is tending away from these intricacies towards the general truth of progressive understanding of meaning. Surah 2: 106 certainly admits of this. The battle itself for apprehension and for *confessio fidei* strips away old meanings, jettisons into 'forgetfulness' terms which cannot further serve the new light, and brings forward 'like' words which hold and convey the meaning more decisively. Abrogation, if less stylized and arbitrary, is a conception which could well fit the actual history of a struggle for minds.

That the Qur'ān reflects such a history is evident, overlaid as it may sometimes be by the more exciting and tangible conflicts of politics and power. Muḥammad is several times reminded, in the Meccan period, that his only task is *al-balāgh*, communication, the causing of the message to 'arrive' (3: 20; 5: 92 and 99; 13: 40; 16: 35 and 82; 24: 53; 29: 18; 36: 17; 42: 48; 64: 12), with the adjective *al-mubīn*, already noted in Chapter 2, used frequently in the same context. He is a man with a verbal work in hand, not dealing in cyphers but obligated, we may say, to what the New Testament calls *parrhesia*, plain and frank expression that is discontent until it is thoroughly apprehended.

[1] E.g., see a summary in Richard Bell, *Introduction to the Qur'ān*, Edinburgh, 1953, pp. 98–9.

[2] As in the matter of inheritance. There was a time just after the *Hijrah* when believing non-relatives were to inherit in place of non-Muslim relatives. The subsequent capitulation of Mecca enabled a countermanding reinstatement of the priority of blood relationship.

The Qur'ān itself is called *al-bayān*, 'the clarifier', 'the explanation' that makes manifest (3: 138; 55: 4). While not all the connotations of that term can be claimed here, they certainly include the labour of language. 'The burden which was breaking your back' is the description in 94:3 of the trust of the Book to Muḥammad, while the Surah cited in the study of his vocation in Chapter 1 (73: 5) reads: 'We shall cast upon you a heavy word (a weighty saying').' Need we exclude a travail of words themselves from the intention of these phrases? It has been argued that the verses 2: 97 and 26: 194, 'We sent it down upon your *heart*', rather than merely 'We caused you to hear it. . . ', indicate that Muḥammad's task entailed genuine effort and anguish and not, as traditional theology has assumed, a 'mechanical' recipience. If we can understand a vigorous engagement of the Prophet with the living meaning and with the opaqueness or stubbornness of human minds and wills, then our point is made and the Qur'ān, in its vital sequences, is indeed a workshop of semantics, an enterprise in clothing truth in recognizability and exposing the false for the falsehood it is.

What of these transactions the other way round—in the hearers' world? Surah 51: 11 speaks of those who are 'perplexed in the depths', but it is difficult to isolate mental wonderment from the turpitude, bigotry and perversity which the Qur'ān passionately ascribes, in characteristic vehemence, to the unbelievers. Despite this charged atmosphere of irreconcilability, there are many traces of essential bewilderment and crises of language proper. Interlocutors are noted as putting questions to Muḥammad, not all of them contentious or, as is the case in e.g. 2: 215 f., relating to practical matters in the new allegiance.

Thus, for example, in 79: 42, 'They ask you about the hour: when will it come to its moorings?' (an intriguing nautical metaphor). Surah 7: 187 renews the enquiry. They ask also (17: 85) about 'the Spirit' (*al-rūḥ*)—one of the deepest of semantic problems for a pagan culture. What is the elusive agency of revelation and how is it related to the unity of God and the individual soul? The Quranic reply introduces yet another taxing word: 'Say: "the Spirit is from the command (*amr*) of my Lord. You have only been given to know a very little." ' Warning thus against excessive curiosity, the passage contents itself with a simple association of the Spirit and the *amr*, just as utterance, breath and authority combine in one *fiat* of effectuation of the divine will. The theme of the *amr* engaged us in Chapter 1 in the context of Muḥammad's commission and the coming down of the Spirit 'for every behest'. Though 17: 35 forbears to answer the interrogative beyond a single phrase, at least it illustrates what preaching involved when it began to be heeded. That the problem was postponed is evidence enough that it existed. It became one of several questions left to the lively speculations of post-Quranic theology—questions which in the Prophet's own day were still too deep and latent to take sophisticated, philosophic form.

Similarly and perhaps most touching of all: 'When my servants question you concerning Me, I am near to answer the call of the caller when he calls to Me; so let them pray and let them believe in Me' (Surah 2: 186). Here, of course, we have to do with believers. Yet they are not without queries and wonderings. The answer is deeply religious: God is known in godwardness. But, in and with that most Muslim posture, go a score of restive questions about words and meaning, names and images, rights and wrongs of belief. We have noted in Chapter 3 the misconception in 49: 14 f. about the nature of faith and the reproach of an *islām* into which no heart-faith had entered. Or, in the verses earlier quoted, 'they did not have the right idea of God' (6: 91).

That very term *qadr*, in 'the right idea' verses, was itself a further example of recurring puzzlement. We have met it already in 'the night of power' passage in Surah 97. But *qadr* as authority, or decisive mind, in the revelatory sense, is also thought of as the determining of fate, or lot, and 'the night of *qadr*' then becomes a divine handing down of human fates on a night in the year that decrees all that will occur until the anniversary returns.

This duality of interpretation persists in the most characteristic of all refrains in the Qur'ān, describing God as *qadīr 'alā kulli shay'in*, 'able over all things', 'the All-competent' or 'the All-disposing'. The phrase may be taken to mean that God effectuates all that occurs, or that nothing is outside the range of his will and power. Since the centuries of Muslim piety and doctrine have been exercised by conflicts between these two contrasted senses, it needs no arguing that the original pagan hearers were no less liable to uncertainty, or that their confusion lay at a point of vital meaning in Islam.[1] Nor was the deeper sense aided by natural attitudes or habits of mind.

[1] See Daud Rahbar, *God of Justice: Ethical Doctrine of the Qur'ān*, Leiden, 1960, pp. 108–19.

It is useful here to emphasize the repeated Quranic prominence of the idea of *Ẓann*, or 'surmise', as obscuring truth and impeding communication. Almost seventy times the root and its derivatives occur, often with the implication of a culpable, as well as a mistaken, quality about men's notions. 'What do you suppose about the Lord of all being?' Abraham asked his idolatrous kindred (37: 87). The same charged enquiry runs through Muḥammad's preaching. The element of reproach is paramount. Men think evil thoughts of God (48: 6). But the frequency of the term indicates that there were also conflicts simply of entrenched idea. Truly 'surmise avails not against the truth' (10:36). But it certainly complicates its task. *Ẓann* is a persistent legacy from the *Jāhiliyyah* (3: 154) and contrasts always with believing cognisance of truth. Most of the areas of pagan obduracy about Muḥammad's words—resurrection, judgment, idols, prophethood—are within these fixed and 'suppositious' attitudes. They were the set thoughts of those who were fortified against the vocabulary, old and new, that threatened to disturb them.

Clear *balāgh*, then, or communication of meaning, had formidable adversaries—apathy, prejudice, naivety, and hesitation. All, and not least the hesitation, were reinforced by the instinct after 'double insurance' in the pagan mind. It stretched, a large and devious territory, between unresponsive heathenism and final maturity in faith. Where idolatry had so long and so far permeated language, usage, manners, customs and the rest, as we saw with Tertullian, it could hardly be wholly banished from the mind or dismissed from the currency of life.

There is ready indication, in the first and subsequent centuries of Islam in expansion, of efforts to extinguish pagan, or non-Muslim, elements in greetings, names, oaths and conversation.[1] There can be no doubt that similar, even sharper, occasions arose within Quranic days and scenes. Old loyalties survived conversion. The new believer anywhere is liable to trust in a both/and mentality, 'clutching his gods' even while he confesses their rejection. Surah 6: 71 seems to hint at such a situation.

[1] See, e.g., Ignaz Goldziher, *Muslim Studies*, ed. S. M. Stern, trans. from the German by C. R. Barber and S. M. Stern, vol. 1, London, 1967, pp. 239–41. Formulae of the *Jāhiliyyah*, in greeting or condolence, were suppressed and, e.g., *Rabb* (Lord) was reserved for God alone and a man should be *'abd* (servant) to no human master. The efforts, not always successful, of theology to make ordinary vocabulary consistent with doctrine merely develop the problems implicit in affirming the doctrine in the first place.

'Say: "Shall we call on that which profits us not, instead of upon God, on that which cannot harm us? Shall we turn backward again after God has guided us, as a man dazed and bewildered in the world, when he has comrades calling him to guidance saying: 'Come our way.'?". Say: "Truly the guidance of God is guidance: we are summoned to *islām* to the Lord of all being." '

Here, it would seem, is the struggle for the operative meaning of conviction, a battle for decisiveness against timidity, and the courage of faith against the drag of the past and of fear.

Further in the same Surah comes a passage reminiscent of the problem of idolatrous meats in New Testament Corinth. Idols are not to be reviled lest the idolaters blaspheme God in return (6: 108). Only meat consecrated in the name of God is to be eaten, for an idol-invocation is a real thing (v. 118). Some pagans make offering of their produce both to God and to idols (vv. 136 f.). But this kind of compromise is to be repudiated. The very vigour of Quranic language in its antipathy to the delusions and conjectures of the heathen is a measure of how strenuous was the effort of mind and will for an effective monotheism. While perversity is no doubt part of the conflict, experience everywhere would seem to demonstrate that opposition and reluctance are not always perverse and that genuine puzzlements and fears have their place. It is these that bring the temptation to want both worlds, the anxiety to be safe with each. Language was the crux of these issues. It was by words that the *Jāhiliyyah* was indicted as such and by vocabulary that its errors, if not its wilfulness, had to be overcome. The very *Jihād* of Islam began and continued as a struggle for meaning within the ambiguities of speech.

From the immediacy of Muḥammad's *balāgh*, this theme moves naturally into the field of exegesis and into the possession by the centuries of the completed Qur'ān. What had been for him the matrix of the Scripture itself became the core of capacious margins, in which the fidelity of the faithful revolved in a wealth of words. The sum of the matter may be found in the two halves of an interrogative in Surah 47: 24: 'Do they not reflect on the Qur'ān, or is it that their hearts have locks upon them?'[1]

[1] The question was first impressed upon the present writer when he encountered it quoted in four languages and inscribed outside the tomb of Muḥammad Iqbāl beside the Badshāhi Mosque in Lahore (cf. also 4: 82).

Chapter 10
THE MAKING OF MUSLIMS

'The progress of religion', wrote A. N. Whitehead, 'is defined by the denunciation of gods.'[1] Defined, but not achieved. The task is bigger than the declamation. That 'there is no god but God' only masters paganism as a denunciation when it transforms the pagan and liberates him into a true worship. Seeing the crux of the Qur'ān, as we have argued, in the end of the *Jāhiliyyah*, our studies in Chapters 3, 4 and 9, are incomplete without an exploration in the text of the actual shaping of Muslim character and conduct out of the raw material of heathen humanity. The semantic question about 'education' into meaning is only the mental dimension of the other struggle—the realization in the concrete of the *islām* it defines.

This is an area of the book which has been frequently neglected, though, in the last analysis, all else is contributory to it. The final battle with paganism is the making of Muslims, the actualization of the divine will in the forms of life which the teaching enjoins, the rituals discipline and the power structure defends. These latter, and especially the statehood, have tended to monopolize the image and the interests of Islam. There is need to retrieve the Qur'ān from that situation and explore it as a document of religious 'progress', in Whitehead's sense, as the arena of 'becoming' in which the instincts and habits of polytheists were effectively transformed into the loyalties of Islam.

Tertullian's world, as we noted in the previous chapter, was in persistent rearguard action with idolatry. The pagan past pursued the new believer even in naming a street, or suggesting a rendezvous or greeting a friend. The process of extrication from its toils in the deeper reaches of the soul was more formidable still. We have a closely comparable scene in the cities, the markets and the tribal societies of Arabia in the Qur'ān. The *Hijrah* in its implications had given a similar dimen-

[1] *Adventures of Ideas*, New York, 1933, p. 12.

sion of personal decision and inescapability to the issue. Once the victories were won in Medina, in Mecca, at Ḥunain, and beyond, the shadow of persecution, which so darkened the early Christian centuries, was banished. Muslim emancipation from paganism could proceed, with the old foe politically prostrate and militarily extinguished. But despite this great lever and sanction for the new faith, pagan psychology was capable of many a recoil and hideout in the emotions and habits of the people. In most of the actual years of the Qur'ān, the outer triumph, it should be remembered, was still to come.

What, then, from its narrative can we discern about the Muslim in the making? What does it disclose of the inner transformation of pagan into Islamic existence? How was the semantic struggle implemented in the moral? The enquiry is meant to relate to the religious dimension in inwardness and integrity, rather than to the actual codification of law or the development of ritual and precept. The latter are no doubt the framework of the other, the anatomy, we might say, of the body of *Din*, or religion. But what of the life itself within the body, the attainment of the new order in the human material nourished, as the Qur'ān so often recalls, in the ways and customs of the ancients and their idols? For this religious achievement is the most vital of all aspects of Quranic events and one that is often merely assumed in the study of legislation and the institutions which were its external fabric. How did the community mature in the discipline of 'the straight path', in the practice of piety and sincerity? To attempt to answer from the Qur'ān is to initiate ourselves, too, into certain of its deepest themes and phrases.

Moments are rare in the book when the reader is suddenly aware of himself as almost an eye-witness, seeing things happen, as it were, from the edges of the crowd, in the very markets or camel grounds of Mecca or Medina. There is one such at the end of Surah 62, which deals with prayer and merchandise and lays down the directive for the Friday congregation in the mosque. Unlike the sabbath, business is proper before and after the assembly. But the pattern was not at once, or always, congenial in the ranks. 'When they see merchandise or fun around, they melt off', says the text, addressing Muḥammad, 'and leave you standing there.' Truly, as the Surah continues, 'with God there is something better than merriment and commerce. For God is the best of providers' (62: 10–11). Imagination retains that glimpse of the Prophet, alone where the audience had been, with prayer and preaching for the moment outbidden by a passing caravan. There is nothing modern in the magnet of the secular. The scene serves as a lively parable of the strains and stresses and distractions in accomplishing *islām*.

It is imaginatively right to invoke it also to focus the fact that the personal element in Muḥammad himself was a paramount factor. He is directed in 6: 163–4 to

> 'Say: "Truly my prayer and my ritual sacrifice, my living and my dying, are God's, the Lord of all being, whom none can equal. Thus was I commanded—I who am the first of Muslims." '

Earlier figures in revelatory history had borne the name of *muslim*, so that 'first' refers, not to chronology, but to initiative, ardour and example. The Prophet is he from whose zeal and spirit all others take their impetus.

Within this crucial personal factor, nevertheless, there moved long stimulus drawn from the patriarchs and, most eminent of all, from Abraham. Their precedents not only gave Muḥammad solace and courage for himself: they brought a long gathering momentum to his community. The passage just quoted is immediately preceded by the characteristic words:

> 'Say: "As for me, my Lord has guided me into a straight path, a right religion, the faith community of Abraham, a true believer he and no idolater." '

The sense of the word *ḥanīf* used here and in eleven other passages[1] indicates at least a distinctive Abrahamic quality of godliness reproduced in Muslims by a true 'facing towards God', a theme which occurs in 3: 95; 6: 79; 10: 105 and 30: 30. In the last passage the phrase *fiṭrat Allāh* is set in apposition to the *ḥanīf* disposition, so that the whole passage reads:

[1] Two being in the plural. They are: 2: 135; 3: 67 and 95; 4: 125; 6: 79 and 161; 10: 105; 16: 120 and 123; 22: 31 30: 30; and 98: 5. Tested by the contexts the word *ḥanīf* points to strong anti-idolatry and the claim to membership in Abraham by devotion, in possible contra-distinction to community in Moses or in Jesus, or community in Abraham by ethnic means. Since the term *muslim* only became current after the *Hijrah*, *ḥanīf* may have served as an early descriptive. In that case its suggested affinity to 'heathen' would derive from a usage denoting those who were 'not for the gods'. (Cf. the early Christians as 'atheists'.)

'Set your face towards religion as a *ḥanīf*. Such in his ordering will God meant man to be.'[1]

It thus finds Abrahamic devotion the essential expression of the divine design for man, unchanging and often unrecognized. Awe and prayer were its hallmarks and solidarity in the repudiation of *Shirk*.

If the great patriarchal figure gave the making of Muslims its commanding precedent, brought to immediate meaning by the call of the Qur'ān, its steady reproduction demanded a patient habituation. There is no single Quranic passage which directs five daily occasions of *Ṣalāt*. But the incidence of prayer and times, lending the aid of regularity, is fundamental. Surah 11: 114 says: 'Perform the prayer at the opening and the closing [lit. 'at the two ends'] of the day and in the last and first watches of the night.' Surah 24: 58 refers to three periods of time as 'privacy', when slaves should not intrude upon the presence of believing masters without leave, namely before the dawn prayer, during the heat of noon siesta, and after the prayer of evening. There may be matters of domestic convenience here, noted in the context. But the periods that greet and farewell the day properly focus the religious will to reverence. 'Glory be to God,' says 30: 17, 'when you [pl.] come to evening and when you come to morning.' These are the elemental realities of life's measure and prayer celebrates them in the same rhythmic loyalty.[2]

The rhythm of the hours was matched by the rhythm of the words. The genesis of the liturgy of original Islam cannot be firmly demonstrated in detail. The role of the *Fātiḥah*, explored in Chapter 4, and of the *Bismillāh*, within it, was crucial in giving both form and vocabulary to Muslim invocation. Something of the semantic question we have considered in the previous chapter.

[1] Translation has to struggle here with a cryptic language almost requiring paraphrase, though the broad implication is clear. Noun and verb in the second half are from one root. Constitution, way, nature, state, true faith, have all been suggested for the noun. God inaugurated man for a certain quality of humanness and the *ḥanīf* attains it, on the model of Abraham. Dawood has: '. . . which God himself has made and for which He has made man'. Arberry has: '. . . God's original upon which He originated mankind'. The true piety achieves what creation intends: man is naturally constituted by divine intention to be as the *ḥanīf* is. But the face must be set and authentic religion obeyed.

[2] 76: 25–6 renews this directive and fills the night also with praise and, being in the singular, may be linked with 73: 6–8, which explains how night is the time of keenest apprehension and which undoubtedly addresses Muḥammad personally. But the event of the Qur'ān, with him, becomes a precedent for the disciple's discipline also. This is explicitly stated in 48: 9. Cf. also 50: 39–40.

'Say: "Call upon God or call upon the Merciful. Make either invocation. For His are the most excellent Names. Be neither strident nor speechless. Set your heart on the due path of prayer." '[1]

So 17: 110, possibly reflecting some confusion of misgiving about the alternative word, and warning against the contrasted temptations of brash vulgarity and secretive timidity. The verse follows a passage of great feeling, describing the awesomeness in the religious sense of the Qur'ān in recital and its invocation of humility.

But these qualities were not attained overnight, nor the rough world easily ordered into reverence. Postulants among the *badū* were were no doubt the extreme in restiveness. Surah 9: 97 describes them as obstinate and wily. The struggle of the sacred text with their unruliness is perhaps best caught in an anecdote of Jalāl al-Dīn-Rūmī:

A certain person was leading the prayers and he chanted: 'The *badū* are more stubborn in unbelief and hypocrisy.' By chance a *badū* chieftain was present. He gave the chanter a good cuff on the ears. In the second genuflexion he chanted: 'Some of the *badū* believe in God and the Last Day.' The *badū* explained: 'Ha! that slap has taught you better manners.'[2]

There were, of course, more subtle menaces than *badū* brusqueness and guile. 'O you who believe, why do you say and do not?' asks 61: 2. Devotion was meant to detect its own discrepancies, not condone or cover them. In particular, the habit of prayer was to involve the habit of social solidarity. Hence the constant juncture of *ṣalāt* and *Zakāt* as the marks of the Muslim: 'Perform the prayer and bring the alms.' Surah 107: 4–7 reproach those who pray in heedlessness, who pray for the public eye and withhold the helping hand.[3] The nurture of such public spirit, whether for the securing or the serving of Islam, meant the taming, the reversing, of customary attitudes of mind. It required to be fostered by common encouragement and the stimulus of fellows. Hence again the injunction to mutual counsel in mercy and

[1] Again, some read the second part of the verse, where the verb goes into the singular, as intending Muḥammad only. 'Say . . .' clearly directs the first half to his auditors. But if not the precept, his example would embrace them too. The verb has the sense of desiring strongly the prayer that is 'right', neither raucous nor inaudible.

[2] *Post hac non propter hac.* The second quotation is v. 99 of the same Surah 9. See *Discourses of Rumi*, trans. A. J. Arberry, London, 1961, p. 191. The date of his story is not clear but its substance is perennial.

[3] (Lit. 'who want to be seen and forbid assistance'.)

steadfastness (90: 17; 103: 3). In their wealth believers must acknowledge the right of the beggar and the destitute (70: 24–5). In the earliest days of Muḥammad's mission the theme of compassion and the care of the needy was a guiding principle, as may be judged, for example, from the ardent language of Surahs 89 and 90. In post-*Hijrah* years the social conscience broadened into state action and official policy and its character changed accordingly. But it is evident that the course of Islam through the years of the Qur'ān not only created community in law by rules of power, but cared for it in spirit by tasks of character. The growth of this quality of discipleship is acclaimed in the closing words of 48: 29. 'Those who are with Muḥammad' it describes as 'hard against unbelievers and merciful among themselves'. After commending their devotion and discipline, it hails them as like to 'a seed of corn, its shoot grown strong and full and tall, delighting the sowers'. The satisfaction this simile expresses hinged on the steady recognition of the Prophet. Surah 49: 7 insists that it would have been eroded if the roles of ruler and ruled had been confused. By firm preservation of the sanctions of authority, 'God caused the faith to be endeared among them and beautified in their hearts.'

That fruitful discipline was toughened as well as endeared. Its personal *islām* was sustained by the awe of vow and pledge. This was not covenant in the sense of ethnic destiny, but of obligation under the shadow of the end. 'They fulfil vows and fear a day . . .', says 76: 7 (cf. 2: 270). 'The hand of God is over their hands', reads 48: 10, solemnizing all compacts within Islam as compacts under God. The root *'āhada* is a frequent one and in 16: 91 is a typical instance: 'Fulfil God's covenant when you make covenant and do not break oaths you have affirmed, with God as your surety.' The fidelity in the devotional sphere, to prayer, alms and fasting, was to generate and fortify fidelity in the social and economic spheres. Trusts and prayers are thus linked in 23: 8–9.

The descriptives that belong with this temper of religious dependability are brought into a single verse in 33: 35 and cited in both grammatical genders to include men and women specifically, and not merely by inference from a common plural. Muslims and believers are characterized by eight terms in apposition, namely, 'devout, truthful, patient, humble, actively compassionate, self-restraining, chaste and ever aware of God'. The first and fourth illuminate each other, their roots *qanata* and *khashi'a* having to do with humility and reverence.

Both are employed of the innate submissiveness of the natural order to the will of God (cf. 2: 116; 30: 26; 41: 39). The second belongs with the hushed voice (cf. 20: 108) and the downcast eye. It has to do with that quality of soul that 'stands in awe and sins not'. There is a clear hint of the struggle towards it in 57: 16:

> 'Is it not high time that the hearts of those who have believed should be hushed to reverence [*takhsha'*] at the remembrance of God and of the truth sent down?'

Was Muḥammad here wrestling with still active vestiges of the *Jāhiliyyah* mind, striving for that conversion in depth, for a progressive realization of *islām* within Islam, for the temperament answering to the allegiance? The roots however do not intend a mere docility. For, as in 33: 35 and also in 3: 17, they are actively associated with social responsibility and self-discipline.

In both those clusters of virtues is the repeated Quranic theme of *ṣabr*, or staying power. The root belongs in a variety of contexts and occurs in verb, noun and participle form. The primary, transitive sense of the verb is to bind or restrain. In religious terms it denotes the quality of tenacity demanded under duress or persecution, the strength of will that surmounts opposition and breaks through to victory. It is the antithesis of petulance, querulousness, repining and indulgence, and it signifies a purposeful indifference to ease and comfort, to circumstance in general. Like the Greek word ὑπομονή it means resolution towards a goal whatever the odds or the stresses. It is thus associated often with prayer. 'Seek help, you believers, in patience and prayer', says 2: 153. 'Truly, God is on the side of the patient'—a refrain that repeated in 2: 249 and 8: 46 and 66.

Ṣabr is that which undertakes what otherwise would be insupportable. Its perseverance is reciprocal to the promises of God (30: 60; 40: 55 and 77). Its temper is near to gratitude and praise (cf. 14: 5; 31: 31; 34: 19; 42: 33). It is an uncomplainingness alerted by the demands of fasting and, indeed, any of the claims of the divine will. In certain situations it might best be translated 'resignation', as in 12: 18, where Jacob invokes 'sweet patience' at the tidings seemingly corroborated by the evidence of Joseph's blood-stained coat. It is the quality of spirit which attains the heavenly reward (23: 111; 25: 75; 28: 54; 39: 10).

Imagination can readily measure the role of *ṣabr* in the making of Muslims. The Qur'ān abounds in allusions to situations that evoked and tempered it. 'Serve him and be patient in His service' was the call to Muḥammad in 19: 65 (here a derived form the simple verb). The staying-power necessary to him had to have its counterpart, appropriately, in those who sided with him. For detractors were capable of turning against Muslims the very arguments of Islam and disconcerting them in their own idiom. Thus, for example, in 43: 20 they invoked the will of God to explain and justify their worship of angels: 'Had the *Raḥmān* willed it, we would not have served them.' Or they demanded the portion of the final reckoning before the last day (38: 16), either in disdain or arrogance. Surah 46: 35 enjoins the Prophet to bear it out through the long interim. For the judgment will not be hastened, either prematurely to confound the foolish or conveniently to relieve the steadfast of their vigil. Whatever the calumnies or confusions, those who serve God must abide unwearied (cf. 21: 19). They neither flag nor fail.

The Quranic *ṣabr*, however, presupposes triumph. It is an outlasting of evil, rather than its transmuting. Its task is to outstay all opposition so that the good of prophecy is not overcome by the enmity of unbelief. Its endurance keeps the cause from capitulation, so that it may anticipate the victory other factors will achieve. It is not, broadly, a suffering which in itself and of itself makes the fabric of the triumph that is to be. This calls for other forces whose opportunity tenacity ensures. It is not, by definition, a patience that forbears, or excludes retaliation. Rather, as Surah 8: 58 observes, treachery must be met in its own coin, and that justifiably.[1] Surah 47: 35–6 puts a steady militancy at the heart of patience, and enjoins no weakening towards peace, with the promise that guts will not lack their fruit and that being the stout-hearted ones is to be the 'upper ones' in the end. It is clear from sundry passages that, within the years of the Qur'ān, Islam was not called to those dimensions of patience in which suffering knows itself perpetual and finds its victory, actual and perspective, in the very fact of knowing it without hate.[2]

[1] Again, the *Discourses of Rumi* conveniently illuminate the assessment. Since the initiators of conflict were the wrongdoers, any retaliation is justified by that initiation and both 'wrongs' are 'on' the original doers. 'When he [Muḥammad] defeated his enemies he was still the wronged party. For in both cases he was in the right [i.e. witnessing and resisting] and the wronged party is who is in the right.' Op. cit., p. 64.

[2] 'Within the years of the Qur'ān' is important here. For Shī'ah Islam, in its subsequent

There are, nevertheless, passages in the Qur'ān which show that this other, and larger, dimension of *ṣabr* was present in the perspective of the whole, and that its potentialities are present even though they do not control the final pattern. Surah 28: 54, already cited, joins to its celebration of the patient the words 'they turn back evil with good', and 41: 34–5 lay down the obligation to 'repel with what is better', or 'fairer', noting how thereby a sundering enmity may be transformed into a loyal friendship. None, it adds, can come by this retrieval of evil by good except those who practice *ṣabr*. Surah 60: 7 is careful to insist that retributive action is right only in respect of explicit enemies and allows no state of hostility against those innocent of such enmity themselves. Surah 16: 126–7 conclude with the directive:

> 'If you take punitive action [pl.] do so proportionately to what has been done to you. But if you endure patiently, that is surely the better thing for patient men. Be patient then [sing.]. Your forbearance [*ṣabr*] is by God alone . . .'

For only thus can the counter-endurance of idolaters and gainsayers be overcome.[1]

Two other familiar Quranic terms are closely related to this concept of fortitude and resilience. They are (in verbal form) *tawakkala* and *itma'anna*, or 'trustfulness' and 'the quiet mind'. The former could in itself comprise a study of personal *islām* coming into being. The root *wakala* has to do with entrustment to another and from it comes one of the most current Names of God, *Al-Wakīl*, 'the guardian' of human interests in responsible charge of human cares. 'Put your trust in the Almighty, the Merciful,' Muḥammad is directed in 26: 217. 'He it is who sees you when you stand and confront the worshippers.' The thought here is of the divine presence as protection and perhaps

experience of unrequited evil, developed its own unique relation to the mystery of tragedy which the rest of Islam eluded by the very philosophy and attainment of vindication. There is, however, a persistent tradition of the Prophet to the effect that 'Islam began a stranger and will return a stranger as it began'. The point is further involved in Chapter 11 below .The critical question at issue within the Qur'ān's justification of militancy (namely that the enemy has properly brought it upon himself) is whether such militancy does not in itself 'confirm' him in the original impulse behind his hostility, namely that he is resisting one he takes to be his foe. Militancy 'justifies' his view. It is a larger duty of patience to 'unjustify' it by love.

[1] Surah 25: 42, for example, uses the same word *ṣabr* in the mouths of the heathen protesting an ungodly tenacity.

also as vindication, in the most solemn occasion of religious leadership. It had also to be the central experience of the congregation. *Tawakkul* is thus very close to the central doctrine of *Tauḥīd*, or unity, since it signifies an inclusive confidence, terminating and disowning all the diversified reliances of fear and ignorance. Men of mature faith who have learned how God suffices say: 'God is all we need, the best of guardians' (3: 173). 'In God let the believers put their trust . . . we will take patiently whatever injury (men) do us. In God be their trust, all those who are entrusting!' (14: 11–12). 'In God let all the believers set their trust' (3: 160; cf. 5: 11; 9: 51; 12: 67; 58: 10; 64: 13). The last of these verses joins the injunction significantly with the confession: 'God, there is none save He.' For the credal avowal was to be worked out in an effective unity of heart, where all practising superstitions have to die out in a single committal. In all altercation and the stress of controversy, this is the security: 'Say: "He is the *Raḥmān*: in Him we believe and on Him we rely" ' (67: 29). The crisis of Islam, we might almost say, was not what to believe but whom to trust.

The verb *itma'anna*, though rarer, is of kindred quality and has to do with the progress of *islām* in the soul. It denotes the calm of mind, the composure, that should belong with belief, in contrast to the restlessness of superstition and the vagaries of unbelief. It is used in a very literal sense in 4: 103, in reference to the security to be had by vigilant precautions against molestation when praying in the midst of foes. By the recollection of God men's hearts are set at rest (13: 28). The larger subtler menaces of the demonic are disarmed and broken for 'the soul at rest'.

It was, then, by the nurture of *ṣabr* and its related attitudes of spirit that personal religion availed against the instincts of the old order and acts of *islām* were multiplied in the sequences of the prophetic years. External events, in their gathering momentum, must be seen to have exercised a double influence upon that inner story. By their very prosperity and efficacy they exposed the cause to dubious recruitment of hypocrisy and its forms and institutions to merely outward service.[1] But this only sharpened the criterion of sincerity and alerted vigilance to its proving. In a situation prone to feigning and pretence the virtues of straightforwardness, of *al-ṣirāt al-mustaqīm*, are the more authenticated and their hallmarks known and scrutinized. Hence the constant

[1] See *Nifāq* and the *Munāfiqūn* in, e.g., Surah 63.

emphasis on sincerity or *ikhlāṣ*, the quality of the *mukhliṣūn*.[1] Its contrast with the insincere was further heightened by the same sanctions of success, as genuine adherence read into their unfolding story the divine imprimatur. The battle for the inward *islām* of the heart had both its counterpart and its comfort and succour in the battle of the outward Islam in the twin cities and the many tribes.

These factors may be seen as integral to the very meaning of faith, or *īmān*. The active participle *mu'min*, or believer, is even more frequent than the word *muslim* itself as the main denominator of the new identity. As evident in 49: 14–15, belief had in essence a more inclusive sense than submission, since it was possible to be outwardly surrendered (*muslim*) without inwardly believing. There is in 106: 4 an early use of the verb *āmana* to denote divine protection: 'God made them secure from fear'—a usage to be linked with the occurrence of *mu'min* in 59: 23 among the Names of God, as the eternal defender, the trustworthy keeper. This original sense of trust and safe-keeping passes over into the more technical and developed meaning of belief or credence. *Imān* is thus the active of personal faith which issues in the personal dependability of the faithful. They hold the faith securely in the double sense that they count it right and are thereby loyalists within it. The sense of 'counting right' or 'crediting' was expressed in the early Qur'ān by the verb *ṣaddaqa*, i.e. 'to account to be true' (cf. 37: 37; 39: 33; 75: 32; 92: 6). But in later years the verb *āmana* became more general in this sense, with the antonyms, *kadhdhaba*, 'to belie', and *kafara*, 'to deny'. In comment on 49: 14, Al-Baiḍāwī joins faith with the *itma'anna* root and defines it as 'holding to be true with a quiet heart.'

We cannot rightly take the measure of the Muslim conviction of truth without also reckoning with that sharp consciousness of contrast. There was vehemence, more than mere distinction, in those antonyms. No doubt the precariousness of Meccan *islām* and the state calculus of Medinan Islam necessitated this vigorous antipathy and the forthright denunciations of unfaith. Surah 111, in its anathema on Abū Lahāb, 'the father of the flame', is the most personal of these repudiations. The total antithesis of belief and unbelief is everywhere explicit.

[1] Used, for example, in 15: 40; 37: 40, 74, 128, 160 and 169; and 38: 83, adjectivally to 'servants of God' and with the noun *Din*, religion, in 7: 29; 10: 22; 29: 65; 31: 32; 40: 14 and 65; 98: 5.

We find it, terse and antiseptic, in Surah 109, with its conclusion: 'To me mine and to you yours.'

There can be no doubt that this posture entered deeply into the making of Muslims, giving them both the strength of simplicity and the vigour of simplification. It was almost as if the immediate making in the assurance postponed or obscured the larger making in ultimate religion. Idolatry and symbol, sin and responsibility, doubt and integrity, the soul and society, all demanded more penetrating reckoning than pressing urgencies allowed or recognized. By the same token, personal religion, steadied and exhilarated by the strong awareness of contrast, had many of its criteria of evil externalized. Its sympathies and instincts lived by and for its antipathies, in sheer confrontation. 'Turn aside from them and wait: they are waiting too' (32: 30).

When the reader looks beyond the evident strength of this assurance to its moral liabilities, and beyond these to its spiritual submission under God, he has to fall back upon the insistence within Islam itself that God only is God—God beyond and over, not merely for and with, Islam. He has to discern the criteria we have already studied, governing even the institution and the conviction that exist to secure and affirm them. He needs also to penetrate into the undergirding sense of gratitude and penitence in the Qur'ān. The Quranic believer, for all his sense of commendable contrast with the infidel, has bound himself over to humility, reverence, patience, dependence and the quiet mind.

It is perhaps well, in this context, to ask also whether, despite the simple enmity of belief towards unbelief, there is not an element of inclusiveness by which the believer represents the human reality on behalf of the unbeliever as well as against him. So much at least is implied in some exegesis, for example, of 2: 251:

> 'Had not God held back humanity by some of its members, indeed the earth itself would have been corrupted. But God is the source of good to all beings.'[1]

[1] Lit. '. . . driven back, or repulsed, the people, some by others . . .'. It seems fair to understand humanity at large, and to take 'some . . . others' to mean believers and infidels. Mazheruddin Siddiqi in *The Quranic Concept of History*, Karachi, 1965, p. 36, says that 'this verse was recited after the Prophet had cited a tradition that God defends the community of Islam from those who do *not* pray through those who do pray, from those who do *not* pay *Zakāt* by those who do, from those who do *not* fast by those who do, through those who do *not* perform the pilgrimage through those who do'. The faith, so to speak is *for* the unbeliever precisely in being *against* him.

Militancy itself holds the ring and by hostility ensures the possibility of good. The community that militates and obeys the law preserves thereby both the clue to, and the chance for, a right humanity. The door of capitulation is always open to the enemy. Though the question must persist whether this handling of the enmity does not retain and toughen the evil, even while it retains the opportunity of good, the Quranic conviction intends incorporation, once its victory has been conceded. Whether this is, or is not, a right exegesis, one thing is clear, namely that Quranic personal religion cannot be understood without this militancy. Islam cannot be defined without non-Islam: nor can it be practised except in the pervasive sense of the distinction.

In this search for the Quranic believer in his time and place, it remains to study the moral obligations of his faith, in and through the fundamental things *Shahādah*, *Ṣalāt*, *Zakāt*, *Ṣaum*, and *Ḥajj*, those five pillars, *confessio fidei*, ritual worship, alms and social conscience, fasting and personal restraint, and pilgrimage in the ordinance of solidarity. The Qur'ān does not contain a single code of ethics, nor a decalogue. The nearest in form to such a codification of moral character is in Surah 17: 22–39—a passage which begins and ends with the claim of the unity against all profanation. Its elements recur elsewhere in numerous passages but nowhere else quite so collectedly. The ethical portrait of the Muslim needs to be seen in full.

> 'Do not set up another god with God, lest you find yourself in shame and desolation. Your Lord has commanded that you serve none but Him. Show kindness to parents, whether one or both of them attains old age with you. Do not be round or impatient with either of them, but speak kindly words to them. Lower to them the wing of humility tenderly and say: "My Lord have mercy on them as they nurtured me when I was little." Your Lord knows well what is in your hearts, if you are true of soul. He is all forgiving to those who seek Him.
>
> 'Give to the kinsman his due, and to the needy and the wayfarer, and do not squander your substance, for squanderers are brothers to Satan. Satan is ever thankless to his Lord. And if you turn from them, anticipating the wherewithal from your Lord's mercy, then at least speak to the needy kindly.
>
> 'Do not have your hand chained to your neck; yet do not be open-handed to utter excess, or you will end up with reproach and bankruptcy.
>
> 'Your Lord gives with bountiful hand and with sparing hand to whom He wills. Truly He knows and observes His servants.

'Do not kill your children for fear of poverty. We will provide both for you and for them. To kill them is a most grievous sin.

'Come not near to adultery, which is foul and an evil way.

'Do not kill any man—a deed God forbids, except for rightful cause. If a man is slain unjustly, We have appointed to next of kin the right of satisfaction. But let him not carry his vengeance beyond the due, for there is counter retaliation.

'Handle the property of the orphan in all integrity, until he comes of age. Keep your bond, for you are accountable.

'Give full measure, when you measure, and weigh with just scales. That is better and fairer in the end.

'Do not pursue things you have no knowledge of. Hearing, sight and heart—all these faculties of a man will be held responsible.

'Do not strut proudly on the earth. You cannot cleave the earth or match the mountains in stature. All such ways are evil with your Lord.

'All this is given you by revelation of the wisdom of your Lord, and set not up any other god beside God, or you will be cast in blame and dereliction into Gehenna.'

Here are most of the elements of Islamic existence, affirming the One Lord, disowning false worships, cherishing human kinships, practising human kindness, keeping human proportions and living with a human integrity—all in the prospect of eternity. Surah 16: 89–97 echoes several of these precepts more briefly and adds its own warning on fidelity to covenants and on the disparity among nations as being no cause for strife or chicanery. Surah 46: 15–19 elaborates the charge to be gentle with parents and measures the length of retrospective gratitude a full forty years.[1] It is clear from the further context that instances where the care of aged parents was repudiated turned on the issue of faith, the parents invoking Muslim assurance of the resurrection as solemnizing family duties during life, and the non-Islamizing children dismissing that belief as idle and the duty as bothersome. It may be inferred from such cases that Islam and its rejection coincided with devotion and neglect between the generations, or that compassion prevailed where faith prevailed.

Surah 25: 63–76 repeat several of these themes—modesty, devotion,

[1] Forty has always been a significant waymark in Muslim biography, no doubt because it was the age at which the Prophet began his Quranic vocation. It was also at just that point that the great Abū Ḥamīd al-Ghazālī, around 489 AH (AD 1095) and Jalāl al-Din Rūmī in 642 AH (AD 1244) underwent their deep conversions.

moderation that avoids extremes, integrity of word and oath and action, gravity that has no truck with idle talk, and domestic joys.

Through all the delineation of the right Islam runs the awareness of eternity and of life as passed in its shadow. Contrariwise, engrossment with the present, with the mortal state, and the impulse to discount personal resurrection—these are the symptoms of *kufr* and unbelief. 'Nay, but you prefer this life present' is the characteristic warning (87: 16). The inward test of Islam in the soul, as the Qur'ān reflects it, was this capacity to say with a later Ṣūfī:

> Servants of God, is it not true
> Where'er I go, whate'er I do,
> I cannot aught, except there be
> A Watcher watching over me.[1]

To set these disciplines and patterns of personal character, with their framework of rite and of community, against the background of the *Jāhiliyyah* and the circumstances of the Quranic years, is to have the measure of the achievement of Islam within the soul. 'Unto God is your becoming' is the steady refrain of the Qur'ān's summary of life, intending in its meaning the climax of eternity. Yet that *maṣīr*, or coming into being of the things that make the end, was a sustained moral struggle with the frailties, the perversities and the potentialities of men—and all within the immediate drama of the Qur'ān's own time and place.

The first mosque built in Yathrib after the emigration had, according to Tradition, a simple roof of intertwined palm branches. It was likened by the Prophet for that reason to Moses' ark of bulrushes. A recent writer takes the likeness to have been inspired by the sense of precariousness which then obtained.[2] If, however, the risk and jeopardy were comparable, no less so was the issue of that survival in the attainment and the identity of a whole religion.

[1] A. J. Arberry, *A Sufi Martyr: The Apologia of 'Ain al-Quḍāt al-Hamadhānī*, with Introduction, London, 1969, p. 21.

[2] Emel Esin, *Mecca the Blessed and Madinah the Radiant*, London, 1968, p. 91.

Chapter 11
THE SENSE OF HISTORY

The event of the Qur'ān and the life of Muḥammad belong powerfully with world history by a sturdy independence of it. There is nothing in religion quite so concentrated as the Islamic Scripture, as a single book, through a single prophet, in a single territory, in a single quarter-century. It was only in the very final years that it began to be related prospectively to the tribes and lands beyond its own borders,[1] while retrospectively its bearing on precedents and patriarchs of the past was always strictly subordinated to its own logic and its own drama. It emphatically took the world to be its province, but nurtured that confidence in a surprising seclusion from it. Its sense of history is at once majestic and quiescent, possessive and yet also indifferent.

We can more effectively study the Quranic focus of history if we first recognize the absence of the historical. It was some time after the expansion of Islam and the Arabicization of scholarship within it that Muslim historians and chroniclers became involved in general history. The time-perspectives of the Scripture, backwards to the prophets and their generations, and forwards to the judgment-end, were as decisive for its contents as the bounds of geography. Events outside its span of vision found only incidental place in its pages. The external world never occupies the Quranic stage. Relationships there undoubtedly were, with Ethiopia, Persia, Syria and India, as the commerce of Mecca, the biography of Muḥammad and the diplomacy of Medina demonstrate. But the revelatory text itself, metaphor and vocabulary apart, hardly reflects, still less records, these factors.

[1] It was some five or four years before his death in AD 632 that Muḥammad began to turn seriously to the frontier tribes beyond the borders of the Ḥijāz. But the Qur'ān remains almost wholly silent here, and the famous six letters to 'world' rulers are traditional only. See W. Montgomery Watt, *Muḥammad at Medina*, Oxford, 1955, pp. 345–7 for a brief analysis of these.

It does not undertake to chronicle or ponder the history of surrounding cultures, except in that far retrospect which sustains its own moral of prophetic sequences. The revelation, we may say, has no articulate external relations. The Ḥijāz suffices for its locale. It will address the world. But it will do so from its own immediacies of time and history.

Thus, a reader anxious to discover what history outside the prophets might have meant to the first Qur'ān-reciters has to be content with the barest answer. If he asks how Athens, Rome or Alexandria, the philosophers and the imperialists of the classic world, or the disciples of Zoroaster, might have seemed to them, the text affords him little or no clue. For these relationships, however tenuous they may have been, are beyond its purpose and foreign to its nature. Nor does the subsequent meeting of institutional Islam with these elements in history fall within the time and scope of its revelatory definition.

The briefest review suffices to cover the rare and incidental references to alien events. Surah 30, with its title 'The Greeks', is the most obvious example. It opens with a statement and a promise.

> 'The Greeks (Al-Rūm) have been defeated in the near land. But a few years hence they will gain the victory after their defeat. For God's is the authority, in the before and the after. Then the believers will rejoice in the triumph of God, who makes whom He will victorious. He is the Almighty and the Merciful.' (30: 2–5)

The struggle between the two great powers beyond the northern borders and the buffer states, the Persians and the Byzantines, had been fluctuating during the years of Muḥammad's life. In the second half of the second decade of the seventh century, the Persians overran Syria and Egypt and Anatolia in a seemingly decisive success. But by AD 627, Heraclius had redressed the balance and carried the war on to Persian territory. The rest of Surah 30 does not concern itself with those opening verses, save for the theme of dependable promises. The passage may indicate a sympathy in Muḥammad with the Christian side against the Persian dualists. Or it may suggest a further historical logic in the see-saw of northern rivalries, whereby the enemies, in weakening each other, were the more exposed to the future eruption of the Muslim armies against both.

Or, more likely, we may understand the reference to suggest a certain parallel between the resurgence of the Byzantine cause against the Persians and the Muslim cause against the Quraish, each of these emerging, by promise, out of seeming failure into success. If so, the sense of larger history is here recruited to the local crisis. The first post-*Hijrah* years in the Ḥijāz coincided with the turning of the tide for the northern monotheists in their cause.[1]

Belonging, as it does, sometime before the *Hijrah*, Surah 30 is notable both for the conviction with which it looks across the frontier and for the angle of its vision. But it is also notable in being isolated. The Greeks do not figure again, nor the Persians, who even in 30: 2–5 remain unnamed.[2] Other allusions to their histories are in the context of parable and legend and cannot be decisively identified. It is widely assumed that *Dhū al-Qarnain*, the two-horned figure in 18: 83, 86 and 94, is Alexander the Great. But it would seem that he appears only because the Prophet was catechized about him by either curious or malicious critics of his preaching, since the passage is prefaced by the phrase, 'They ask you about *Dhū al-Qarnain* . . .', and the directive, 'Say: "I will rehearse to you what is said of him."' It then goes on briefly to describe his rise to power and his empire. 'We set him up in strength and facilitated his whole advance,' his westward success, presumably into Illyricum or regions beyond Macedonia and 'the dark water' where he exercised a discerning clemency. Turning eastwards into the sun-rising, he came in his conquests to a ravine between mountains where he erected a rampart to defend the suppliant population from marauding 'Gog and Magog'. The rampart was an effective piece of engineering that could be neither scaled nor pierced, but whose solidity could not endure beyond divine dispensation.

Strenuous efforts have been made to identify the locations and incidents in this paragraph of history. Persia seems certainly to be meant in the eastward journey. The iron wall may perhaps belong in the Caucasus, or the Caspian Sea area, or Bukhara, or Turkestan, or elsewhere, with 'Gog and Magog' taken as the Mongols. Some commentators dispute the Alexander identification altogether and refer the

[1] Al-Baiḍāwī explains that the idolaters in Mecca welcomed news of the Persian victory and exulted over the Muslims, saying: 'Our brothers who are *ummiyyūn* (unscriptured) have triumphed over your brothers and we shall indeed overcome you.' He adds that the number of years between the defeat and its reversal would be between three and nine, and goes on to note that later on the Muslims themselves had the better of the obdurate Meccans. The parallelism, therefore, seems close.

[2] Except that the Persians are no doubt in mind in the term *Al-Majūs*, the Magi or Mazda-ites, in 22: 17.

central figure, and Gog and Magog, to the Book of Daniel. From the ample conjecture and discussion it seems wisest to be content with the Qur'ān's own use of the moral of the story, rather than to search for a historical precision which need not and cannot be reached. The Alexander theme had long been current in the lore of many lands and peoples. The form in which it stands in the Qur'ān, elusive and incidental as it is, belongs wholly with the express concerns of Muḥammad's mission. It witnesses to the Muslim sense of history, not to history itself. In so far as it is responsive to curiosity, it is the curiosity of unbelievers.

It is similar with all the other echoes of the outer world. Surah 18 derives its name, 'The Cave', from the legend of the Seven Sleepers of Ephesus, whose story it notes in vv. 9–25. Clearly, the parallel with the Islamic situation explains its presence, bearing as it does on the themes of fidelity and the resurrection. Fot it has to do with loyal souls, set against idolatry and surviving by divine protection to be a perpetual parable of constancy and providence.[1]

Many problems arise for Quranic students in respect of the sources and the shape of these items of historical material from beyond Arabia.[2] Into these our purpose here has no duty to enter. It is the elusiveness of the historical interest and its steady relation to internal issues which are the significant things. The case is much the same with the several instances of historical memory in areas closer than Greece, Ephesus and the Caspian. The Surah of the Elephant (105) relates to the advance of Abraha from the Yemen against Mecca, in the year of Muḥammad's birth, and its sudden disastrous conclusion in the onset of plague or other catastrophe. Surah 34: 16 and 'the flood of the dam' have been taken to refer to the collapse of the irrigation systems at Ma'ārib around AD 450—an event, or series of events, well fitted for awed

[1] The young men fled during the persecution of Christians by Decius (AD 201–51), who revived a militant idolatry. They sought shelter in a cave in Mount Anchilus, where a deep sleep overcame them. After some three hundred and seven years, during a period of heresy over the resurrection, God awakened the youths and a nearby builder took away the stones from the mouth of the cave to build a fold. One of them goes down to the city, resolved to bear faithful witness, only to find the idols gone, the cross in evidence as a symbol, and nobody recognizable. The coins he offers to purchase bread are assumed by the vendors to be part of an ancient treasure. The governor, the bishop, and later the Emperor come to the cave and register the wonder before the youths pass into a final sleep.

[2] Using 'historical' to refer to the currency of tradition as well as actual fact. For currency is certainly factual!

recollection down the generations. The context rehearses also the breakdown, by wilful over-extension, of the caravan system or the selfish manipulation of the caravanserai. Surah 85: 4–9 are taken by some to allude to a great persecution of Christians in Najrān in AD 524 when the bodies of the victims were mutilated and burned in the trench or *ukhdūd*.[1] Again the precise history is open. What matters is the burden of the preaching that recalls it.

It is likewise with the frequent allusions to 'Ād and Thamūd, the distant ancestor tribes of Arabian memory who figure prominently in numerous Surahs. The former seem to have been denizens of the great Al-Ḥijr, the famed Petra, where the inhabitants had hewn the very mountains into dwellings yet 'cried lies to Our messengers'. Surah 15 bears their rose-red city as its title, while Surah 54: 18–31 reproach both peoples for their recalcitrance and 69: 4–8 celebrate their overthrow. Whether the rock architecture of Thamūd or the tent-pitching of Pharaoh (89: 9–10), there is no staying the divine nemesis.[2]

When we turn from these echoes of general history, within or beyond the island of the Arabs, to the broad panorama of the Biblical and the prophetic, it is the same criterion of Quranic immediacy which governs the whole. What we may perhaps call Semitic memory in the Qur'ān is always a present summons to God. The perspective from Adam and Noah to Moses, David and Jonah provides its solemn commentary on the sequence of Muḥammad's own struggle, especially through the middle years.[3]

The heroism and the vindication of Noah, Abraham, Joseph, Moses and the rest, in their generations, in comparable circumstances of idolatry, ridicule and enmity, had a double implication for the Quranic story. They served notice on the Prophet's detractors and

[1] The persecutor was Dhū Nuwās, last king of the Himyarites, who sought to will Judaism on to the people of Najrān. Their refusal is said to have provoked his punitive attack. Axel Moberg, in *The Book of the Himyarites*, which he translated from the Syriac, with an introduction, Lund, 1924, pp. xliii–xlvii, is doubtful of this view of Surah 85, though he does not exclude it. Richard Bell upheld it in *Origin of Islam in its Christian Environment*, Edinburgh, 1926, pp. 38 and 68, but he rejected that earlier view, without elaboration, in his translation of the *Qur'ān*, vol. 2, Edinburgh, 1955, p. 646.

[2] Charles Doughty (*Arabia Deserta*, vol. 1, 1921, pp. 95–6, and 188) locates Al-Ḥijr at Mada'in Sāliḥ in north-western Najd. Some derive 'Ad and Thamūd originally from the south of Arabia.

[3] Details of the patriarchal narratives can be readily found, for example, in H. U. W. Stanton, *Teaching of the Qur'ān*, London, 1919, reprinted 1969; or J. Jomier, *Bible et Coran*, Paris, 1959.

they encouraged and steadied his own fortitude and tenacity. These predecessors in a common struggle had wrestled against obloquy, prejudice, superstition and tradition, and had come through to manifest triumph, with their foes and hostile conspirators disowned and broken. So it would be again and the assurance gave strength to the beseiged and embattled cause of Islam in the Meccan years, while the movement towards victory in the Medinan 'turn of the tide' took momentum from the precedents of flood and exodus and rule, as the patriarchs had known them.

The divergencies in the narratives from the Biblical counterparts can best be understood within this didactic purpose. There were no doubt historical factors also at work, arising from the circumstances of Muḥammad's contacts and his familiarity with oral tradition.[1] Whatever conclusions Muslim, or other, opinion may reach about these, the sense of history, not the sources of the historical, is the finally important thing.

The wide canvas from Adam to Jesus depicts for Muḥammad's people the meaning and destiny of their own cause. Biblical material, in independent shape, is rehearsed in lively corroboration of Quranic authority. All prophecy accumulates towards it, so that revelation may culminate. Other Scriptures are mentors, not masters. It is the ruling theme of prophecy as crisis which they consistently serve. The patriarchal retrospect witnesses to a continuity of truth and multiplies the signs by which the Meccan/Medinan situation must be read both in conflict and prosperity. All is historical prelude to a biography and a biographical conflation of history. The patriarchs find Arabicization in the Qur'ān, not merely in the literal sense that they are now heroes for Arab listeners and told on Arab lips, nor yet in the literary sense that they have found celebration in a new and Arabic Scripture, but in the ultimate sense have become elements in a religious crisis by which Arabia 'turns to God from idols', through the energies of a final and universal prophethood.

It is this historical review of the past in the present which gives to the

[1] The suggestion has become popular of late in *some* Muslim circles that Quranic narratives diverge from earlier sources through conscious literary adaptation on Muḥammad's part, much as Shakespeare's genius touched his material to a finer power. But such theories cannot be reconciled with orthodox understanding of *waḥy*, as precluding deliberate authorship or conscious artistry. In any event, what matters finally is not whether Surah 12 makes a better story than Genesis 39–45, but that Joseph through adversity and triumph was an instrument of the providence of God.

Qur'ān and Islam the characteristic quality of *Jihād*, or struggle, in the deepest and non-technical sense of that term. The very sequence of the prophets is a sequence of law and claim, of insubordination and nemesis. The logic within it is the unremitting necessity of struggle and the necessary sinews of strength. To bring a divine message is to incur a human enmity and so, in turn, to enter a trial of stamina and resolve, of the will and the means to outstay the opposition. Noah at length rides securely over the inundation of ridicule. The lonely Abraham, breaking down his people's idols, incurs and survives persecution. The maligned and rejected Joseph finds a providence in his tribulations which brings him to the seat of utmost power. Joseph and Moses especially, with David, are exemplars of the conjoining of prophecy and power, of the representative of the divine will properly becoming the holder of the human government. In this logic, suffering is present as a preliminary to its redress. It is that which has to be endured before it can be terminated. It bears the odds until they can be evened and reversed. The successful eventuality is held open by the refusal to be denied it, and this demands persistence and non-compromise. History, then, by this toughness of will and under the divine hand, will yield the proper verdict.

'A historical defeat is also to Islam a metaphysical scandal', wrote Professor N. Bammate.[1] History owes prophecy vindication.[2] Events must sustain it after due occasion and encounter, since otherwise its divine *imprimatur* would be proved unreliable. Existence is poised, so to speak, between prophecy and eschatology, in that the prophetic address to humanity must have, in token and in fact, that writ of success which eschatology brings to final authenticity in the last judgment. The utter unambiguity of the eschatological must belong suitably and surely with the interim evidence of prophetic standing in time and in power.

The simple Quranic statement that 'God is with those who fear Him and are doers of good' (16: 128), is taken by some to mean that

> The course of history is a moral agency through which the morally superior elements rise to the top, while those who are morally inferior

[1] In 'Islamic Tradition and the West', in Charles E. Moore, *Philosophy and Culture, East and West*, Honolulu, 1962, pp. 726.

[2] 'Prophecy' here, of course, not in the (very) secondary sense of foretelling, which would, at length be discredited by non-fulfilment, but in the essential Quranic sense of witness, law and ethical claim.

> sink to the bottom . . . That virtuous living, which is the outcome of a healthy religious faith, must inevitably lead to success.[1]

But that inevitability—if such it be—is properly served, as well as anticipated, by political action. The same writer adds that 'the possession of political power has been repeatedly stressed by the Qur'ān'. Such possession and the quest for it, as argued in Chapter 3, is no more than the sincerity, the integrity, of the prophetic vocation itself. The historical order which the word addresses the will must also subdue. Meaning is at work in it unrealistically, and therefore insincerely, unless it is ready for action in its cause. Indeed, loyalty could be defined here as message becoming a mission and its confession a campaign. Only the endeavour and the struggle guarantee the intention. The *Jāhiliyyah* or insubordination is only rightly countered in the *mujāhadah* or enterprise of which the *Hijrah* is the symbol and the twin cities are the two poles.

Islam, therefore, expects history's corroboration and sees its historic role as encompassing what it expects. It can perhaps be defined as an optimism of the intentions, with a realism of the acts. There is no gainsaying the vigour of the case it makes and its assurance that it has the patriarchs and the precedents with it. Indeed, the questions that might give it pause, or interrogate its confidence, only emerge when we ponder the contrasted, other, precedents of prophecy. To do so, we must abandon our general principle here of studying the Qur'ān *vis-à-vis* the predominant paganism, and not the minority monotheism of its setting. But in doing so, we argue from its own significant silence—a silence which would seem to indicate a deep instinctiveness in its historical sense of necessary success.

While the patriarchs are vigorously Quranic figures, the great prophets of the Bible from the eighth century BC onwards, are entirely absent.[2] The sequence stops with Elijah and Elisha. It does not include Amos, Hosea, the Isaiahs or, supremely, Jeremiah. The explanation may simply be that these did not come within the range of *Waḥy* as Muḥammad received it. But certainly they could not have been unknown in the Meccan and the Medinan *milieu*, however we finally

[1] Mazheruddin Siddiqi: *The Quranic Concept of History*, Karachi, 1965, pp. 7–8.

[2] Jonah, the Quranic Yūnis (Surah 10), is a specia lcase, depending on where he, and his book, should be placed chronologically.

assess the Jewish presence there. Evidence exists that the *Ka'bah* itself may have housed pictures of the Quranically absent prophets of the Old Testament.[1] Whatever the circumstantial factors in their exclusion, the fact of it is a symbol, whether deliberate or unconscious, of a view of history from which the consensus of those Old Testament heroes very deeply diverged.

For, with the greatest of them, suffering is not merely endurance until there is a contrasted success. Indeed, it is not endurance at all in the rugged and resistant sense. The interpretation of the experience of rejection does not merely argue retribution and reach for the consistent means to it. It somehow takes that hostility into the mystery of vocation, as a token of the evil which must be mastered, but mastered in terms other than its own. For these have a way of perpetuating the deeper antipathies and even confirming them. Then there is a toughening, rather than a retrieving, of the inner wrongness. Or the success hypothesis leaves its full task unaccomplished, and perhaps also unknown.

The supreme tradition of Hebraic prophecy, therefore, senses and accepts suffering as a vocation to redeem. It sees the consistency of loyalty, not in the determination to win but in the willingness to sustain fidelity even through total loss. It faces and takes a view of history where its fidelity does not of necessity prevail. Yet this is not a pessimism, since it is rooted in longer purposes and endures by the vision of God rather than by the visibility of time.

This is not to say—and it is important not to say—that Hosea, and the Isaiah of 'the suffering servant', and Jeremiah, came to this sense of things by abstract reflection. On the contrary, it was the living circumstances of their experience of multiple wrong, of human sickness of will and mind, of the compromises of power, which required the obedience in which they learned and exemplified the lessons we discover in them. It was that they wrestled with divine Lordship through autobiographies of pain and through collective tragedies of exile and of evil. To serve, and even to address, this world, they had to retain a freedom of utterance which alliances of power would have curbed or silenced.

[1] The *Ka'bah*, as it stood when Muḥammad was young, seems to have been reconstructed by an Ethiopian, Christian, architect and tradition is clear that there were Biblical murals adorning the interior of the shrine and depicting the prophets, of whom only Mary and Jesus remained after the Muslim conquest.

But the price of that circumstance was their defencelessness, as both the condition and the cost of their calling. Their suffering was their partnership in the uncompulsiveness of the divine claim. There had to be a place for vulnerability, if there was to be a ministry to truth. And it could not be required that the place for it should be only temporary or transitional. Times were when it became total and unrelieved, except by the assurance that in its meaning lay the very reality of hope. Suffering might in this way become as inclusive of prophetic biography, and of life itself, as the evil was inclusive against which the prophecy was set. For there is a prophetic declarative, a definitive we may say, which is not in word alone, but in sign and in the very travail of the spirit unto death. It is precisely this that activism may foreshorten or exclude, in its confidence over the struggle that is geared to the necessities of success.

Thus the Biblical prophets we have here in mind know themselves more effectively with the counsel of God because they refuse to be with the patterns of men. Or they are alive to dimensions of good and of evil in history which they sense to be beyond the reach of the order of the political and requiring to be distinguished from it. So it is that, in this perspective, prophecy becomes the critic and the accuser of the state, and cannot achieve itself in coalition. It keeps a liberty of judgment against all the orders of human existence, as spokesman of the transcendent sovereignty of God alone, whose purposes it does not presume to negotiate nor to precipitate, but only to affirm and love. Hence the perpetual quality of exposure, in such service, to the full antipathy of man. The fact that the Qur'ān does not include these representatives of a suffering prophethood, whatever the explanation, may be seen as congruent with its own different assurance and with the centrality of its sense of history as manifest success.[1]

These reflections do not imply that power is ever an irrelevant issue, or that the state has no proper role in the economy of history understood as providential. Power, plainly, is an inescapable historical reality and the political order crucial to the human condition. It can well be argued that Islamic realism at this point is a sounder reckoning with what we mean when we say: '*Magna est veritas et praevalebit*' (Great is the truth and will prevail). But the issue here about history is

[1] In comparable sense, it also presents the climax of Jesus 'prophethood' as a vindication which succeeds by the frustration of the hostile world and the divine intervention which bypasses the otherwise certain suffering as loyalty girds itself to meet it.

whether the prophetic ultimate and the political realm, the religion and the state, can be so confidently allied. Or is history altogether more equivocal in its content and tragic in its nature? The prophets who interpret it for God are the very nerve of the problem. For their calling is precisely at the intersection between history and eternity.

There were pressing circumstances of time and place which certainly conduced to this Quranic pattern of confident realism. But the assurance within it bears upon another aspect of the Quranic text and its relation to history. This is the completeness of the book within the lifetime of its single Prophet, a completeness fundamental to its very nature. The Qur'ān cannot be conceived of as other than singular to Muḥammad, its only recipient. But it means that while there is a long backward retrospect to Adam, there is no forward incorporation into the scriptural of what might be called experience in its meaning, outside, that is, the years when Muḥammad was alive. The Biblical Scriptures, coming into form over long periods, enclose within themselves the relevance of their own currency. The Old Testament comprises the protracted lessons of the law's demands and follows its sequences through many generations. The New Testament presents its message out of the decades of apprehension in which it was authenticated to its people. Islamic experience in the centuries beyond the Qur'ān likewise incorporated the trust of it into tradition, theology and consensus. But those acts of appropriation and achievement remain outside the Scripture itself. Ongoing history did not enter into the fabric of the definitive thing. The twenty-three scriptural years of revelation and accumulation, with their vivid themes and crises, were the only revelatory media. They did not and could not contain issues which only emerged when the faith had passed out of their immediacies. It is as if the Old Testament were all at Sinai or the New Testament only in Galilee.

To note this is not to think that we could have it otherwise or to call in question the Qur'ān's sufficiency to itself. But the sharp focus of those near 300 months in the coincidence of revelation and corporate time operated for exclusion as well as for intensity. Many points in the Islamic sequel would have been different could they have been also Quranic, and the document itself by its very completeness excluded the relevance of its own impact. There is no Quranic measure of Quranic consequence.

Prominent among areas of later experience was the whole Shī'ah dimension of failure and tragedy, with the sense it generated of vicarious suffering and representative atonement, finally enshrined in Shī'ah liturgy and ritual. These belonged with deep religious emotions in the Shī'ah soul. But they lacked explicit and unequivocal sympathy from the Quranic text,[1] though their fervour and perpetuation bear witness to realities in history which time within Islam as far as AD 632 had not compellingly known or suffered. To imagine a Quranic range extended to contain them is to realize how contrasted they are with the ruling confidence of the Scripture that though adversity needs to be patiently endured its pain is not perpetual and its reversal is sure. It was out of long denial of such solace that Shī'ah Islam was born.[2]

There are many lesser examples of what was disallowed, of historical perplexity, by and within the Quranic delimitation of historical experience. While history certainly sustains what we may call the event-texture of the Qur'ān, it also eludes it in those darker reaches where enigma and tragedy cannot be comprehended within the formulae of just reward and due victory.

These thoughts relate, of course, only to post-Quranic history and to the forward direction of Quranic relevance. The backward direction reaches to creation itself and the entrustment of the world to man which Islam sees as the meaning of civilization (Surah 33:72).[3] The Qur'ān is the culminatory truth from all that past, enfolding God's education of humanity through the prophets, of whom Muḥammad is the seal. Thus it sees history as the preparation for itself. Those earlier prophets, with their 'pages' and pledges from heaven, had often lesser audiences or more partial commissions. The named Scriptures

[1] Shi'ah exegesis of the Qur'ān is a vast and intricate study and the authority of the Imāms and the perceptions of the *mujtahids* could go far in discerning congenial meanings in arguably uncongenial texts. These matters are a complex study, outside the present scope. But it can hardly be doubted that the consensus of the Qur'ān is towards the triumphant and away from the tragic. One single, but vital, example of Shi'ah commentary involves the words in 33:33: 'People of the house, God only desires to put away from you abomination and to purify you', on which a belief in the immaculate house of 'Alī has been based and associated with vicarious suffering. Sunnī exegesis disallows this sense. But the very form of the debate shows that there are deep questions between what *is* there in the textual history and what is *wanted* there.

[2] The Old Testament, for example, knows and is known, from its extending into exile, and the New Testament by its incorporation of its meaning from Galilee and Jerusalem into the markets of Corinth and the retrospect of Patmos.

[3] This passage about man accepting 'the trust of the heavens and the earth' is at the centre of Islamic thought about man. Surah 2:30 likewise. On the latter, see, for example, Ibn Khaldūn in *Al-Muqaddimah*, vol. 1, p. 85, 'this is the meaning of civilization'. Trans. by F. Rosenthal, New York, 1958.

are those of Mūsā, Da'ūd and 'Isā, with the *Torah*, the Psalms and the *Injīl*, and the great prototype is Abraham. All past history is comprehended in their education of mankind and there are many unnamed and unremembered prophets. For 'every age (*ajal*) has its book' (13:38).[1]

This sense of the cumulative past, wrought into its own finality, gave to the Qur'ān its characteristic confidence. History as prophecy means history as accountable, history as probationary, history as morality. It means humanity mentored by great personalities and God served by human guardians of the right. It means history proceeding, under reiterated reminder, towards its reckoning. As N. Bammate has it, 'history for Islam is in suspense between a past conceived as prophecy and a future which is constructed around Judgment Day'.[2] What that suspense meant in the hearing of the Qur'ān's first listeners we have already tried to apprehend. It is strangely close, both in meaning and in metaphor—changing only the *Qāri'ah* (Surah 101) for the trumpet, to the familiar negro song:

> My Lord, what a mourning when the stars begin to fall!
> You'll hear the trumpet sound
> To wake the nations underground,
> Looking to my God's right hand,
> When the stars begin to fall.

It is appropriate to conclude these paragraphs with a final reflection on the finality of Muḥammad—a conviction in which so much about history is implied. For the immediacy of his own generation, it could be understood, as the present tense of all history is understood, while it is being lived. For every significant present is an ultimate, a climax. To live with the event of the Qur'ān was to believe it the crisis of history.

But as the centuries have lengthened into almost fourteen, there are many in Islam who read it, not in static and rigorous terms, but as dynamic and potential. The seal of prophecy, they point out, is not the closure of science and knowledge. The first of mankind, who gave names to things and so inaugurated the rational relation to environ-

[1] *Ajal*, meaning 'term' or 'period' is sometimes taken with the other noun in the sentence, *kitāb*, to mean 'everything has its prescribed term', understanding 'book' in the sense here of 'destiny'.

[2] In Charles E. Moore, (ed.), op. cit., p. 728.

ment which is the heart of culture may be, thereby, the first of the prophets. But the technology which he thus initiated goes progressively forward and, so doing, returns back ever more vitally to his meaning as man.[1] Its achievements and confrontations may even be seen as in some sense revelatory. What the finality of prophethood means is, then, no harsh veto on this further, and ceaseless, discovery, but rather the definitive religious principle by which it must always be guided and interpreted. And even that moral finality, in its spiritual discipline of man's restless estate, may be seen as abiding only because it is ever renewed. Its finality is its creative relevance, its vital applicability, in the reverent trust, not of craven or timorous custodians, but of responsible and lively disciples. To these, the Qur'ān could not be final as a past perpetuation but only as a perpetual present. To allow this is surely the deepest recognition of the sense of the Qur'ān for those among whom first it was history.

[1] The author has tried, at greater length, to study Semitic (and Islamic) man in relation to modernity in *The Privilege of Man*, London, 1968.

CONCLUSION

'You who believe,' says Surah 5: 105, 'on you are your souls.'[1] The responsibility of faith as an identity rests with faith as an activity. The believing that responds to truth is a self-possessing in the truth. The institutions of faith live in the commitment of the faithful. The community is liable for the doctrine by which it is defined. Religion can only live in religiousness and its central document mediates the one and anticipates the other.

It is out of this sense of the Qur'ān as both original and contemporary, as both at the source and in the trust of Islam, that we have ventured our study of its eventfulness in the seventh-century. Such study historically is complete in itself. What it means in the present requires another, and in many ways a larger, enterprise, which cannot well begin in a Conclusion. There is place only for a few reflections emerging from all the foregoing and pointing forward to the contemporary concerns. It was suggested at the outset that historical perspective and religious authority in the Qur'ān were properly seen as belonging together, relevant now in the understanding of the relevance then—an understanding alive to the past authentically because it lives in the present.

To move from and with the event of the Qur'ān in this double quality of mind means, for our purposes here, three things. These in the retrospect of our studies are the immediate, the intensive, and the extensive, Qur'ān. There is the psychic-prophetic experience in the personal immediacy to it of Muḥammad himself. There is the corporate confession of it in the inward possession of Islam and of Muslims.

[1] Translating with the literal sense of the preposition. 'Your souls are your own charge', 'take heed to your selves', 'for your selves (alone) you are accountable', are other renderings. The context has to do with pagan obduracy in disbelief which should not dismay the faithful, and with the reality of returning to God which should reassure them. Faith, we might say, is the crux of personal existence and the person the crux of faith.

There is the fact of the Qur'ān in the cognizance of general human history outside the community of interior faith. Our concerns have to do with the mutual bearings of these three realms, with the Qur'ān as act in Muḥammad, with the Qur'ān as fact for Muslims, and with the Qur'ān by virtue of both of these in the diffused participation of the wider world. The Qur'ān is the Islamically received revelation: Islam is the Quranically guided religion. What is, what will be, the quality, the dynamism, of this interrelationship? How does it, how will it, belong with the manifold of human experience around it and with the diversity of contemporary religious and secular life? Islam, as the allegiance and existence of Muslims, is always the middle term, mediating the first to the third.

We can usefully focus this situation in the words of Surah 33:56, noted in Chapter 1 above: 'Truly God and His angels celebrate Muḥammad. You who believe call down blessing upon him and salute him with peace.' The verb *ṣallā 'alā*, here translated 'celebrate' and 'call down blessing upon . . . ', is the one which yields the vital term *Ṣalāt*, or ritual prayer, and the phrase accompanies every devout mention of the Prophet's name. To ascribe to God an activity denoted by the word which, for the human creation, means 'prayer', seems initially puzzling. But its significance is clear. God acclaims or 'celebrates' in Muḥammad, that by which the human acknowledgment of God is rightly wrought. The angels concur in the divine design and pleasure in the prophetic personality. What happens in the immediate instrumentality of the Prophet is saluted with a divine satisfaction. The actual, we might say, serves the cosmic and so doing is cosmically greeted.

The receiving community is therefore bidden to follow suit. 'O you who believe, you also celebrate and greet with peace' the Prophet of God. The imperative, we may note, is the plural of incorporation. The gathered faithful echo the divine mind and, so doing, receive and express its claim and message. The immediate act of the Qur'ān becomes the fact of the Qur'ān they have received. Their very identity, as the context shows, is constituted in their confession and sharpened by the contrast of unresponsive unbelief around them. The Quranically given is the Islamically recgnized. What is immediate to Muḥammad becomes inwardly characteristic of his people, with faith as the criterion. What thus differentiates them from the world around engages them with the divine initiative. Their faith corroborates a heavenly verdict. The event of the Qur'ān, prophetic to Muḥammad, has become participation for them.[1]

Their 'celebration', however, manifestly relates them to the external society. Their allegiance cannot be hid. The devotion that responds and incorporates also discriminates. 'O you who believe' (a most frequent Quranic refrain) is a powerfully selective salutation. So the event in the Prophet and within the community reaches extensively into the wider history. The interior awareness shapes the exterior challenge.

In all the foregoing chapters we have surveyed the circumstantial details of this triple eventfulness of the Qur'ān—the charisma, the geography, the poetry, the local idiom of folk and metaphor, the tension and travail that belonged with it, the circumstances of tribe and tongue and territory that made its setting. We have seen how forthright and combative were the relations of its inward allegiance with the outward scene. Within its own span of years the Quranic drama is decisive and definitive. In the sequel of its vast imperial expansion into the eastern and the western world it steadily recruited the cultures of other history for its own finality. It was secure enough to absorb into its own authority what it held compatible with its charter of ultimacy and habituated itself thus to a mastery which could at once both mould and receive the world. It is the historian's job to ponder and reckon with those centuries as in their turn a measure of what happened in the Qur'ān.

Our business is with the present, when the Islamic relation to the rest of humanity, broadly speaking, is neither so combative as was the Qur'ān's strife with the pagans of its incidence, nor so ambitious and spiritually imperial as its authority in the prime of the Caliphs. We have all survived into a much tauter, confused and plural scene, with religion itself as a viable human dimemsion doubted and daunted by the sheer complexity of the time and by the pride of technology. In the mood of the age, which we need not here stay to analyse or to document, what should we expect of the event of the Qur'ān, or of the trust of it in the souls of Muslims, in a reckoning, theirs and ours, with the world as we know it around us?

The question grows in the very asking. It is sensible to limit it here to the two areas we have noted, that relate what we have called 'the possessed Qur'ān' to the prophetic immediacy as history knew it and

[1] In the sense, that is, of experience received. There is no communal participating in the prophetic action itself, for this is inalienably and uniquely Muḥammad's.

to the external setting of current history. 'We have made you a middle people,' says Surah 2: 153 in a much debated verse—'a mediating people' could it be?—a community standing between the 'guidance' revealed and the 'guidance' commended in witness and warning?[1] However we take this significant verse, there is no doubting this triple eventfulness of something given, something apprehended and something confessed, and, therefore, no doubting the mediating trust of the *ummah* in between. This concept sufficiently defines and delimits what we need to have always in view and in focus.

The sense of the Prophet in Islam is a field of deep and broad diversity in unity. There remains in full vigour and authority the traditional understanding of Muḥammad as the locus of a wholly arbitrary, wholly external, intervention of celestial inspiring, made the more miraculous by the absence, or the abeyance, of natural capacities. This concept of the *ummī* speaker, given voice and giving voice to the wholly miraculous substance of the Book—miraculous both as to language and content—has long satisfied and assured the generality of Muslims. Its insistent quality, however, need not deter the outsider from deeper and more enquiring attitudes of mind. It can well be seen as the shape of the Islamic confidence about the Qur'ān, the dogmatic form of its final values and their *imprimatur*, and, in that sense, be respected even where it is not shared. Merely to deplore or to accuse it for excess of simplicity would be to miss the religious necessity by which the sacrosanct is popularly identified. What ultimately matters is the reality residing within the formulation. Doctrinal structure is for the sake of doctrinal content, despite the danger that the one may be complacently or vulgarly taken for the other. This is not, of course, to say that the duty of intellectual exploration is rightly to be excluded but only that its pursuit must first acknowledge a religious actuality secure in its own significance.

But the traditional and authoritarian pattern of Islamic relation to the Qur'ān is not without important and sustained exceptions. There have long been attitudes which possess the Scripture in a different temper. In these, if he is perceptive and patient, the outsider can often discover accents and interests he, from without, would be most liable to assume. Thoughts that naturally attract him about the Qur'ān have in measure

[1] It could be a merely geographical middle position in the earth, or a 'moderation' in ethical terms that refuses the extreme either way. But these conjectures do not readily fit the context which adds '. . . in order that you might be witnesses to men.'

been long articulate or latent among Muslims also. His concern for a penetrating and imaginative relation to it need not see itself as venturing where Muslims have not gone at least in part, nor as lacking significant precedents of thought from the domestic thinking of the house of Islam.

There are many examples in the middle centuries of Muslim thought of interpretations of the phenomenon of the Qur'ān which linked prophetic instrumentality with superlative endowment of reason and spirit. The Prophet was then understood in his Quranic role as pre-eminently rational. The status of *Al-Rasūl* could be seen as the dogmatic account describing and attesting an inherent excellence of soul. Despite their obvious tension with traditional assumptions about the meaning of *al-nabī al-ummī*, these views, if in an esoteric way, could well exist within an orthodox profession. The familiar denial of natural aptitudes as accounting for the Qur'ān could readily be accommodated to a view of *waḥy* which saw them conferred. It could always be said that the popular form of the belief was necessary to popular mentality, while philosophic thought cared for the essence of the matter with a more perceptive competence.

The way was then open for men of reason to hold the significance of the Qur'ān in easy relation with the activities of reason in other spheres of culture and history. Dogma, at least in these circles, could be saved from the exclusivism, which would otherwise have isolated it, by this kind of reconciliation—a process facilitated by the possibility of including such extra-Islamic sources of wisdom within the conception of prophets having visited all peoples. This allowed the great names, Socrates, Plato, Aristotle and the rest, to be in some sense conjoined with the Quranic ultimacy of truth.

It is from the hints, indeed the solid liberties, of the middle centuries in these ways that contemporary Muslim possession of the Qur'ān can relate itself to the wider obligations of belief. It can and it does. Qur'ān-consistency will always be the criterion of the Islamic. But the criterion of the consistency will always be a Muslim decision. That it should be so is the mark of a living religion. The principle of non-repugnancy to the Qur'ān, so often invoked in constitutional, political, legal and social thinking in the last few decades of Islam, suggests even in its negative form a broad opportunity for initiative and flexibility. There are a variety of factors loosening the still formidable influence of official religion and as it were laicizing the concerns that Quranic loyalty must register and satisfy, The Scripture has proved and will continue to prove susceptible of an impressive responsiveness to the human necessities of faith and to the currents or situations that shape them.

This conviction is not a religious romanticism, nor is it a convenient opinion designed to comfort religious complacence or evade stern tasks of mind. It is rooted in the sense of the inclusive relevance of that passion for unity which, as we have seen, is the essence of the Quranic drama. The struggle against the plural deities contains within itself the urgent negation of all ultimates but the one that is worthy. *Lā ilāha illā-llah* is a principle which disqualifies every pseudo-absolute and allows race, nation, state, wealth, knowledge, properly to be themselves because they are denied the absolutism which makes them demonic. The core of man's problem and of his existence is a right worship and it is for this, beyond all its localisms and particulars, that the Qur'ān cares. Those very localisms and particulars, as we have here explored them, have their datedness or transience taken up and made perennial in the significance that transcends them. It is that education of man into his true authority of surrender which abides in the unique idiom of Muḥammad's 300 months of Quranic experience. The immediacy of that phenomenon as it was in those decisive days, determining its continuing community of possession through the document, makes the document and the community in turn partners, in whose mutuality the meaning belongs.

This brings us to our second sphere of enquiry. The Qur'ān in the inwardness of Islamic experience and apprehension relates to the larger world on the outer side of that experience wherever man, either in his religions or his secularity, is found. It belongs more widely than the boundaries of Islam. For it is part of human religious history. Non-Muslim reckoning with the Qur'ān must have its due place and so also must an Islamic relation to such external bearings of their Scripture. When, to use our earlier terminology, the intensive passes over into the extensive—the possessive into the diffused and the committed into the neutral—sensitive areas of life and psychology are aroused. But in the developing commonness of the human situation and its contemporary travail, there can be no evading or disallowing this sort of external cognizance, however delicate its implications. Diversities of religious experience can not well, or longer, retreat into their own privacy. But they face difficult adjustments of mind when they confront their own image in the mirror of another. Much here depends on the temper with which Muslims will allow the Qur'ān to be possessed from without—possessed, that is, not by the propagandist who wishes to decry or the dilettante who wills to sentimentalize—for these invite an easier reaction—but by the seriously concerned who has at once both yearning and reservation, both attraction and misgiving.

We can surely expect this kind of religious mind-in-meeting to quicken and deepen in our day. The indications that it may be so are as welcome as they are varied. Perhaps our soundest comment here in relation to Islam is that the reactions are liable to be those which the quality of external interest deserves. The issue, therefore, returns back to the quality of thought and apprehension the outsider is prepared to bring.

Is it fair to observe, in this connection, that western scholarship in Islam has often come with overly academic canons of criticism, sometimes impatiently applied, or with a failure of imaginative reverence for the religious reality with which it had to do? Other forms of interest have created barriers to their own access through persisting suspicion of their motive. Often even right intentions have been impeded by the hard going of the road with them. Thus, for example, there has long been a Muslim plea for a Christian recognition of Muḥammad, a plea which saw itself asking for an attitude reciprocal to its own veneration of Jesus. But it did not realize how far short of a Christian relation to Jesus such veneration fell, nor how painful was the disparity to the Christian mind. Christians, for their part, have in general hesitated to grapple with their side of this problem or have left it to controversies alone.

Examples of the exactingness for all parties of this 'external' Qur'ān —as we are calling it, this Qur'ān outside the interiority of Islam in the hands of the unpredictable stranger, this Qur'ān beyond the explicit faith-community—these are too numerous to rehearse. Without immodesty the present study may perhaps be seen as a venture in answer, a venture in the positive. As explained in the Introduction, we have deliberately excluded the themes of Muslim Christian polemic within the Qur'ān in order to concentrate on what we have recognized to be the central thrust of Muḥammad's *Risālah*. This has disencumbered our task of much controversy. But, more specifically, it has allowed the emergence of a certain fundamental 'sympathy' with the original 'cause' of Islam—a sympathy which has the greater hope of integrity because it does not silence the basic Christian disquiet about the power-equation of Islam, as the Qur'ān formulates it, in the pursuit of that 'cause'.

Surely this is the sort of religious openness we must be set to seek and to give. It is an openness where the themes of legitimate question and reserve of commitment—such as the foregoing—relate positively to the central issue of a recognized and, indeed, a shared objective. For it is only when faiths are taken in their own seriousness that even controversies begin to be urgent. Where they are not so taken, any controversies proposed will remain idle, or tendentious, or academic.

It is to thoughts like these we come if it is asked why a venture such as this book has attempted should be made religiously from within one faith about the centralities of another, and made without retreat into academic indifference and without contention for religious claims. It is inspired by the belief that Islam has a task of the spirit in the contemporary world, which the alert Christian must acknowledge and serve, without abeyance of themes which, precisely because of that partnership, are the more authentic and searching. For they are only discovered to be so within the sincerity of the partnership by which we see what they are. What, for the committed Muslim, is the interiority of Islam, is still in that sense external. But it is no longer alien or unknown territory. A frontier marks it, it is true. But it does not only divide. We are not always sure where it runs. At points we lose it altogether, only to find it again as a formidable thing. The map itself reads differently for the inhabitant and for the traveller.

Moved by its fascination, we have aimed in these chapters to take the measure of what happened in the Qur'ān, and so doing to penetrate where Islam belongs. To know that event as it was is a goal of study. But the goal of study is an open country of relationship.

Glossary of Quranic Terms

The sense of words and phrases in, or relating to, the Qur'ān is central to the concern of the foregoing Chapters and may best be sought there, with the help of the Index. The brief notes here are intended only to facilitate study and cannot capture the range and variety of contextual usage. We follow the English alphabetical sequence and give the Arabic consonant indicated by ' the place determined by its following vowel and we merge in one English equivalent the differentiated 'light' and 'heavy' consonants, noting the latter only by the dot below, thus ṣ, ṭ, ẓ, etc.

'abd. The status of man as servant of God as *Rabb* or Lord. The root verb joins the twin ideas of 'worship' and 'service'.

Allāh. The Name of God in His Essence, to whom all the attributes belong. The word signifies the force of the English word 'God' without definite article and it should not, with its long syllables, be vulgarized into the short-syllabled English 'Alla'. The Arabic term is usually, though not unanimously, interpreted as a conflation of the common noun *ilāh* and the Arabic definite article *al*, eliding the 'i' syllable.

amr. The command or *fiat* of God which gave being to the worlds, the divine initiating by which all things are, understood as descending on creative and legislating 'errand' from heaven to earth. The term is extended to embrace both moral obligation (*al-amr bi-l-ma'rūf*) and human destiny.

Al-Asmā' al-Ḥusnā. 'The beautiful Names' of God, recalled in Muslim recollection and central to Islamic theology. They number ninety-nine, of which some seventy are Quranic. They point to the attributes and activities of God but, being involved in human language, cannot be thought of as describing Him.

āyah (pl. *āyāt*). The term for a verse of the Qu'rān, but more importantly the 'sign quality' of events in nature and history in which men—or, at least, grateful and perceptive men—can read the divine power and mercy.

asbāb al-nuzūl. Lit. 'The occasions of the descent', the points in circumstances to which, or in which, the contents of the Qur'ān belonged in their sequence, and in reference to which they should be understood. The events with which *waḥy* coincided.

balāgh. The communication of the message, its content and import, the revelation as something to be uttered to its constituency, irrespective of the *ḥisāb* or reckoning with its reception.

barzakh. The bar or barrier that marks the frontier of death, which the departing cross and become, beyond it, irretrievably the departed (Surah 23: 100). Used alone of the physical bar of the sea, the strand that guards the land and the fresh waters (Surah 25: 53; 55: 20.)

bayān. One of the titles of the Qur'ān, the disclosure, the manifest, the revealing which illuminates and clarifies (Surah 3: 138; 55: 3). Related to the very frequent adjective of the Qur'ān for itself, *al-mubīn* (q.v.), the clear, or perspicuous.

Bismillāh. The invocation of the divine Name, in the words: 'In the Name of God, the merciful Lord of mercy'. The phrase prefaces every Surah of the Book, save Surah 9, and every act of Muslim devotion or intention.

dīn. Religion, in correlation to *īmān*, faith, the ritual acts and moral duties of the faithful Muslim. The term also denotes the last judgment, the final reckonong by which all acts are sifted and weighed.

falāḥ. Well-being and prosperity, the true good of life to which Muslims are summoned in the call to prayer. Those who know it are the *mufliḥūn*, in contra-distinction to the *khāsirūn* or losers.

fasād. The corruption or disorder which men do in the earth, an active perversity which degrades things and depraves men.

Fātiḥah. The opening Surah of the Qur'ān, in which the quintessence of Islam is expressed. The verb, to open, has also the sense of to open up, to provide the clue and to prevail.

fitnah. Initially persecution, ultimately sedition, a word that develops in meaning as the Qur'ān proceeds. It denotes what is a test or trial to the faith and community.

fiṭrah. The natural constitution of man, the innate disposition as divinely designed (Surah 30: 30) and thus fitted to the right and ultimate religion of Islam.

furqān. One of the names of the Qur'ān, as the criterion or that by which truth is distinguished from falsehood and right vindicated against wrong. The Battle of Badr is described as *yaum-al furqān*, the day which demonstrated where right was (Surah 3: 4 and 8: 41).

ghazwah. The depredatory raid erupting in tribal quarrel.

ḥadīth. The Tradition of Muḥammad as treasured and recorded, his words outside the Qur'ān, his deeds, manners, habits, opinions, carefully memorialized, and leading to the *Sunnah*, or pattern of Islamic conduct and law, complementary to Quranic legislation.

ḥanīf (pl. *ḥunafā'*). A word of much debated origin, traditionally denoting the pure faith of, for example, Abraham and other anticipators of the final Islam. Etymologically it may be much closer to the general sense of 'pagan.'

ḥanafiyyah. The collective identity of the *ḥunafā'*.

Hijrah. The emigration of Muḥammad and his community from Mecca to Medina in AD 622. The initial event of the Islamic calendar and the watershed of the event of the Qur'ān.

ḥisāb. The reckoning which ensues upon men's reaction to the *balāgh* (q.v.), the divine judgment of men.

ḥukm. Judgment or decision, arising from the power and wisdom (*ḥikmah*) of God, one of the titles of the Qur'ān itself (Surah 13: 37).

I'jāz. The matchlessness or inimitability of the Qur'ān as a literary and spiritual miracle, the demonstration that its form and content are beyond natural, human, personal origins and accountable only by divine bestowal of word and meaning in *waḥy* (q.v.). An Arabic phenomenon attesting a universal Scripture.

Ijmā'. Consensus, the collective mind of the Islamic community which *Itjihād* (q.v.) must develop and by which it is controlled. *Ijmā'* is a source of law, according to some schools, and is an effective principle of development by which, in the end, 'Islam is what Muslims believe it to be'.

Ijtihād. The endeavour, or initiative by which the rightly qualified Muslim(s) may elaborate law and opinion consistently with the Qur'ān.

ikhlāṣ. Sincerity, the worship of God that is free of all taint of *shirk* (q.v.) or pluralism and diversion of heart (cf. Surah 39: 2, 3, 11 and 14; Surah 112).

īlāf. The composing or assembling or the caravans and so the ventures and enterprises, of the merchants of Mecca, trading from the Hadramaut and Aden to Damascus and Byzantium (Surah 106).

īmān. Faith or reliance, complementary to *dīn* or religious performance, the act of credence and conviction towards doctrine, as it may be distinguished from the act of submission or *islām* (cf. Surah 49: 14 f.) though true *īmān* and *islām* are one.

islām. The act of submission, or recognition of the unity of God and the *rasūliyyah* of Muḥammad. The due subordination of all things to the divine sovereignty and will.

iṭmi'nān. A settledness of spirit and heart, resultant upon faith and prayer, the awareness of the divine sufficiency, inner tranquillity.

isnād. The support that warrants *ḥadīth* (q.v.) consisting in the chain of attestation, reaching back dependably to the Prophet through his immediate companions. The science of *isnād* became quite complicated and gave rise to many main collections of warrantable tradition.

Jāhiliyyah. The state of uncouthness and disorder traditionally associated with the pre-Islamic scene. It denotes the related ideas of 'ignorance' and 'wildness', lacking both the light and the order of the régime of the Qur'ān.

Ka'bah. The central shrine, of cube shape, in the great mosque at Mecca and the centre of Islamic pilgrimage, as it had been previously of pagan veneration and circumambulation.

kāfirūn. See *kufr.* Those who deny or belie the revelation and reject or discredit the authority of God and Prophet.

khāsirūn. The losers, a Quranic descriptive of unbelievers in contrast to the state of *falāḥ* (q.v.): those who in unbelief make a bad bargain of life.

kitāb. Book, a term applied to the Qur'ān but also to previous scriptures given to earlier prophets, notably Moses, David and Jesus. In some contexts the volume of destiny under God.

kufr. The state of repudiation of God, His law and His messengers, the inclusive ground-sin of man, the ultimate atheism by which God is both denied and disregarded. Sometimes contrasted in the Qur'ān with *shukr* or gratitude.

al-mubīn. See *bayān.* An addjectival title of the Qur'ān, the book which clarifies and illumines.

mufliḥūn. The prosperers, those who in well-being have the divine favour, responsive to their faith. (cf. *falāḥ*).

mukhliṣūn. The sincere ones, the folk of integrity, who eschew *shirk* (q.v.) and worship only God and God alone, without anything ulterior in object or motive.

mu'min. One of the Names of God who responds to faith (Surah 59: 23). Of men, the believer, the keeper of *īmān* (pl. *mu'minūn*), as opposed to the *kāfir* and the *mushrik.*

munāfiqūn. The hypocrites who figure strongly in the post-Hijrah struggles of Muḥammad. They are the people of *nifāq.* It is not possible to tell whether they were an organized political party or simply people of moral turpitude and dissembling. The very prosperity of Islam in the days of success contributed to the calculating insincerity sometimes present in outward submission.

mushrikūn. Those who commit *shirk* (q.v.).

muslimūn. The true submitters, acknowledging both Muḥammad's message and his rule and therein the divine will and sovereignty: those who enter into the peace of submission, in *Dār al-Islām* ('the household of Islam') as contrasted with *Dār al-Ḥarb*, 'the household of antipathy' yet to be subdued.

nifāq. See *munāfiqūn*.

qadr. The divine decree arising from the divine will. Originally the measure, and so the determinant, and so the destiny determined. Also the aegis of Quranic revelation given on 'the night of power' (Surah 97).

qāri'ah. See Surah 101. The knocking, or cataclysmic summons which inaugurates the last assize.

qist. Fairness of dealing and that which measures it, the justice which the Qur'ān teaches and identifies (cf. Surahs 7: 29; 57: 25), the scales of truth.

qisṭās. The instrument of *qisṭ*, the balance of truth, the test of integrity.

Al-Rabb. The title of God as Lord, most frequently with the conjoined *al-'Ālamīn*, 'the Lord of the worlds'. The word has the co-ideas of authority, power, nurture and control.

Al-Raḥmān al-Raḥīm. The two most notable of the divine Names, or *Al-Asmā' al-Ḥusnā*, always found in the *Bismillāh* (q.v.). The root verb denotes mercy and the progression in meaning is that between mercy in character and mercy in excercise.

Rasūl. Apostle or messenger, a title used of many prophets, though in measure distinguished from that word. With the definite article (*Al-Rasūl*) denotes Muḥammad, 'the apostle of God'.

Al-Rasūliyyah. The commission of Muḥammad as *Rasūl Allāh*, the dignity and authority of the Prophet of the final revelation.

Al-Rūḥ. The spirit, or Spirit, of God, that breathes in or through the archangel and other emissaries of the throne. (Surah 17: 85 answers what may be asked of the Spirit.)

ṣabr. The quality of patience, or endurance, or composure which characterizes men of faith and prayer, the faculty by which the difficult and the puzzling become feasible.

Ṣalāt. Ritual prayer performed in Islam five times daily with a liturgy of adoration and rhythmic prostrations of the body. This (lit.) bowing symbolizes and focuses the reality of submission and Godwardness.

Ṣallā 'alā. Lit. 'to pray upon', the verb denoting the calling down of blessing upon Muḥammad, the celebration of the Prophet which both God and believers make.

Al-Ṣamad. One of the divine Names occurring in Surah 112 only, denoting the utter non-contingency of the divine, the entire self-adequacy of One whose resources are entirely in himself. Hence, by derivation, the Eternal. (Surah 112: 3 is the best commentary.)

Shahādah. The act of witness or confession by which one becomes and remains a Muslim. The confession of God as God alone and of the Apostolate of Muḥammad, with intention.

Sharī'ah. The sacred law of Islam, (lit.) the path. Its sources are the Qur'ān, the *Sunnah*, analogical derivation from these and (in some schools) *Ijmā'* (q.v.). The sanction is wholly revelational—God so wills.

Sakīnah. The *Shechinah* of the Old Testament, the token of the divine presence and so, derivatively, the peace it brings. (Surahs 48: 4, 18 and 62; 9: 26 and 40.)

shirk. The cardinal sin of worshipping other than God, whether crude idolatry or the pseudo-absolutes of modern man. 'Having other gods.'

tanzīl. The verbal noun denoting the sending down of the Qur'ān upon Muḥammad, so that the heavenly Book became the earthly experience and its Arabic form and content vouchsafed to the world.

Tauḥīd. The affirmation of the divine unity, the effective assertion of the God to end gods.

tawakkul. Reliance or trust in God, the state of mind and will for which God is all-sufficient.

Ta'wīdh. Seeking refuge in God, the verbal noun relating to the refrain (e.g. Surahs 113 and 114): 'I take refuge in God.' In adversity, controversy, malignity, the believer looks for his security, his vindication, and his 'cause', to God. There is also refuge from the inner evil of the self.

Ummah. The 'nation' or community of Islam, the corporate faithful in their religious identity, transcending merely ethnic distinctions and constituted in contra-distinction to other religious collectives. (cf. Surah 2: 143: *ummatan wasaṭan*, 'a people in the middle').

ummī (pl. *ummiyūn*). An important descriptive of Muḥammad (Surah 7: 157 and 158) often taken to mean 'unable to read or write', but much more likely denoting one 'unlettered' in the vital sense of not having Scriptures and called to be the means to Scriptures to those (i.e. the Arabs) who lacked them.

waḥy. Revelation-inspiration understood as one, the enabling, by *tanzīl* (q.v.) of that awareness and utterance by which Muḥammad was instrumental to the Qur'ān, as its sole spokesman and means. The state of *waḥy* was accompanied by psychic phenomena which made it readily discernible.

Zakāt. One of the five duties of Islamic *dīn*, the payment of alms in the cause of the faith and in expression of its sense of a responsible society.

Ẓann. Supposition or conjecture, usually perverse, such as accompanied the controversial attitudes of Muḥammad's detractors.

Ẓulm. The inclusive Quranic word for wrong-doing, wrong-thinking and wrong-willing. The root sense is to deny true place to a thing, and so to pervert, to oppress, to distort, to belie, to malign. There is also *ẓulm al-nafs*, by which men degrade their own selfhood.

Numerous less prominent terms and ideas occurring above in the text can be identified by the Index and studied in context. Quranic references in the Glossary are not meant as complete.

Index

forty, age of, 164 n.
French, T.V., 73 n.
Frost, Robert, 74 n., 75 n.
āl-Furqān, 75, 118, 189

Gabriel, 32, 43, 51, 52
  wing of, 58
Galilee, 176, 177 n.
gardens, 89, 90
Gaza, 100
Gehenna, 164
Gentile, 60, 61, 75
  as translation of *Ummī*, 61
geography, of the Qur'ān, 86 f., 99, 166
Al-Ghafūr, 77
Al-Ghazālī, Abū Ḥamīd, 164 n.
ghazwah, 92, 106, 189
Gibraltar, 90
God, 52, 74 n., 80, 112, 132, 148, 150, 155, 156, 162, 175, 181
  sole worship of, 14, 78, 150; bounty of, 63; doctrine of, in the Qur'ān, 73 f., 162; face of, 107; hand of, 156, 163; and his apostle, 32, 36, 37, 43, 71, 131 f; and man, in revelation, 22, 141 f., 173, 175; Names of, 52, 63 f., 101, 103, 133, 148, 155, 159, 161; non-contingency of, 80
goddesses, the three, incident of, 141 f.
Gog and Magog, 168, 169
Goldziher, I., 50 n., 149 n.
Gospel, 57, 63
gradual principle, in Qur'ān, 113 f.
gratitude, 24, 157, 162
Greeks, the, 167, 168
Grünebaum, G. E. Von, 96 n.
guidance, 57, 74, 75, 78, 90, 150, 183

ḥabil Allāh, 92
Al-Hādī, 52
Ḥadīth, 121 f., 189. *See* Tradition
Ḥadramaut, 100
Ḥajj, 163
Ḥamāsah, the, 69
ḥanīf, 30, 153, 190
Ḥanafiyyah, 30, 190
hardness, of life in Arabia, 86, 87
Harries, Lyndon, 42 n.
Hāshim, 30
Al-Ḥashr, 127
Al-Ḥāsib, 101
Hawāzin, the, 118
Heaven, 157
Heraclius, 167
Ḥijāz, the 24, 35, 59, 65, 86–97, 138 167, 168
Al-Ḥijr, 94, 170
Hijrah, the, 15, 18, 23, 38, 55, 65, 66, 67, 98, 111, 112, 117, 126 n., 146, 151, 168, 173, 190
  religious implications of, 129, 130
Hinduism, 73 n.
Ḥirā', Mount, 28, 34, 58
ḥisāb, 101 f., 133, 190
history, in Islam, 62, 67, 72, 112 f., 166 f., 172
  in the Qur'ān, 23, 55, 67, 112 f., 121 f., 166 f.
  and triumph, 172; contemporary, and the Qur'ān, 21, 22, 23,
Hosea, 173, 174
Al-Ḥudaibiyyah, Treaty of, 99, 118, 128, 131
ḥukm, 190
human relations, 163, 164
humility, 108, 155, 156, 162, 163, 164
Ḥunain, battle of, 118, 152
hypocrisy, 118, 160 n.

Ibn Ḥanbal, 105
Ibn Khaldūn, 52, 177 n.

Quraish, 16, 30, 35, 92 n., 99, 104, 118, 127, 131, 141, 144, 168
finances of, 98 f.
merchandise of, 98 f.
and usury, 105 f
Qur'ān (throughout), 13, 15, 17, 19, 20, 23, 27, 28, 31, 38, 43, 51, 75 f., 90, 115, 141, 145, 172, 176, 179, 180, 182, 186, 187
and abrogation, 146
and Arabic, 13, 18, 40 f., 50
Arabic letters in, 50 f.
chronology in, 14, 16, 74, 111 f.
contemporary world of, 16, 81, 82, 83, 98 f., 116, 151 f.
eloquence of, 13, 47 f.
encounter with pagans, 16, 82, 83, 100, 140, 146, 151 f., 162, 165
eternity of, 17, 19
ethics of, 163 f.
as event, 13, 17, 18, 20, 24, 25, 45 f., 84, 166, 177, 180 f.
events in, 13, 112 f., 141 f., 172 f.
and evil, 158 f., 174 f.
experience of, 26 f., 43 f., 83, 180, 181, 183
finality of, 178
foreign words in, 138
and the *Hijrah*, 126 f.
as history, 114 f., 171 f.
I'jāz of, 21, 43 f.
incidence of, 34
intelligibility of, 40, 141 f.
invocations in, 86 f., 181, 182
as literature, 40 f.
location, 14, 86 f., 98 f.
margins of, 150, 180 f.
metaphors of, 14, 82, 83, 90, 98 f., 147
miracle of, *See I'jāz*
nature in, 24, 68, 74, 86, 94, 97
non-autobiographical, 27
and the non-Muslim, 20, 183 f.
non-poetical, 41 f.
order of, 112 f.
parables in, 14, 87–97, 109
perspective of, 166, 181 f.
political aspects of, 13, 54 f., 135
popular world of, 83
the Prophet in, 26 f., 43 f., 176, 184
prose in, 49, 50
questions in, 13, 24, 26, 27, 84, 91, 141, 147, 148, 150
recital of, 26, 115
relation to history, 16, 17, 111 f., 166 f., 181 f.
repugnancy to, 123
revelation in, 13, 21, 22
sacrament of Arabness, as, 54 f.
significance of, abiding, 17 f.
silences of, 173 f.
situational character of, 112 f., 151 f.
spiritual dimensions of, 13, 81, 82, 180 f.
territory of, 14, 86 f.
and Tradition, 121 f.
universalism of, 55, 181 f.
vocabulary of, 138 f., 149, 150
Quranic scholarship, 18, 138 f.

Rabb al-'Ālamīn, 75 f.. 149, 192
Rahbar, D., 148 n.
Al-Raḥīm, 52, 76, 77, 192
Al-Raḥmān, 52, 76, 77, 158, 160, 192
rains, 89, 97
Rasjidi, Muḥammad, 123
Al-Rasūl, 36, 120, 184, 192
Rasūl-Allāh, 116, 192
the Arab, 55 f.
Al-Ra'ūf, 77
ra'y, 123

Vaughan, Henry, 31
verbal inspiration, 46 f.
vindication, 55, 133, 172
vindictiveness, issue of, 69, 70
vision, in revelation, 25–6
vocation, of Muḥammad, 25, 29, 85, 133, 138, 181
vulnerability, in service to truth, 175 f.

wadis, dry, 86, 88
Al-Wadūd, 77
Waḥy, 17, 21, 22, 36, 43 f., 51, 58, 61, 113, 115, 124, 171 n., 173, 184, 193
Al-Wakīl, 159
Al-Wāqidī, 142
water, 89, 90, 110
watering of pilgrims, 30, 91
Watt, W. Montgomery, 142 n., 166 n.,
west, and 'wests', 95, 96
western scholarship, 20, 84
whisperers, 81, 84
Whitehead, A. H., 151
Williams, T. H. Parry, 54
winds, 89, 90, 91, 97
word, the, 32, 44 f.
words, 137 f.
Wordsworth, William, 25, 26
worship, 23, 24, 73, 76, 94, 116, 134, 151, 163
  care for, 15, 185
  and nature, 94, 185
  pagan, 29, 149, 150, 185
  unification of, 68, 71, 149
wrath, in the *Fātiḥah*, 78, 79

Yathrib, 65. *See* Medina
Yaum al-Ḥisab, 101
Yemen, 87, 96, 169
yusr, 104, 108

Zakāt, 106, 155, 162 n., 163, 193
Zamzam, 109, 110
ẓann, 149, 193
Zaynab, 120 n.
Zoroaster, 167
ẓulm, 193

Quranic Verses Cited

(References below are to verses quoted or used in the text. Numerous other verses merely listed in support of the argument are not noted here.)

Surah	passage	page	Surah	passage	page
51	1–8	97	80	25–32	89
51	11	147	81	8–9	95
52	29–30	41	81	17–24	32, 49
52	49	91	84	19	91
53	4–12	25, 44	85	4–9	170
53	19–30	140 f.	86	1	90
54	18–31	170	86	11	89
57	16	157	87	16	165
57	29	63	88	3–6	88
58	22	108	88	26	101
61	2	155	89	9–10	170
61	10	104	90	1–3	86
62	2	60, 61	90	10	88
62	5	109	91	1	32, 91
62	10–11	152	92	8	108
64	13	160	93	3–4	117
64	15–17	103	93	6	28
65	7	104	94	1–4	37, 49, 147
67	29	160	94	5–6	104
67	30	88	95	1	92
68	17–32	88	96	1	26, 27
69	4–8	170	97	—	31, 36
69	19–26	102	100	—	92
69	40	41	101	—	109, 178
70	—	90	104	—	108
70	24–5	156	106	1	92
73	1–10	33, 95, 126,	106	3	79
		130, 132, 147	106	4	161
74	1–7	33, 130,	107	4–7	155
		132, 133	109	—	116, 162
74	51	90	111	—	109, 161
75	16	114, 115	112	—	80
76	7	156	113	—	80, 81, 82,
78	6–7	90			91
79	42	147	114	—	81, 83
80	—	120, 121			

(verses numberings as in the Egyptian Edition.)